Jonah's Arguments with God

The Honeymoon Is Over!

Jonah's Arguments with God

The Honeymoon Is Over!

T. A. PERRY

HENDRICKSON PUBLISHERS

Jonah's Arguments with God—The Honeymoon Is Over!

© 2006 by Hendrickson Publishers Marketing, LLC
P. O. Box 3473
Peabody, Massachusetts 01961-3473

ISBN 978-1-61970-489-3

Previously published in 2006 as *The Honeymoon Is Over: Jonah's Argument with God*.

Printed in the United States of America

First Printing New Hendrickson Publishers Edition — May 2014

Cover Art: The cover artwork entitled "Jonah & the Whale" was produced by He Qi in 1998 using ink and color on paper. The vibrant colors and thoughtful interaction with the subject matter caught our eye and we are pleased to feature his work on the cover of our book. Photo credit: He Qi. Used with permission. www.heqiarts.com.

This book is dedicated to my beloved grandchildren, Noah, Caleb, Ezra, Jacob, Atarah, Andrew, Daniella, Asher.

וראה בנים לבניך שלום על ישראל:

Ps 128:6

Bible study, a prominent Jonah scholar has reminded us, is a social activity. I have been blessed to participate in the New Haven Shabbat Study Group for many, many years. Each week we gather and puzzle over Tanakh with energy, creativity, and love. I here wish to express my gratitude and admiration for all those who have shared their insights and motivated my learning. Eric (*z"l*) and Marcia Beller; Neil and Nanette Cogan; Donald and Phyllis Cohen; Stanley and Donna Dalnekoff; David Dalnekoff; Toni and David Brion Davis; David and Ina Fischer; Rabbi Lina and Linden Grazier-Zerbarini; Yonatan and Adina Halevi; William Hallo and Nanette Stahl; Hannah Sokol and Oliver Holmes; Jay and Marilyn Katz; Michael and Rebecca Konigsberg; Dov and Nechama Langenauer; Arthur and Betty Levy; Bob and Adina Lieberles; Joe and Hadassah Lieberman; Daniel Nadis and Sally Zanger; Esther Nash; Howard and Willa Needler; Pamela Reis; Sydney A. Perry; Michael and Barbara Klein (*z"l*) Schneider; Heni and Mark Schwartz; Ina Silverman and Jay Sokolow; Shai Silverman-Sokolow; Michael Stern and Kathy Rosenbluh; Michael and Elise Wiener; Steven Wilf and Guita Epstein.

We have also had the privilege of outstanding Israeli scholars who have made New Haven their temporary home over the years and joined our study. They include Moshe and Nechama Bar-Asher; Al and Rita Baumgarten; Corey Brodie; Jonnie Cohen; Richard and Shlomit Cohen; Steven M. Cohen; Arnie and Malka Enker; Hillel and Rochelle Furstenberg; Moshe and Evelyn Greenberg: Ze'ev and Nurit Harvey; Ranon and Charlotte Katzoff; Danny and Debbie Lasker; Charles Liebman (*z"l*); Alex and Yardena Lubotsky; Uri and Reena Levine Melamed; Chaim Milikowsky; Bezalel and Debbie Porten; Jacob and Tamar Ross; Eliezer and Sabina Schweid; Shmuel and Hava Shulman; Uri and Shula Simon; Susan Wall.

Yagdil Torah ve Ya'adir!

TABLE OF CONTENTS

PART ONE
THE OCEAN EXPERIENCE: Jonah 1–2

PART TWO
THE DRY-LAND EXPERIMENTS: Jonah 3–4

PART THREE
THE THEOLOGY OF THE BOOK OF JONAH

PREFACE

> I'm not going to stop loving you, Silly!
> But I am not going to cut myself off from
> the rest of the world either! Enough of
> this King Lear "we two alone" stuff!
>
> Molière, *The Misanthrope* (free adaptation)[1]

What is the book of Jonah about: a whale? Well, at least about a large fish, but also about a *kikayon* (Heb. *qiqayon*), or gourd tree, and a Thoreau-like hut on the edge of civilization. Is it history? If so, its literary form comes eerily close to what are known today as tales of the fantastic. Is it about Jews? Well, it is indeed preserved in Hebrew and is included among the prophetic books of the Hebrew Bible. Yet, with the sole exception of the hero, no Jews appear, and Gentiles are the focus of at least half of the book. But if Jonah is a prophet, what is his prophetic message? A paltry five words, as against the pages of prophecy in other prophetic books, and these spoken reluctantly, between angry teeth. Of course, other prophets were also disinclined and argued against the Lord, but in the end they all gave in. Jonah's rebellion is more original: instead of the usual

---

[1] Molière, *Le misanthrope* (London: Bristol Classics Press, 1996). All translations are mine unless otherwise indicated. Since my purpose is to explore various possible readings of the book of Jonah, translations of the same words and passages may vary, depending on the meanings and contexts under consideration, and one is warned not to expect rigid consistency.

arguing and trying to stay his ground, he simply shuts up, makes an about-face, and flees. The main question of the entire book is why, and the writing delights in delaying and even in confusing expectations. Jonah himself does not say why, at least not right away, and the narrator does not tell either. Only towards the book's end does the prophet seem to offer a deferred excuse, one that shocks our sense of religion and, for some readers at least, reduces Jonah to the level of a comic character. His complaint seems to be that God will let the repentant Ninevites off the hook because He[2] is too *merciful!* The truth is that this is anything but an explanation, for, as Ben Zvi explains, Jonah 4:2 does not really resolve the question. "The reason for his flight is not textually inscribed in the book."[3] But already at the start, Jonah's attitude raises serious questions, for can one hope to escape from God:

Whither shall I flee from Your Presence? (Ps 139:7)[4]

And if God's prophets can be expected to know this better than anyone, then what on earth—or on the seas—can Jonah possibly have in mind? The proverbial "strangeness" of the book of Jonah thus challenges simple solutions.[5] Its close reading may bring us to understand and even approve Jonah's deep religious and existential rebellion. And from the book there is some evidence that God, too, comes around to His prophet's point of view. That does not mean, of course, that Jonah is off the hook. It does, however, intimate that standing up to God is necessary both for humans and perhaps for God too.

We might begin by offering that the book of Jonah is existential in a most elementary way, since all the protagonists—God

---

[2] In this book I regularly use uppercase—He and not he—to refer to God. My purpose is purely to maintain the distinction between the divinity and humans and certainly not for purposes of one-upmanship with atheists. Similarly, I use the masculine gender for pure convenience.

[3] Ehud Ben Zvi, *Signs of Jonah: Reading and Rereading in Ancient Yehud* (JSOTSup 367; Sheffield: JSOT Press, 2003), 59. This remarkable study, written by an historian of ancient Israel, is a promising sign of a new wave of fresh readings and broadened perspectives on the book of Jonah. It requires close study.

[4] In addition to Ps 139, the *Mekhilta of Rabbi Ishmael* (Tractate *Pisha*, 3) cites Zech 4:10; Prov 15:3; Amos 9:2-4; and Job 34:22.

[5] The epithet took hold due to Elias Bickerman's catchy title, *Four Strange Books of the Bible: Jonah, Daniel, Qohelet, Esther* (New York: Schocken), 1967.

included—have to survive a major threat to their very existence: the Ninevites because of their evil deeds, the sailors because they happen to be in the wrong place at the wrong time, Jonah because death is what he wants, and God because He disregards Jonah's threat. In the words of the poet Rilke:

"What will You do, God, when I die?"[6]

Jonah might thus be considered a salvation narrative. Just as Job is rescued from pain and accusation, Jonah is saved from suicide, the sailors from drowning, the Ninevites from annihilation, and God from the loss of His beloved prophet and possibly His reputation. But what survives for the generations is what was fully sought and only partially obtained by Job, and only partially sought and fully obtained by Jonah: a frank dialogue on the way the universe works and in particular on where humans who try to be "good" fit into the world order.

My excuse for adding yet another to the several good books about Jonah is to remain faithful to the obligation to recover for our own generation more of the seventy faces of scriptural interpretation. These seem to me at present stalled at two levels: on the one hand, a widespread refusal to "loosen the fixities, the ossifications of preconceived readings,"[7] and, on the other, a failure of imagination to explore other literary and theological agendas. For example, it is painfully obvious that important ideas in the book of Jonah do not often come up for discussion and yet are of great interest to our contemporaries. I refer to such questions as suicide (and assisted suicide, its Jonah variant), near-death experiences, mere survival and existence conceived as a theological imperative, the moral capacity of animals, erotic theory, the possibility that God can not only change His mind but even be educated, universalism or outreach to Gentiles, and of course more standard issues such as the nature of repentance and prayer.

---

[6] Rainer Maria Rilke, *Rilke's Book of Hours: Love Poems to God* (New York: Riverhead, 1996), 30.

[7] Aviva Zornberg, *Genesis: The Beginning of Desire* (Philadelphia: Jewish Publication Society, 1995), xii. The perspectivism implied in the many faces of interpretation will be in evidence throughout this study. Thus unresolved contradictions (e.g., did Jonah repent?) must be fully discussed but not forced into resolution.

A second excuse is to question some trivializations of the book of Jonah that have become fashionable. The following seem to me the most problematic:

a) mainly because of the giant fish, a generic fairy-tale ambience is read into the book, leading to a hovering suspicion that the whole thing is not all that serious. But if Jonah is as serious as fairy tales, then it is very serious indeed.

b) demeaning personal ascriptions, such as the claim that Jonah's grief over the death of the *kikayon* plant that provides him shade is based on a concern "for his own comfort level."[8]

c) psychological theories about Jonah's clinical depression or insanity or just plain foolishness. For example, it is complacently asked how anyone could try to run away from God, least of all a prophet, forgetting that, as the Vilna Gaon remarks, "Everyone flees from the presence of God; no one wants to stand in His presence."[9]

d) comic theories that trivialize the prophetic calling, for, as Kenneth Craig puts it, "the story is too earnest for laughter."[10] Even Jonah's putative plea for justice has been ridiculed, forgetting it to be but a variant of Abraham's own exclamation before God: "Shall the righteous and the wicked be treated equally?" (Gen 18:25).[11]

---

[8] James Limburg, *Jonah: A Commentary* (Louisville, KY: Westminster John Knox, 1993), 97. A low point is reached in such statements as Jonathan Magonet's: "Yet for all his selfishness and absurdity, even Jonah has an inner life" (Magonet, *Form and Meaning: Studies in Literary Techniques in the Book of Jonah* [Sheffield: The Almond Press, 1983], 53). Or, yet more breathtaking is dubbing Jonah a "mantic bumpkin," so B. Halpern and R. E. Friedman, "Composition and Paronomasia in the Book of Jonah," *HAR* 4 (1980): 89.

[9] This appropriate antidote to such naiveté is quoted in Zornberg, *Beginning*, 24.

[10] Kenneth Craig, *A Poetics of Jonah: Art in the Service of Ideology* (Columbia: University of South Carolina Press, 1993), 143.

[11] I leave aside the more grievous anti-semitic issues, which have been adequately dealt with by Yvonne Sherwood, "Cross-Currents in the Book of Jonah," *BibInt* 6 (1998): 49–79; *A Biblical Text and Its Afterlives: The Survival of Jonah in Western Culture* (Cambridge: Cambridge University Press, 2000). I am especially indebted to these brilliant and spirited studies, which saved me loads of time, cleared the way for more balanced and accurate assessments of the book

e) stylistic assumptions that God's treatment of Jonah is basically ironic, as if parody and satire were the appropriate tone and means to conduct a serious discussion about crucial theological issues.[12]

It is a fortunate and astounding fact of literary history that Jonah has not only survived such assaults but continues to thrive, for, as Meschonnic triumphantly puts it, "Jonah has swallowed up his critics like the fish swallowed up Jonah."[13] As against these and similar reductive tendencies, we recall the Christian identification of Jonah with Christ's descent into hell only to rise again (Matt 12:39–41), or the Rabbinic conviction that Jonah ascended to Heaven without suffering death.[14] For if Jonah "ups and runs away from God's Presence" merely because he is depressed or foolish or crazy, one might wonder why God would invest such quality time in a basket case. One thinks of God's extensive dialogue, its tender humor, the impressive battery of tricks used to bring Jonah around: the large fish, the storm, the *kikayon*, the worm, the east wind. It would seem that, for whatever reason, Jonah is, at the very least, worthy of God's attention. For, as Sherwood has argued, "marginalising Jonah's perspective" is tantamount to "banishing his potentially explosive challenge to the deity from the text."[15] Perhaps a more interesting question, though—all the way from Jonah's startling refusal to his climactic silence at the end—is why God is worth Jonah's. For if Jonah's only lesson from God is "might is right," then Scripture has canceled its own moral authority in favor of common lawlessness.

---

of Jonah, and helped to restore for biblical studies that "fundamentally experimental character of interpretation," *A Biblical Text*, 6.

[12] Satire has in fact become the locus of both moral evidence and uncontrollable eloquence, as I. J. Spangenberg: "Evidently the author of Jonah wanted to expose and elicit public contempt for the behaviour of a self-centered, lazy and hypocritical religious person" ("Jonah and Qohelet: Satire versus Irony," *OTE* 9 [1996]: 509).

[13] Henri Meschonnic, *Jona et le signifiant errant* (Paris: Gallimard, 1981), 77.

[14] "Jonah never died but entered the Garden of Eden alive" (Midrash Shoher Tov, section 26; quoted in Ze'ev Haim Lifshitz, *The Paradox of Human Existence: A Commentary on the Book of Jonah* [Northvale, NJ: Jason Aronson, 1994], xxi).

[15] Sherwood, "Cross-Currents," 56.

This book is conceived as a prolegomenon to the reading of the book of Jonah. Its focus on the requirements of reading arises from the impression that we have become too fixed in our ways, too convinced that we already know what the book says. We tend to forget that a fresh reading—and every reading should be that—requires bracketing out inherited truths and preconceptions. At this simplest level, this requires going back again and again to our, yes, our dictionaries. This basic necessity for any sophisticated literary text is especially crucial when these texts are foreign and ancient. As the classicist and poet Anne Carson put it:

> Sometimes when I am reading a Greek text I force myself to look up all the words in the dictionary, even the ones I think I know. It is surprising what you learn that way. Some of the words turn out to sound quite different than you thought.[16]

At another level of our attempt to untangle and recover some of Jonah's meanings, the popular generic puzzle—is the book a fable or a history or a parable or a satire or a prophetic account or something else—must be dislodged or expanded. One way to do this is by following hints from the book of Jonah itself, to broaden the text's imaginative context, to approach Jonah from a fresh reading of such texts as Toni Morrison's *Beloved*,[17] Shakespeare's *King Lear*, the pastoral, the Song of Songs, and the literature of the fantastic. Another way to raise this question, if we remain (quite sensibly) attached to the prophetic genre as our model,[18] is to be willing to retrieve earlier understandings of prophecy, to follow such thinkers as Maimonides in regarding the essence of prophecy as, beyond the usual religious and political interests, an intense and passionate clinging of the soul to the divine Presence, of Lover to Beloved. I shall suggest that erotic theory may open doors to Jonah's mysticism and contemplation that have been

---

[16] Anne Carson, *Glass, Irony, and God* (New York: New Directions, 1995), 136.

[17] Toni Morrison, *Beloved* (New York: Knopf, 1998).

[18] "In terms of its ancient literary critical classification, there can be little doubt that it [the book of Jonah] was understood as a story about a prophet" (John Day, "Problems in the Interpretation of the Book of Jonah," in *In Quest of the Past: Studies on Israelite Religion, Literature, and Prophetism* [ed. A. S. van der Woude; OTS; Leiden: Brill, 1990], 39).

avoided by modern inquiries but that were perhaps at the heart of Rabbinic speculation about Jonah's "dying without dying."[19] As an epigraph suggesting the erotic aspect of my argument, I refer to the central love-relationship of Molière's *Misanthrope*, whose subtitle *l'atrabilaire amoureux* designates the male lead as a black-biled or melancholic lover. In my free adaptation the coquettish female lead Célimène is speaking to her hopelessly enamored and very jealous Alceste. For whatever reason—his sincerity, passion, devoted attachment, hatred of hypocrisy, to name a few—Célimène still loves the grouchy misfit. But she is quite unprepared, for all that, to renounce an imperfect world and the enjoyment of the flattery it affords. In this analogy, the Lady is, as was the case in the old courtly tradition, God Himself (or Herself), and the misanthrope is, yes, Jonah.

My final and really primary excuse for writing this book is so that somewhere a thirteen-year-old will write that I have helped her or him to read Jonah a bit better. For, speaking from personal experience with my own kids, at that age the mind is vigorous and the heart is pure; the imagination can still range the seas and the dry land, and the intentions are uncluttered, existential. I mean that at that age it is still possible to have a personal reading, or at least one not totally subserviant to the usual. My suspicion is that our hero will no longer be regarded only as Jonah-the-Jew but also as Jonah-Everyman.[20]

Put differently, turning from trivialization may help us recover what Wallace Stevens has called "the freedom to yield ourselves" to the ancient Ur-images that still haunt us, help us to penetrate the utter simplicity and modesty of the narration. Again, Stevens:

> A force capable of bringing about fluctuations in reality in words free from mysticism is a force independent of one's desire to elevate it. It needs no elevation.[21]

---

[19] John of the Cross's "muero porque no muero"; see Concluding Midrash I below and the Yehudah Halevi verse quoted there.

[20] See Sherwood, *A Biblical Text*, 280. For "adults," however, Sherwood's sobering sarcasm proffers its challenge: "How is one to read, and teach this text, at the turn of the millennium," in *Higher Education*, 87.

[21] Wallace Stevens, *The Necessary Angel: Essays on Reality and Imagination* (New York: Vintage Books, 1951), viii.

The challenge to the modern reader is, behind the strange and atypical folk-images of fish and *kikayon*, to perceive the intimations of epiphany, to recover, behind the imagined appearances of an egoist, the Hebrew Bible's sketch of God's intimate friend.[22]

New Haven and Beer-Sheva

---

[22] As this book was already on its way to press, Ehud Ben Zvi's *Signs of Jonah: Reading and Rereading in Ancient Yehud* appeared on Jonah, and I was so impressed that I was tempted to rename this work "Rereading Jonah." Ben Zvi has identified the book of Jonah as metaprophetical (i.e., not only concerned about single prophetic events but also about how prophecy itself works). In so doing and true to his source of inspiration, he has written the manual not only for rereading Jonah but also for what rereading Hebrew Scripture itself can mean. Most important for my own work, Ben Zvi gives a theoretical basis for authenticating both interpretations long in service and really new understandings of familiar passages.

ABBREVIATIONS

AB	Anchor Bible
BDB	Brown, Driver, and Briggs, *Hebrew and English Lexicon*
BibInt	*Biblical Interpretation*
b.	Babylonian Talmud
CAT	Commentaire de l'Ancien Testament
CC	Continental Commentaries
ConBNT	Coniectanea biblica: New Testament Series
GKC	*Gesenius' Hebrew Grammar*. Ed. E. Kautzsch, rev. A. E. Cowley. 2nd English ed., Oxford: Clarendon Press, 1910.
HALOT	Koehler, L., W. Baumgartner, and J. J. Stamm, *The Hebrew and Aramaic Lexicon of the Old Testament*. Translated under the supervision of M. E. Richardson. 5 vols. Leiden, 1994–2000
HAR	*Hebrew Annual Review*
HBT	*Horizons in Biblical Theology*
Int	*Interpretation*
JB	Jerusalem Bible
JBL	*Journal of Biblical Literature*
JPS	Jewish Publication Society
JSOT	*Journal for the Study of the Old Testament*
JSOTSup	Journal for the Study of the Old Testament Supplemental Series
ms(s)	Manuscript(s)
MT	Massoretic Text (the standard Hebrew version)
NCB	New Century Bible

NJPS	*Tanakh: The Holy Scriptures: The New JPS Translation according to the Traditional Hebrew Text*
NovT	*Novum Testamentum*
NT	New Testament
n./nn.	note/notes in the Commentary
NRSV	New Revised Standard Version of the Bible
OTE	*Old Testament Essays*
OTS	Old Testament Studies
RelArts	Religion and the Arts
RHR	*Revue d l'histoire des religions*
RSV	Revised Standard Version of the Bible
SBB	Stuttgarter biblische Beiträge
SCR	*Studies in Comparative Religion*
v./vv.	verse/verses
VT	*Vetus Testamentum*

Biblical books are abbreviated according to guidelines published in *The SBL Handbook of Style*. All references to the Bible and to classical texts give chapter followed by verse or appropriate subdivision. I cite Hebrew Scripture according to the chapter and verse of the MT and give the English when different. All biblical and other translations are mine unless otherwise noted.

For the transliteration of Hebrew, since in all cases the goal is less to reproduce the exact spelling of the MT than to recall the shape of the Hebrew words, vowels are transliterated as they would sound in an English reading. Consonants are transliterated according to the "General Purpose Style" in *The SBL Handbook of Style*.

Introduction

A Dialogue of Silence

If in our reading and study of the book of Jonah we are looking for "the central theme that unites all the elements of the story
into a literary and conceptual whole,"[1] then we might say, at least
stylistically speaking, that the constant element throughout the
book is the dialogue—really a series of arguments—between
God and His prophet Jonah. This feature in itself is of course not
distinctive to our story, since dialogue characterizes the entire
Hebrew Bible and is especially definitive of the prophetic relationship with God. The Jonah dialogue is so deviant from this model,
however, as to seem to constitute its own genre.

As is typical in prophetic stories, it is God who initiates:

Now the word of Lord [came] unto Jonah, etc.

When we reach the very end, the dialogue rages on, God and His
prophet still locked in argument. Between start and finish, it is
true, the dialogue takes some remarkable turns, but in so doing it
merely remains true to the double surprise that encapsulates the
entire book. At the start, God's word to Jonah evokes the response
not only of flight but of silence—thus a dialogue aborted at the
very onset.[2] Not differently at the end, God asks a question that,

---

[1] Uriel Simon, *Jonah: The Traditional Hebrew Text with the New JPS Translation* (trans. Lenn J. Schramm; JPS Torah Commentary; Philadelphia: Jewish
Publication Society, 1999), vii.

[2] According to George M. Landes ("The Kerygma of the Book of Jonah:
The Contextual Interpretation of the Jonah Psalm," *Int* 21 [1967]: 14), however,

within the pages of the text, is left unanswered—thus, again, a frustrated exchange.[3] Analogous to what the French would call a dialogue of the deaf, the book of Jonah takes on the quality of a dialogue of silence. It is this dialogic silence—which is anything but a silencing of dialogue—that we would like to explore.[4]

The concept of dialogue most valuable here goes far beyond mere exchanges of words, if only because, as pointed out, many of the responses from both sides avoid the verbal.[5] Yvonne Sherwood has proposed a Bakhtian model, a shift from a satirical mode of reading, in which Jonah is seen as particularistic and selfish, to an open form of carnavalesque parody where both parties—Jonah but also God—get their come-uppance and neither gets the last word.[6] Indeed, our text takes pains to stress the impossibility of knowing for sure, by pointing out both our ignorance of God's mind ("who knows?" 3:9) and also the possi-

---

Jonah did react verbally to God's initial charge, but the response was delayed for greater dramatic effect. Thus 4:2 ("was this not *my word* while still in my land?") would not mean "what I thought" but rather "what I said."

[3] But an exchange or dialogue nevertheless. See below, Conclusion. For the possibility that the book does *not* end on a question, see below, "The Double Ending, . . ." in chapter 8.

[4] The rabbis, sensing a similar argumentative scenario in Hosea's silent compliance with God's outrageous command to "take to himself a wife of harlotry and children of harlotry" (Hos 1:2), fleshed out the controversy in *b. Pesahim* 87a–b.

[5] This needs to be asserted against those who seek to limit divine communication to the verbal, as for example Landes ("Kerygma," 20–21): "Jonah experiences no word from Yahweh all the time he is on the ship, in the sea, or within the great fish." On the contrary, all of God's "appointees" (the fish, *kikayon*, worm, east wind) embody divine messages. As for Jonah, his actions speak as loud as his words—for instance, his trance while in the belly of the ship reaches up to God (see below, "Jonah's Trances," in chapter 5). It is important to see Jonah's words and actions as *integrated or coordinated* parts of an ongoing and developing dialogue with God, as against those critics who see a disparity. Steven Weitzman (*Song and Story in Biblical Narrative: The History of a Literary Convention in Ancient Israel* [Bloomington: Indiana University Press, 1997], 110), for example, thinks that Jonah's deeds "reveal that Jonah does not fully understand the implications of what he said." Or, more stringently and parochially, Samuel E. Balentine (*Prayer in the Hebrew Bible* [Minneapolis: Fortress 1993], 71–80).

[6] Yvonne Sherwood, "Cross-Currents in the Book of Jonah," *BibInt* 6 (1998): 49–79. Bakhtin's work on Rabelais had an important influence on literary studies in the early '60s and, as Sherwood brilliantly shows, still has enormous potential for liberating biblical texts from petrified readings.

bility that God can change His mind and even repent. This approach, especially welcome in the present climate, rids us of what is often poor psychology or—worse—grim theologizing about Jews behind a comic mask. What needs to be incorporated into this method is an awareness that Jonah's issues are as real and important and worthy of discussion as God's own. And if the notion of parody is to be retained, this should be with full awareness of heroically held and principled positions. To return briefly to the paradigm of *The Misanthrope*, it may be that Molière was indeed making fun of Alceste, at least of his lack of sociability. But Alceste's grandeur is also recorded, his fervid attachment to principles, his heroic love attachment reminiscent of outmoded but grand courtly ideals. Few mockers of Alceste are able to withstand Rousseau's withering scorn, and one wonders whether Jonah's detractors might not merit similar treatment.[7]

Symbolizing Something

> There was grace and mystery in her attitude, as if she were a symbol of something. He asked himself what a woman standing on the stairs in the shadow, listening to distant music, is a symbol of.[8]

Consider the following three scenarios, all variants of a single pedagogical method:

  a) A sage and member of the community goes out and marries a whore, and everyone asks why. And, indeed, the prophet Hosea wants to help folks imagine that they are themselves behaving like whores with other gods.[9]

---

[7] Rousseau's essay on *The Misanthrope* can be found in his "Lettre à d'Alembert sur les spectacles."

[8] James Joyce, *The Portable James Joyce* (New York: Penguin Books, 1976), 227.

[9] For the dramatic aspect of such symbolic actions, I like Marvin A. Sweeney's discussion of Hosea in *The Twelve Prophets* (2 vols.; Collegeville, MN: Liturgical, 2000). See also my remarks below ("Pastoral Pedagogy," in chapter 9) on the prophetic project of being a "visible saint."

b) A distinguished intellectual ups and leaves town, withdraws to the edge of civilization in order to build and live in a hut, and folks are curious. And, again, people come to understand that Thoreau's cabin at Walden Pond, perched at the meeting point between the civilization of Concord and wild nature, is a visible figure of that pastoral inner landscape where humans should establish their primary residence.[10]

c) A leading member of the religious establishment, during an intensive campaign to reach out to outsiders, suddenly gets up and runs away. Local curiosity is piqued not only by the contradictory behavior but also by the ostentatious style: the departure is unannounced, sudden, even mysteriously precipitous (according to some, Jonah buys up the entire escape ship). What on earth are people to make of such provocative behavior? For there are no words to help unravel the puzzle, only silence and gestures that seem to signify. Later, in a symbolic move that recalls the first in its style, Jonah withdraws from the target city "in order to see." Yes, to see and perhaps, as God Himself is fond of doing, to be seen as well.[11] Again, the demonstrative behavior seems intended to teach something. But what?

In this last scenario, Jonah's two silences that bracket the book at both its extremities do not frustrate the dialogue but give it extraordinary resilience, thus remaining true to its prophetic underpinnings. For the strong debate that occupies the entire book is conducted not only by words but also, when these do not perform their service, by a whole battery of means and tricks. Jonah, in addition to silence and flight, uses behaviors that, if only because of their strangeness, seem symbolically intended: a precipitous descent from God's Presence to the mountains' very roots; rushing through the city—a three-day journey—in a single day; building himself a pastoral hut on the edge of the

---

[10] See below, "A Pastoral Perspective," in chapter 9.
[11] Deuteronomy 16:16 and Jeffrey H. Tigay's comment (*Deuteronomy* [JPS Torah Commentary; Philadelphia: Jewish Publication Society, 1996], 159). The active/passive crux of seeing/being seen seems to be based ultimately on Gen 22:14.

city to monitor its . . . annihilation? compliance? It is as if Jonah were trying to teach—us? God?—something, rather than the other way around. God, for His part, also has means beyond the verbal: the windy storm, the great fish, the worm, the *kikayon* bush. Beyond their specific mission, these messengers or "appointees" are usually thought to be sent to teach Jonah a lesson, but we shall see that their impact on Jonah is intended to be argumentative as well as pedagogical. As Montaigne said about educating children, Jonah's God—contrary to the usual view—would rather be loved than feared, rather teach and persuade than constrain, with all the risks of refusal that this may entail.[12]

Thus each one of God's and Jonah's actions seems intended to persuade the other, to win an argument. About what? That is the single issue of the book of Jonah, the central factor motivating Jonah's flight. It soon becomes patent that the narrative voice does take God's side against Jonah, thus further motivating readers to do likewise. But the narrator also carefully records Jonah's point of view. And it is especially this latter voice that, in a more sympathetic mode, we must try to recover.

Why Did Jonah Flee from God's Presence?
Four Hypotheses

Jonah's strange behavior as a prophet has inspired a wide range of explanations. Focusing on what he sees to be the basic puzzle of the book—Jonah's refusal to preach repentance to the Ninevites—Uriel Simon has summarized the following four possible motivations:[13]

Repentance or Punishment

For Yehezkel Kaufmann, as well as for Jews generally, Jonah is the book of Repentance, designated to be read liturgically on

---

[12]"Even if I could make myself feared, I would much rather make myself loved" (Michel de Montaigne, *The Complete Essays of Montaigne* [trans. Donald Frame; Stanford: Stanford University Press, 1976], 285).

[13]Simon, *Jonah*, vii–xiii.

Yom Kippur.[14] Kaufmann's particular view of the book's argument is that Jonah's antiquated concept of necessary punishment for sin is replaced by the possibility of repentance and thus represents a theological advance. According to this view, repentance is to be learned from the Ninevites, and Jonah is not an example to follow. This argument strikes me as most powerful according to Simon's own criteria in that, as I shall argue, it unifies all parts of the book under a single theme. Simon thinks otherwise, since he finds the repentance theme restricted to the Ninevites and thus the focus of only the third chapter. As we shall see, however, repentance is not so confined but is rather a strong focus of attention from the very first to the last verses of the book. For the sailors in chapter one are also involved in repentance, and Jonah himself, in the entire second chapter, undergoes profound regret— otherwise, how does he come to accept, at the start of chapter three, the mission that he rejected from the start? And, finally, the Jonah of chapter four is once more challenged to rethink his ways, mainly by choosing life over death both for himself and the Gentiles.

Israel and the Gentiles

A stronger objection to Kaufmann would be that the theme of repentance does not concern Israel, at least not explicitly. And even taking Jonah as a figure for Israel, one wonders whether Israelites could learn of God's mercy from such an example—maybe for them God has higher standards! According to this argument of chosenness, Jonah doesn't want to preach to Gentiles because he knows that they will repent and this will make Jews (who presumably, as in Ezekiel 1–15, don't repent) look bad.

The first problem with this argument is that, although the lesson of Gentile repentance is a good one, the modern wish to use it to make Jews look narrow-minded[15] is contradicted by its

---

[14] Yehezkel Kaufmann, *The Religion of Israel* (trans. Moshe Greenberg; Chicago: University of Chicago Press, 1960), 283, 285; see also Jeffrey H. Tigay, "The Book of Jonah and the Days of Awe," *Conservative Judaism* 38 (1985/86): 67–76.

[15] On this whole question see Sherwood, "Cross-Currents," and Bickerman, *Four Strange Books*.

inclusion in the Jewish biblical canon. The second problem is that Jews are nowhere mentioned in the book, with the single exception of Jonah's self-identification as a Hebrew to the sailors (1:9). The third reason is that neither the sailors nor the Ninevites are depicted in such positive terms: the sailors, as we shall see, are guilty of assisted suicide, and the Ninevites are likened—albeit in a somewhat positive sense—to animals (4:11).

The Validity of Prophecy

According to this argument, Jonah is angry that, if the Ninevites do repent, then he will be proved wrong and thus a false prophet: he predicted a destruction that didn't happen (see Deut 18:21–22). But, surely, the purpose of preaching repentance is to bring about . . . repentance! And in such cases, both alternatives—the Ninevites repenting, or not—are clearly fulfillments of prophecy.

To save this argument, Sasson[16] finds Jonah a victim of oracular ambiguity: In announcing that Nineveh would be overthrown, Jonah saw only destruction, whereas the opposite possibility— "overthrow" by repentance—was also intimated. When Nineveh is indeed not destroyed and Jonah finally sees the paronomasia, he is upset not because of his faulty understanding or God's trickery, but rather because God didn't observe proper etiquette in now allowing him to prophesy Nineveh's weal.[17]

The problems with this position are multiple. First of all, announcing weal is a prophetic possibility but certainly not a necessity and not even widespread (Sasson cites only Isaiah). And if Isaiah can indulge a basically decent king, requiring an Israelite prophet to congratulate Nineveh would be quite another matter. On the matter of paronomasia, the failure to perceive ambiguity is never a simple case of linguistic incompetence. Jonah does not see the (linguistic) possibility of Nineveh's salvation because he is presumably not interested in its salvation, not believing it to

---

[16] Jack M. Sasson, *Jonah: A New Translation with Introduction, Commentary, and Interpretation* (AB 42B; New York: Doubleday, 1990), 294–98, 346.

[17] For a discussion, see my forthcoming study (T. A. Perry, "Cain's Sin in Genesis 4:1–7 and Oracular Double-Talking," *Prooftexts* 25 [2006], 259–76).

be possible. This could mean that, as the rabbis projected, Jonah doubted that their repentance was sincere. Or, alternatively and as we shall argue, it means that Jonah does of course see the ambiguity but holds that the Ninevites are not yet deserving of God's *full* love.[18]

Justice or Mercy?

Simon's own explanation of Jonah's anger is that Jonah is a law-and-order man, that in the perpetual tension between God's compassion and justice Jonah is overprotective of the latter, feeling that mercy can mean overindulgence with the wicked and absence of justice. But one must notice that Abraham, the grand patron of mercy over justice (see Gen 18), concedes the destruction of the wicked and does not preach repentance. Terry Eagleton said it best: "If disobedience on the scale of a Nineveh goes cavalierly unpunished, then the idea of obedience also ceases to have meaning. God's mercy simply makes a mockery of human effort, which is why Jonah ends up in the grips of *Thanatos* or the death drive."[19]

Moreover, if Simon is correct, then we must reconsider one of the rabbis' most famous judgments of our prophet, according to which Jonah cared for the honor of the child (Israel) but not of

---

[18] There are, of course, instances in the Hebrew Bible that smack of classical oracular ambiguity (see the previous note). Here too, God, unable to speak an untruth, proffers words that have opposite meanings. Thus *hpkh* can mean either be literally overthrown and destroyed, or spiritually transformed through repentance. One must occur—actually, over the course of time, both can occur—but humans can influence which. Similarly, Jonah is invited to speak initially *against* the Ninevites and then *to* them. In the first instance, he infers from the preposition "against" that the meaning has to be physical destruction and he refuses. When this is revised as "to" them, he can at that point see the second meaning and on that basis accept the mission to preach their repentance. There is thus no ambiguity in the classical sense and this is not merely another instance of poor Jonah's stupidity. Rather, he does make the two options clear to the Ninevites: they are going to be "overthrown" one way or another, the choice is theirs; either they do it or God will do it for them. If the choice seems easy, change is not. Recall Lot's wife, who just couldn't avoid her clinging gaze backward. Or even Lot, on the edge of annihilation and still bargaining for yet "a little" of the old stuff.

[19] Terry Eagleton, "J. L. Austin and the Book of Jonah," in *The Book and the Text* (ed. Regina Schwartz; Cambridge, MA: Basil Blackwell, 1990), 231–36.

the Father (God). It would seem, rather, that Jonah's entire purpose was quite the opposite: disregarding the honor of all human beings (including the Israelites, who do not appear in the book anyhow), Jonah's total preoccupation was with the honor of God, for the total integrity of the divine Being, which includes justice as well as mercy (see below, "Conclusion").

The matter of the Ninevites' repentance as the book's central focus is problematic, however, since the book is not at all about Gentiles—in fact, they don't even appear in chapters 2 and 4. Thus, for example, the argument that "it was the belief that the Ninevites would repent that prevented him [Jonah] from going to Nineveh in the first place"[20] is to be rejected, not because Jonah hates Gentiles but because God's edict of annihilation is incomprehensible, both in terms of what Jonah knows about the divine attributes and because of his prophetic understanding of the goals of human life, as we shall discuss in chapter 8 below.

A Fifth Hypothesis: The Love-Plot

Now the word of the Lord [came] unto Beloved.[21]

The book's simple words of prophetic opening are actually among the most mysterious in the Bible, and yet we behave as if they were perfectly clear and obvious. One typical reaction: "How could Jonah have even thought of refusing? God told him to do it!" But the period of prophecy is past; God no longer speaks directly to humans, not even to His prophets. By this we do not engage the nature of prophecy but rather observe that we simply may have neither experiential nor conceptual bases for grasping what is being said. All we surmise is that Jonah himself—whether through dreams or inner inspiration or whatever—was convinced that the order was from God. And that is enough to follow his psychology and even try to penetrate his lofty perceptions. But

---

[20] John Day, "Problems in the Interpretation of the Book of Jonah," in *Quest of the Past: Studies on Israelite Religion, Literature, and Prophetism* (ed. A. S. van der Woude; OTS; Leiden: Brill, 1990), 45.

[21] I.e., Jonah or dove or, as per Cant 5:2, "Beloved"; see below, "The Opening Scene," in chapter 5.

it does not authorize assertions about God's nature, nor does it set immutable parameters for the ensuing dialogue.[22] By this I mean something quite simple but essential for today's human being, whether religious or totally secular in outlook. Jonah was convinced that he had a personal experience and dialogue with God and this experience is somehow reported by what we have of Scripture. Through this writing we can now try to reconstruct his concept so that we can decide whether the experience is worth the pursuit.

In the matter of Jonah's motivations we thus wish to put forth a fifth hypothesis, one that combines elements of the other four but looks single-mindedly neither to the theological issue, nor to the secondary characters, nor to Jonah's professional responsibilities as a prophet, nor to the psychology of the other major player— God. To be sure, what all of these have in common (except the last one) is a focus on the *message* of prophecy, in this case the call to Nineveh to repent. However, I see the problem as one of a threatened *relationship* (between God and His messenger) that involves all of the above but that is distinct, enmeshed in the very fabric of the prophetic dialogue.[23] To see the matter clearly we must stay as close to the words of the text as possible and be attentive to every possible nuance of meaning. For example, the book's main problem has been presented as Jonah's refusal to preach to the Ninevites.[24] This may indeed be a correct inference

---

[22] Current understandings of the book of Jonah are typically reductive, reading the exchange between God and Jonah as entirely uni-directional and monologic (God has to convey a lesson, convince Jonah of some important truth, and the like). However, "the primacy of the signifier [the entire Jonah story] goes beyond theology as such. The Book's language, which is history and the relation to history, is sufficient. Even God is part of the signifier, since that is where dialogue occurs" (Henri Meschonnic, *Jona et le signifiant errant* [Paris: Gallimard, 1981], 86). Thus God does not have anything like a privileged position but is rather conceived as merely part of the total signifier.

[23] Alexander Rofé (*The Prophetical Stories* [Jerusalem: Magnes, 1988], 175) cogently argues this point in the case of the Man of God at Bethel (1 Kgs 13): "the prohibitions [against eating and drinking] are related to the Man of God's role as messenger, rather than to the message." Rofé also makes a good case for viewing Jonah and the Man of God story as belonging to the same literary genre, that of a parable whose dynamics focus on the relationship between the prophet and his God (173).

[24] Simon, *Jonah*, vii.

from his flight, but it does not tell the whole story. The text says, rather, that Jonah attempts to "flee from God's presence," which is a rather more complex matter.

We may begin by asking: What, then, is God to Jonah? The answer, according to the prophet himself (4:2), is that He is a patient and merciful God such as is mentioned throughout the Hebrew Bible. Now this God, whose mercy is said to be "upon all His creatures" (Ps 145:9), tells His servant—if he wants to be His servant—to bring the immoral Gentiles back to proper behavior and He will let them live. That is to say, Jonah's belief in God requires him to leave the security and joy of the divine Presence (the Holy Temple) in Jerusalem and journey to an unclean land and a wicked people. But why should he? Because God commands! But why on earth, on the basis of his experience and expectations, should God so command?! For Jonah regards God as primarily the One who has a special relationship of *love* towards His *servants*, who "watches over those who love Him and that He loves, and destroys the wicked" (Ps 145:20). We often conclude from that—somewhat hastily—that Jonah is to be thought of as a law-and-order man, one who is jealous of God's Justice, which in this case would mean deserved retribution against the cruel and the wicked. But a different focus is possible since, surely, the wicked, if not through divine agency, will *self*-destruct if given a decent chance.[25] No, Jonah is concerned about the implications of God's mercy less towards the wicked than towards God's own beloved, such as he feels himself to be. Let's be clear about this: Jonah does not complain that God loves, only that He loves "too much," without discrimination or faithfulness, showing *rab khesed*, "too much"[26] love for the wrong people (sinners), undoubtedly, but by that very fact *not enough love for his Beloved*.

In our search for the book's unity there are also matters beyond thematics to consider: literary questions of tone, levels of dialogue. My hunch, to repeat, is that Jonah's upset is less that of

---

[25] As per Ps 9:16: "The nations drown in the pit which they made; in the net that they hid their own foot is caught."

[26] For this meaning of *rab* see Num 16:3; Ezek 45:9; and Qoh 1:18, as I argue in T. A. Perry, *Dialogues with Kohelet* (University Park, PA: Penn State University Press, 1993), 72.

a false and/or unsuccessful prophet or law-and-order man than of a jilted lover. There are many reasons why this thesis is preferable as an explanation of the work's unity. First of all, it views the main problem dialogically, providing a more realistic explanation of the relationship between God and His beloved prophet, while saving the story from the temptation to view it as merely or basically parody, or irony, or even comedy. Secondly, it unites not only all the major themes but also those otherwise unexplained and unexplainable elements such as both Jonah's strange behaviors and God's playful irony. It enables us to understand these as amorously motivated and thus vulnerable and tender rather than simply ridiculous. It also encourages us to notice that Jonah and God have some serious issues to work out before their relationship can get back on track; and, as in such circumstances, the matters must be worked out not by put-downs but rather by patient dialogue. Let us now proceed to some of these issues, in more or less the order in which they are presented in the text, indeed in the very manner of their presentation.

Structure and Plot: Two Equal Parts, Delayed Plot

A rather unique feature of our book is that, of all biblical prophets, Jonah is the only one who "needs to have his assignment from the Lord given to him a second time," suggesting to this critic that Jonah's mission to Nineveh was "very important indeed":[27]

> *The word of the Lord came to Jonah son of Amittai: "Go to Nineveh, that great city, and proclaim . . ."* (1:1–2; emphasis added)

> *The word of the Lord came to Jonah a second time: "Go to Nineveh, that great city, and proclaim . . ."* (3:1–2; emphasis added)

Before jumping ahead to interpretations—or getting bogged down on the mission itself—however, certain stylistic implications must

---

[27] James Limburg, *Jonah: A Commentary* (Louisville, KY: Westminster John Knox, 1993), 22.

be noticed, and these will in fact be important for interpretation. This repetition, quite astonishing for both its length and verbatim precision, focuses attention on structural features even more astonishing. Notice both the distance of the repetition from its pattern and also its location: it occurs precisely at the midpoint of the book, thus yielding, even on first reading, the correct impression of a perfectly balanced two-part composition, its four chapters being divided into two equal parts:[28]

Part One = chapters 1–2;
Part Two = chapters 3–4.

The Lord's repeated command thus marks both an ending, bringing closure to Part One, and a beginning to a new part.

Such a repetition of words—variously called *inclusio*, or *Wiederaufnahme*, or repetitive resumption in literary parlance, occurring often but not necessarily at the start of a verse or section—is a frequent feature of biblical style, its function being similar to that of a bracket or parenthesis. For example, Gen 22:6 closes with the observation "So the two of them went together." There ensues a brief dialogue between father and son, followed by the verbatim repetition "(s)o the two of them went together" (v. 8), indicating that the parenthetical dialogue is now closed. The text then resumes where it left off before the interrupting dialogue, which, from the point of view of plot, could easily have been omitted, the reader skipping ahead to where the action resumes.

If this simple stylistic rule is now applied to Jonah, then we must consider that the entire first half of the book is somehow bracketed. For the repetition of the opening verse at 3:1 stylistically sponsors the argument that the long parenthesis opened at the outset is finally closed. At the start of Part Two Jonah is simply brought back to square one, so to speak, where the aborted plot can resume or, rather, so that it can finally

---

[28]Other divisions have been suggested. Jacob Licht (*Storytelling in the Bible* [Jerusalem: Magnes, 1978], 122), for example, sees three "episodes" (corresponding to chapters 1, 3, 4) rather than two parts, but his analysis has two disadvantages: loss of the parallelistic implications of two equal parts (see below), and dismissal of Jonah's psalm (chapter 2) as a mere "poetic intermezzo."

commence.[29] Thus, quite astonishingly, Part One represents such a notable lack of progress as to be merely parenthetical, and half-way through the book the story has not advanced; indeed, since nothing has yet happened, the story has not even begun, and some readers might wish to have been warned to skip ahead to the real action!

Such a compression or postponement of the plot is further exaggerated, this time at the end. It has been accurately observed that, as a prophetic work of Hebrew Scripture, the book of Jonah's four chapters could have been condensed into one, the third.[30] The remainder of the book is quite subsidiary to the prophet's call and mission, both fully described in chapter 3. Thus, the entire rest of the book, chapter 4 as well as the first two, focuses merely on Jonah's psychological reactions to his prophetic call: his refusal of the mission before the fact (chapters 1–2), and his regret or reaction over having succeeded (chapter 4). Three-fourths of the book, in other words, presents (merely!) the emotional problems, as it were, that God and prophet are having with one another.[31]

However, if the parallelism of Jonah 1:1 and 3:1 demonstrates the sheer excess of the first half of the book—that the entire bulk was simply a false start and that the plot is brought back to degree

---

[29] It is thus imprecise to say, with Phyllis Trible, that "the plot *continues* by beginning a second time," since the plot has not even yet begun. See her *Rhetorical Criticism: Context, Method, and the Book of Jonah* (Minneapolis: Fortress, 1994), 109; emphasis added.

[30] André LaCocque and Pierre-Emmanuel Lacocque, *The Jonah Complex* (Atlanta: John Knox, 1981), 137.

[31] If the comparison between simple or local *inclusio* and the extended one in Jonah seems strained, Job's Prologue in Heaven can be seen as a bridge between the two:

One day, the sons of God came to present themselves before the Lord, and Satan came along with them. (Job 1:6)

One day, the sons of God came to present themselves before the Lord, and Satan came along with them to present themselves before the Lord. (2:1)

In terms of the plot, nothing has happened between the parentheses, except a nice chat and an aborted attempt on Job's honor: the satan's plan has failed and things are back to square one. If indeed the satan's first experiment was even necessary is a question that seems a strong provocation to clever exegesis, since, upon appearance, it could have been skipped, with little lost in the bargain. See Meir Weiss, *The Story of Job's Beginnings: Job 1–2, a Literary Analysis* (Jerusalem: Magnes, 1983), 62.

zero—we are similarly provoked to ask why the chapters that make up Part One have been included. What else does the book of Jonah attempt to represent, beyond the prophetic goal of saving Nineveh? At the start of Part Two Jonah now knows that the previous option has been exhausted, that in reality something new is about to unfold. Before examining the progress of this awareness, it is worth sketching out ways in which such a binary and symmetrical organization—especially as reinforced by the *inclusio*—can help us conceptualize how meaning is structured in Jonah.

The Two/Four Settings

Critics have interpreted these two equal parts to the book of Jonah in a variety of ways: as complementary, as parallel or mirror-like, and as contrastive.[32] For the moment, let us take note of several ways in which such a partition distributes meaning and suggests interpretations:

a) Each part sponsors its own mode of what we might call dialogic behavior, distinct but parallel, as it were:

Part One: Jonah goes down into a boat, God takes him into a fish;

Part Two: Jonah goes into a *succah*,[33] God lures him under the *kikayon*.

b) Each part presents its own Group of Gentiles. The focus, in traditional discussions, is on the Ninevites (chapter 3), with the sailors (chapter 1) playing at best second fiddle, providing a kind of weak parallel or anticipation. The balancing of parts, however, suggests that the sailors play a

---

[32] There is a considerable body of critical writing on this mirror effect, most of it belaboring the symmetries between the parts. Whereas Sasson (*Jonah*, 16) considers the listing of such parallels as superficial, the opposite extreme (e.g., Trible, *Rhetorical Criticism*, 109–17), through excessive multiplication, actually has the effect of reducing both parts to a single one. We shall later have more to say about how the two parts of Jonah mirror one another.

[33] Heb. *sukkah*, hereafter using the Eng. succah.

more central function, as we shall see in our examination of chapter 1.

c) Each part focuses on alternate psychological motivations and presents distinct episodes in Jonah's relationship with God. In Part One the focus is on Jonah's reasons (or lack thereof); in Part Two the focus is on God's motivations. Stated differently, in Part One God saves Jonah for his sake, in response to his prayer; in Part Two, God saves Jonah for His own sake as a Creator or, alternatively, as a Lover.

d) There is a studied, parallel alternation between the social and the highly personal. Thus each part opens (chapters 1, 3) with a stress on Jonah's service to and/or relations with other people. These are then followed (chapters 2, 4) by scenes in which only God and Jonah are the interlocutors. Here each chapter opens with a personal prayer and expands from highly personal communication with God (through the fish and the *kikayon*) to highly abstract theological matters relating to creation and divine mercy.

e) Finally, each part—quite independent of the prophetic plot but crucial to the meaning—has its own distinctive setting. The alternate geographical settings of Parts One and Two have been characterized as the sea and Nineveh.[34] More accurate would be Jonah's own focus, for when the prophet first opens his mouth, it is to acknowledge his allegiance to the Lord "who made *the sea* and *the dry land*" (1:9; emphasis added). This declaration also has structural import, since it forecasts in a very precise way what will prove to be both the geographical and symbolic environment of the entire book:

Part One: the sea;

Part Two: the dry land.

A second and finer distinction can also be made. Just as the dry land has two aspects, each occupying its own chapter, the sea

---

[34] E.g., Sasson, *Jonah*, 16.

setting also moves from the boat to the deep. We thus have, to use a Rabbinic expression, a situation of "two that are four":

> Two symbolic settings: The sea and the dry land;
>
> Two variants of each:
>
>> the sea: the boat (chapter 1) and the deep (chapter 2);
>>
>> the dry land: Nineveh (chapter 3) and the desert (chapter 4).

This carefully elaborated structure has major implications for the understanding of the concluding chapter 4, as we shall see.[35]

This study, following the structure of Jonah, is divided into two sections that mirror one another to some extent. The first (chapters 1 to 4: The Ocean Experience and The Dry-Land Experiments) follows the order of the four chapters of Jonah, attempting to identify and elucidate the main issues of each. The second section (chapters 5 to 8) returns to these materials in roughly the same order, attempting to extend the literary discussion in more theological directions. The final chapters project the generic and pedagogical possibilities of viewing Jonah as a pastoral or, alternatively, a tale of the fantastic.

Let us, in concluding these observations on the structural parallelism of parts and settings, mention a final nuance that will come up later for discussion. Like Job and Faust, the book of Jonah also has a Prologue in Heaven, albeit only a trace. If Jonah's two settings are to be seen as contrastive,[36] these may be less so to one another than to Jonah's point of departure and ultimate destination: the place of the Lord's Presence, since for the prophet both Tarshish and Nineveh are places of exile. Before proceeding to these important nuances, however, we must focus on how the particular setting of each literary part—the sea in the first case, the dry land in the second—creates its own distinct symbolic environment. Let us then proceed to the first of these.

---

[35] See below, "The Structure of Jonah 4," in chapter 8.

[36] Sasson, *Jonah*, 16. See also Harold Fisch, *A Remembered Future: A Study in Literary Mythology* (Bloomington: Indiana University Press, 1984), 133.

PART ONE

THE OCEAN EXPERIENCE
Jonah 1–2

. . . Who made the sea . . .

(Jonah 1:9)

If I am not for myself, who is for me?

(Mishnah *Abot* 1:14)

The creature that swallows and then vomits Jonah has excited the imagination of countless generations and is most certainly one key to the book's universal appeal. The very generality or generic nature of its presentation—simply a "great fish"—has empowered readers to imagine a whale or even the leviathan, and those who prefer an allegorical reading have also had ample room. Common to all readings is an awareness of the fish's awesome power, as precisely that creature who can range across all vertical dimensions of that great flux/void of our consciousness, rising to the surface and plumbing the depths beyond which lies unconsciousness and a death that may also be a rebirth. For the great fish has the power both to kill and give life, thus a worthy messenger of the Supreme Being who has similar powers (1 Sam 2:6).

It is worthy of note that the "great fish" is mentioned four times by the narrator but not at all by Jonah. What does have a powerful hold on Jonah's attention throughout Part One is rather the fish's medium, the mighty sea and its waters:[1]

---

[1] The Targum unfailingly renders Tarshish, Jonah's supposed destination, simply as "the sea," thus suggesting that its particular identity is of less import

*The Lord God of the heavens I fear, who made the sea and the
dry land. (1:9)*

*Pick me up and throw me into the sea so that the sea will be
quieted for you. (1:12)*

*And You cast me out into the depths,
into the very heart of the sea:
The current enfolded me;
All Your breakers and Your waves
passed me over. (2:4)*

*The waters choked me to my very life,
Tehom enfolded me.
Seaweeds closed upon my head.
To the base of the mountains I descended,
the underworld. . . . (vv. 6–7)*

*If it is true that we are dust and there shall return, this re-
gards only the physical body, for in terms of our biological life and
perhaps our consciousness as well, our myths would have us arise
from water. In the Genesis account (1:2), the earth itself is originally in flux, enclosed or engulfed, as it were, by both Tehom (the
cosmic deep) and the waters. Beyond his personal demise, Jonah's
engulfment seems to undo the very act of creation. For Daniel Lys'
beautiful reading of Cant 8:7[2] can also be applied to Jonah's plunge:
"C'est plus qu'une simple mort, c'est l'engloutissement dans le Chaos
originel."[3] Let us, with Jonah, traverse this watery space and try to
describe its project.*

---

than its symbolic value. Put differently, is Tarshish Jonah's real destination or
rather, as we think, a negative one, any place away from the "Temple of Your
Holiness" (2:8)? On the Targum of Jonah, see Eytan Levine, *The Aramaic Version
of Jonah* (Jerusalem: Jerusalem Academic Press, 1978), 57.

[2] 8:7: Many waters cannot quench love / Nor can rivers sweep it away
(Daniel Lys, *Le Plus beau chant de la création: Commentaire du Cantique des
Cantiques* [Paris: Cerf, 1968], 291).

[3] "It is more than a simple death, it is the engulfing in the original Chaos."

CHAPTER ONE

Going Down Under: Jonah 1

> Rabbi Nathan says: "Jonah went to the
> sea only in order to commit suicide."
>
> Mekhilta of Rabbi Ishmael[1]
>
> There is only one truly serious philosophical
> question, and that is suicide.
>
> Albert Camus[2]
>
> He is a priest who has left the world to itself, truly.
>
> John L'Heureux, "Departures"[3]

Jonah's Suicide

Camus' dictum on suicide and the proper pursuit of philosophy is best conceived not as an all-or-nothing affair, a kind of
personal final solution, as it were, but rather as a question that
gnaws at us daily and requires constant attention. Do I like my
life; do I accept it as given? Why on earth am I here; by what cause
and to what purpose? With what level of wakeful attention am I
required to rivet myself to my existence as such?

---

[1] Tractate *Pisha*, 4. Similarly, Ibn Ezra on Jonah 1:12: "He desired and sought
to die."

[2] Albert Camus, *Le Mythe de Sisyphe* (Paris: Gallimard, 1942), 15.

[3] John L'Heureux, "Departures," in *The Vintage Book of Contemporary
American Short Stories* (ed. Tobias Wolff; New York: Vintage Books, 1994),
308–19.

Or to use Jonah's own words in the form of a question: Isn't my death better than my life (Jonah 4:3, 8)? Job, in an attempt to ground the question theologically and protect God, in fact may have had just the opposite effect, since his formulation sends the whole question upstairs, so to speak, by referring the problem to the Creator: why did God create us in the first place; and, by extension, why does God sustain us in being? Hardly embarrassed by such speculations, some midrashists even imagined previous creations that apparently weren't up to snuff and were consequently snuffed out (measure for measure?) by the Creator Himself.[4] Does ours merit the same fate? And, if so, maybe it is our privilege—even responsibility—to decline what is euphemistically called the gift of life, to withdraw and, at whatever level one deems appropriate, to "brown out" or "go dead" or even, literally, to die.

The question that plagued both Camus and the rabbis was also raised by key figures throughout Hebrew Scripture.[5]

Rebecca:

If such [is to be my suffering], why then do I exist? (Gen 25:22)

Moses:

But if not [i.e., if You will not forgive their sin], erase me from the book [of life] which You have written. (Exod 32:32)

Job:

Why is light given to him that is in misery,
and life to the bitter of soul? (Job 3:20; also Jer 20:14–18)

Elijah:

[Elijah] came to a broom bush and sat down under it, and prayed that he might die. "Enough," he cried. "Now, O LORD, take my life. . . ." (1 Kgs 19:4)

---

[4] George Foot Moore, *Judaism in the First Centuries of the Christian Era: The Age of Tannaim* (3 vols.; Cambridge, MA: Harvard University Press, 1966; repr. in 2 vols.; Peabody, MA: Hendrickson, 1997), 1.382.

[5] See especially David Daube, "Death as Release in the Bible," *NovT* 5 (1962): 82–104.

Such reactions to life's problems provide a compelling perspective for rereading Jonah, since the hero of this book, whatever his particular difficulties may be, wants out; he has had it with life; it is all just too much. Let us listen again to Jonah's theme song:

> Please, Lord, take my life from me, for my death is better than my life. (4:3)

> He requested from his soul to die, saying: "My death is better than my life." (v. 8)

> "I am distressed unto death." (v. 9)

One might speak only of a "swan song," positing that, since these explicit examples occur only in the final chapter, they may reflect less a permanent disposition than a change of attitude on Jonah's part. It is rather the case, however, that Jonah's suicidal wishes are fully operative from the very start.

Let us begin at the beginning, with Jonah's refusal to go to Nineveh at God's behest. Interpreted as a reluctance to prophesy, Jonah's refusal is not unique in the Hebrew Bible. What *is* unique is the peremptory nature of the rebuff, first in the absence of any argument or even reply whatever—a mutism stressed even further by the narrative's conniving delay of explanation until much later—and secondly in the seeming compliance followed by an abrupt about-face:

> God: *"Get up and go* to Nineveh!"
> *And Jonah got up* . . . and fled!

Although the reasons for his "wanting out" are unclear, the abruptness of his response points not only to a flight but also to what Uriel Simon has called a "rebellion."[6]

Jonah's flight is conveyed by the verb *yarad*, to "descend" or "go down," which, through insistent repetition, moves from being a mere geographical notation to a metaphoric suggestion of intent:

---

[6] Uriel Simon, *Jonah: The Traditional Hebrew Text with the New JPS Translation* (trans. Lenn J. Schramm; JPS Torah Commentary; Philadelphia: Jewish Publication Society, 1999), 3.

He *went down* to Joppa. (1:3)

He *went down* into it [the ship]. (v. 3)

When the sea storm, God's agent, starts to act up, Jonah descends even further into withdrawal:

Jonah *had gone down* into the hold[7] of the vessel. (v. 5)

As a further and fitting conclusion to Jonah's descent:

. . . he *lay down* and fell asleep. (v. 5)

The Hebrew for "fell asleep," *yeradam* (also v. 6), is a superb word-play or sound repetition of Jonah's successive descents (*yarad*), stressing "Jonah's flight from YHWH's presence as a descent into unconsciousness."[8] As Ackerman further observes, "our prophet is taking a path that leads to death as he seeks to avoid the road to Nineveh."

Jonah's "descent" has been frequently noticed by critics, but its full range and deep implications need to be grasped. In its intensity and pervasiveness, in its repetitive insistence that is literal as well as metaphorical, it means that Jonah *wants to die*, to be relieved of living, since he can no longer accept life on its present terms. No better proof of this than his own request to be thrown into the deep and thus disposed of:

[To the sailors:] "Pick me up and throw me overboard!" (1:12)

It should also be carefully noted that, had Jonah not wanted to die, he would instinctively have prayed, during the storm, to be saved. Even though requested to do so by the ship's captain, however (v. 6), his first uttered prayer occurs only from the belly of the fish (2:2).

---

[7] *yarktei-*, usually rendered "hold" (NJPS, NRSV), "the farthest end" (Simon, *Jonah*), "inner part" (RSV) or, even better, "innards," as Phyllis Trible, *Rhetorical Criticism: Context, Method, and the Book of Jonah* (Minneapolis: Fortress, 1994), 166. It is equated with "*She'ol*, the depths of the pit" in Isa 14:15 (see also Ezek 32:23). In Amos 6:10 the image seems to be that of solitary confinement in the house of the dead.

[8] James A. Ackerman, "Jonah," in *The Literary Guide to the Bible* (ed. Robert Alter and Frank Kermode; Cambridge, MA: Harvard University Press, 1987), 235.

Thus the death wish does not need to be "read back" into Part One, since it is pervasively there from the very start. But we are further invited to consider Jonah's extended prayer in chapter 2 as part and parcel of that wish, as required by the culmination of the ongoing wordplay that occurs in that very prayer:

> To the base of the mountains I descended [*yaradeti*],
> the underworld,
> its bars around me, forever. (2:7)

It is difficult to read this without recalling Jonah's death wish, which now comes almost as a fulfillment. He asks to be relieved of living and the sailors, albeit reluctantly, oblige (see below). God does not acquiesce quietly in His servant's demise, however, but rather calls his bluff, as if to say: "You want to 'go down'; well, I'll really take you down":

> Now the Lord appointed a large fish to swallow up Jonah. (2:1)

The complementary process is thus symbolized in our text by the successive agents of descent: it is Jonah who initiates the process, by going down to his sea-death, where he is assisted by the sailors. Now God goes one better by appointing the fish, which takes His prophet to the point at which death becomes palpable (v. 7). The surprise is that the great fish, besides being the agent of death, is also the means of rescue,[9] and *both* functions come from the Lord. The dual valence of this great fish points to the dual argumentative burden of Jonah's prayers, to which we shall turn in chapter 2 after considering a most interesting variant of the suicide question.

Assisted Suicide: Jonah and the Sailors

The details of Jonah's flight—what we have termed a suicide, if only symbolic—can be rehearsed in a few sentences. Jonah goes

---

[9] So George M. Landes, "The Kerygma of the Book of Jonah: The Contextual Interpretation of the Jonah Psalm," *Int* 21 (1967): 13: "the fish has essentially a salvatory function."

down to the seaport of Jaffa and takes a place on a ship; in fact, according to a close reading of "he paid *its* price" rather than *his* price, some even conclude that he bought up all remaining places so that he could leave right away.[10] A violent storm comes up and the lots point the guilty finger at Jonah, who declares that he is fleeing from God and suggests that the storm will subside if the sailors throw him overboard.[11] The sailors are reluctant and make valiant efforts to row to safety, all to no avail. Believing there to be no alternative, they throw him overboard. To make the standard moral reading even more obvious, the rabbis came up with the following scenario:

So they took up Jonah and cast him into the sea. (1:15)

First they threw him in up to his knees and the storm let up, but when they took him back on board the storm started up again. So they lowered him into the sea up to his navel and the storm again let up, but when they again took him on board the storm resumed. They then lowered him into the water up to his neck, and again the storm abated. As soon as Jonah was brought back on board, however, the storm resumed in all its fury. They then threw him completely into the deep. (*Pirkei de-Rabbi Eliezer*)[12]

The storm does abate—whether instantaneously, as such readings would favor, or at some later time. The sailors in great fright of the Lord offer sacrifices and make vows, and Jonah is swallowed up by a large fish.

---

[10] All citations in Jack M. Sasson, *Jonah: A New Translation with Introduction, Commentary, and Interpretation* (AB 42B; New York: Doubleday, 1990), 83. Alternatively, Jonah's motive, seldom imagined, could also be to reduce the number of lives about to be put at risk.

[11] According to the interpretation that Jonah bought up all the places on board, the sailors' plan to cast lots seems disingenuous at best, for on whom other than Jonah were the lots to fall? Surely not on the sailors themselves, who just returned *from* Tarshish (see below, "The Mediating Narrator" in chapter 10) unscathed.

[12] Quoted in M. Zlotowitz, *Jonah: A New Translation with a Commentary Anthologized from Midrashic and Rabbinic Sources* (Brooklyn: Mesorah, 1980), 103.

Of the number of interesting and tough questions to be put to this text, let us focus on the sailors' participation. Here, at least, there is universal agreement with the rabbis' attempt to exonerate. Let Jerome's assessment stand for all the rest:

> The sailors refused to spill blood, choosing rather to die. . . . The sea is in turmoil, the storm is overwhelming, and here they are forgetting their own danger and only think of saving another.

Citing this text, Sasson also finds proof on the sailors' part of a "demonstration of their humanity beyond normal expectations."[13]

To be sure, the narrative voice supports such an evaluation of the sailors, who are made to sound not only decent but like downright righteous chaps. At one point, in fact, their idiom sounds like God's very own: "Get up and call" (1:6), harking back to the divine call in 1:2. And, to be sure, the sailors throw Jonah overboard only with great hesitation and after trying alternative measures. But—and this is the important point—they do throw him overboard! And to argue that committing murder under duress is not really murder is a bit like the claim, cited by William James, that adultery is not only mitigated but removed when the baby is only a small one! At least under Jewish law, if someone tells me that I must kill him or he will kill me, I am allowed to kill that person. But if someone tells me to kill another or I might die, I am under no obligation. On the contrary, if I do kill that person under the guise of saving my own life, then I am guilty of murder.[14]

---

[13] Sasson, *Jonah*, 141. The sailors were not always so positively viewed however. As Yvonne Sherwood summarizes, "The sailors become variously the Apostles, steering the ship of the church (*and sleeping in Christ's hour of need*), or the Roman authorities who condemned Christ to death, or the Jews who opposed Christ, or Pontius Pilate, washing his hands of Jesus-Jonah's death." See her *A Biblical Text and Its Afterlives: The Survival of Jonah in Western Culture* (Cambridge: Cambridge University Press, 2000), 15; emphasis added.

[14] Scholars are wont to wax eloquent on this subject. James Limburg (*Jonah: A Commentary* [Louisville, KY: Westminster John Knox, 1993], 56) notes, quite gratuitously, that "the Israelites have had a history of taking innocent blood" and concludes that these non-Israelites are most concerned not to do such a thing. The critic has considered all pieces of evidence except the crucial one, since taking innocent life is precisely what the sailors do!

But why not state the matter in the sailors' own words of prayer:

Please, Lord, may we not perish because of this man's life.[15]
Do not put innocent blood upon our heads. (1:14)

Indeed, this is why the sailors are filled with such fear, because they know that it is not legitimate to take another's life to save one's own, and because they are indeed guilty of taking innocent blood.[16]

The very structure of the text brings subtle but firm confirmation of this point in the conclusion. Notice, first of all, that in their prayer the sailors express not one but two concerns:

Please, Lord,
may we not perish because of *this* man,
        and
may we not be guilty of shedding innocent blood (1:14).

Despite the tease of semantic parallelism here, which would collapse the two segments into a single meaning, the matters are quite distinct: may we not perish either because of his guilt or because of ours. In perfect consonance with this dual concern, the sailors, upon being saved, make two distinct acknowledgements to the Lord:

They offered sacrifice to the Lord
        and
they made vows. (v. 16)

Commentators typically conclude that both of these are but variant forms of thanksgiving, the one on the spot to be followed up, as per their vows, by others on land. And, to be sure, the form of sacrifice (*zebakh*) frequently refers either to peace offerings or offerings of thanksgiving. But another linguistic tradition points in a different direction. Here God is speaking to the budding prophet Samuel:

---

[15] Rashi makes clear the sailors' perception of their own guilt: "because of the sin of having laid a hand upon his soul," *nfsh*, meaning life, as in 2:6: "The waters choked me to my very *nfsh*" = life.

[16] The objection that Jonah himself confessed his guilt is no objection, since self-accusation is without value in criminal cases (see *b. Sanhedrin* 9b): perhaps the defendant is crazy or depressed.

I have sworn to the house of Eli that the iniquity of Eli's house will not be *expiated with sacrifice* [*zebakh*] or offerings forever. (1 Sam 3:14)

The sacrifice thus has a role distinct from the vows, since, beyond their thanks for being saved, the sailors still had to atone for taking innocent blood.[17]

Another question that has received scant attention is the form of Jonah's suicidal flight, his decision to take a sea voyage, for, surely, suicide does not need such contrivance. One must at least ask the simple question: if, beyond the hypothesis of his suicide, Jonah was so persuaded of his own guilt,[18] then why didn't he throw himself overboard, if not to take his own life, at least to save the crew? Why involve presumably innocent sailors? And, indeed, the success of such a procedure is not guaranteed. For, surely, the sailors are under no obligation to assist Jonah. To his command: "throw me overboard" they might—indeed should—have responded (especially if, as Jerome would have us believe, the sailors did in fact refuse to spill innocent blood): "throw *yourself* overboard!" Why does Jonah put the sailors into a situation of human sacrifice?[19] Or, for that matter, why does God?

The question of Jonah's mysterious motivations for flight/suicide—this time in involving the sailors—must again be postponed until a fuller picture is painted, but we may here outline the matter from the perspective of the book's discussion concerning the moral status of Gentiles. The matter is complicated by the fact that God Himself changes course at the end. At the start, God plans to destroy Nineveh because of their Sodom-and-Gomorrah-like

---

[17] When, later, Jonah also offers a similar sacrifice (*zebakh*, 2:10), it thus seems also possible to extend the sense beyond that of simple thanks and to include also the notion of atonement, in this case for having attempted suicide.

[18] As Jonah's prayers in chapter 2 make perfectly clear, Jonah does not have any sense of having sinned by running away; see below, "Jonah?" in chapter 7; "A Modern Fantastical Reading," in chapter 10.

[19] One interesting theory (see discussion in Kenneth Craig, *A Poetics of Jonah: Art in the Service of Ideology* [Columbia: University of South Carolina Press, 1993], 132–33) is that, knowing that the ship's troubles are due only to his rebellion, Jonah commands the sailors to throw him overboard out of compassion for their lives. However, to upgrade the sailors' status from innocent victims to murderers hardly qualifies as an act of compassion.

wickedness. After their repentance, however, He is willing to let them off the hook because they are not really wicked but like innocent children or animals. What matters to God, in the long run, is whether their evil deeds are corrected or not. But this remarkable aspect of the book—that God Himself can change His mind—will be convincing only to those who have read ahead to the end and who, moreover, think that God necessarily has the last and convincing word, which is far from the case in the book of Jonah, as we shall see. Earlier in the book, Jonah knows this tendency of God (4:1-2)—is it mercy or mere divine credulity?—and therefore tries to convince Him that the book's Gentiles are much worse[20] than He might come to think. The scenario could be sketched as follows:

> [God to Jonah:] "Go preach to Nineveh!"

> [Jonah to God:] "But the Gentiles are wicked, as You Yourself admit, and I can prove it. They would, for example, have no hesitation to take an innocent life to save their own."

> And Jonah went down to Jaffa and found a boat. . . .

In brief, in pursuing his (still unexplained) suicide, Jonah chooses to involve Gentile sailors in order to conduct an experiment for God's sake—a test, really.[21] And, as we have seen, God in fact loses the argument, since the sailors do commit murder or at least assist a suicide! God's only way out, at this point, is to resort to the fish trickery, as if to claim:

> See, they didn't actually commit murder since you are still alive!

God thus appears to save Jonah principally in order to protect His own reputation. But God also saves Jonah for more responsive and altruistic reasons as well, as the so-called Psalm of Jonah now brings to our attention.

---

[20] Or much better; see below, chapter 8.

[21] Alternatively, in asking to be thrown overboard, "Jonah offers his life to save the sailors." So Marvin A. Sweeney, *The Twelve Prophets* (2 vols.; Collegeville, MN: Liturgical, 2000), 323. This of course does not explain why Jonah had to involve the sailors in his suicide in the first place.

CHAPTER TWO

JONAH'S PRAYERS AND NEAR-DEATH EXPERIENCE: JONAH 2

We must beware when we pray, because all prayers are granted.

Emerson[1]

That which we have chosen is given to us, and that which
we have refused is, also and at the same time, granted us.

Isak Dinesen, *Babette's Feast*[2]

Both doors—to death and to life—can be opened only by prayer.

Uriel Simon[3]

The Issues

Critics have had difficulty with Jonah's "psalm" or "prayer" that
occupies virtually all of chapter 2, and although their objections

---

[1] More assertive than the current proverb but of the same cloth: "Be careful
of what you ask for because you may get it." Quoted in Robert D. Richardson,
Emerson: The Mind on Fire (Berkeley: University of California Press, 1995), 64.

[2] Quoted in Dennis Taylor, "The Need for a Religious Literary Criticism,"
RelArts (1996): 124–50.

[3] Uriel Simon, *Jonah: The Traditional Hebrew Text with the New JPS Trans-
lation* (trans. Lenn J. Schramm; JPS Torah Commentary; Philadelphia: Jewish
Publication Society, 1999), 15. The ambivalence to be studied in this chapter—
Jonah's descent into the great fish as representing *both* death and life—prevailed
in the early Christian understanding of the "sign of Jonah" found in Matt 12:40.
For further elaboration see Simon Chow, *The Sign of Jonah Reconsidered: A Study
of its Meaning in the Gospel Tradition* (ConBNT 27; Stockholm: Almqvist &
Wiksell International, 1995).

do not seem conclusive, a brief review of the major ones can provide a useful introduction to our discussion.[4]

To some, the prayer is seen as *extraneous to the plot*, a mere pious poetic distraction inserted rather artificially into a prose story.[5] But to decide that it is "incongruous" because it is not part of the plot would justify declaring the entire Part One extraneous (as well as chapter 4), since from the parallelism of Parts One and Two and the repetitive resumption of the opening statement we learned that the plot remains at degree zero halfway through the story. It would be naive to conclude, however, that in fact nothing has "happened." Quite the contrary, a return to square one means that Jonah's two "descents" or defections, let us call them—his refusal of God's mission and his desire to die—have been redirected and that, for reasons still to be explored, he is now ready to assume the burdens of prophecy. In other words, the focus of the book of Jonah is less on plot itself than on the emotional and legal encounters between God and His prophet, and until these are put into some kind of order, then the plot cannot properly even begin. For what has indeed happened between the two parts? What now leads God to expect that Jonah has had a change of heart and is now willing to assume the burdens of prophecy rather than simply to flee again? Only Jonah's prayer gives a clear, sequential account as to why Jonah can make it to chapter 3, thus giving both himself and the book a second chance.

Another critical issue of Jonah's prayer is the *formulaic nature* of the poetic speech, as evidenced by both style and numerous parallel passages from Psalms and elsewhere. Distinguished scholars such as Bickerman have wondered whether this prayer is in fact Jonah's and have declared it to be simply imported from liturgical sources and transplanted into this context because of the allusion to the fish.[6] In reply, although it is readily admitted

---

[4] For a comprehensive and interesting study of Jonah's "psalm," see Hermann Opgen-Rhein, *Jonapsalm und Jonabuch* (SBB 38; Stuttgart: Katholisches Bibelwerk, 1997).

[5] E.g., George M. Landes, "The Kerygma of the Book of Jonah: The Contextual Interpretation of the Jonah Psalm," *Int* 21 (1967): 3–31.

[6] Unable to deny that the prayer at least "sounds" pious (after all, it is just stuffed with quotes from other psalms), Steven Weitzman (*Song and Story*

that the impression of importation is made by the formulaic nature of the language, such borrowings do not obviate the need for *contextual* interpretation.[7] On the contrary, they require heightened attention to minor variations, since these are often the carriers of essential meanings. To impose modern criteria of originality upon traditional texts is anachronistic—one might as well level the same charge against icons or epics. Our attention should be focused less on originality than on organic relevance to the context of our present text.[8] The approach in this study, far from disregarding the psalm or wishing it away, locates it at the very center of Jonah's problematic dialogue with God, the one time that the reticent Jonah speaks his entire mind about his existential dilemma.

---

in Biblical Narrative: The History of a Literary Convention in Ancient Israel [Bloomington: Indiana University Press, 1997], 109–13) observes that it was the expected literary norm that salvation narratives sing about God. Arguing both sides of the coin, he posits that if the prayer was originally part of the work, the intent was to satirize Jonah's character by contrasting his (apparently pious) prayers with his later (supposed) recalcitrance. However, if the prayer was secondary, then, again, the tactic was to accommodate earlier narrative tastes, this time in order to gain acceptance in the emergent canon. Both attempts, Weitzman claims, are really parodies of earlier biblical narratives. If such is the case, however, then Jonah's spiritual quest is swallowed up in the belly of literary concerns, and his much touted hypocrisy is really but a cover for the writer's (or the interpolator's) own.

[7] See Landes' important corrective, "The Kerygma of the Book of Jonah," appropriately subtitled "The Contextual Interpretation of the Jonah Psalm." Judah Goldin's defense of the authenticity of the ethical wills genre in Hebrew literature is relevant to the context of prayer in Jonah as well: Although "all the moral testaments are a reaffirmation of what all moral writers and preachers have emphasized and defended in their treatises," each testament "becomes a unique statement. He may even knowingly say what others have said, but because *he* says it and wants to say it, and may say it with an accentuation of his own, his message is genuinely him." See his New Forward to *Hebrew Ethical Wills* (ed. Israel Abrahams; Philadelphia: Jewish Publication Society, 1976), 16–17. For a balanced appraisal in terms of traditional understandings, see also Leslie Allen, *The Books of Joel, Obadiah, Jonah, and Micah* (Grand Rapids: Eerdmans, 1976), 184: "That the author did not take liberties with the psalm shows his respect for the original composition and for conventional psalm language."

[8] Meir Weiss makes a similar observation with regards to the presence of Satan in the book of Job: "Even if it were to be proven that Satan is not an original part of the story, he is nonetheless an *integral* part of the story in its extant form." See his *The Story of Job's Beginnings: Job 1–2, a Literary Analysis* (Jerusalem: Magnes, 1983), 34.

A third problem is that of *verb tenses* in Jonah's prayer, which to one major critic constitute a "smorgasbord" of confusion.[9] It seems to us, rather, that careful analysis here will help uncover the finely layered character of Jonah's prayers (in the plural).

The fourth and perhaps central issue concerns the nature of Jonah's invocation, in particular whether it is a *prayer of petition or of thanksgiving.*[10] Critics have pointed to the prayer's possibly ambivalent nature, alternating between the petition suggested by 2:2, 3, on the one hand, and thanksgiving, as projected by the "voice of thanksgiving" and the vows in v. 10, on the other. We are thus invited to decide whether *yitpalel* (v. 2) refers only to prayers of petition, as it does later in our own text (4:1), or whether it has the more general meaning of thanksgiving, as in Hannah's prayer in 1 Sam 2:1. One could plausibly opt for the latter, for, to put the matter squarely, what did Jonah have to ask for? Surely not his life, since he had already given it up, not only by his exit from the land and escape from his divine mission, but also in his declaration to the sailors: "Throw me into the sea!" However, if we decide that Jonah's prayer is one of thanksgiving, then we conclude that he thanks God for being saved from a death that he himself desired!

Postulating the prayer as one of petition, however, we should try to settle on what exactly that petition is. What is most difficult for the supplication theory is that, with the unlikely exception of Jonah 2:3, the "prayer" has no language of request; indeed it is entirely a detailed *narrative* of a near-death experience. The very abundance of detail, especially in the description of Jonah's descent, points rather in the direction of thanksgiving, but would one give thanks for being lowered into the underworld?! The answer is yes, if that voyage is in response to a request.

It thus appears that the paradox inherent in each approach argues the insufficiency of an either/or solution.[11] Critics who

---

[9] Jack M. Sasson, *Jonah: A New Translation with Introduction, Commentary, and Interpretation* (AB 42B; New York: Doubleday, 1990), 170, n. 10.

[10] It should be carefully noted that this formulation misses what Simon (*Jonah*, 15) calls "the main point," which is "an entreaty to be forgiven for his flight and a promise to repent and undertake his mission to Nineveh." For an explanation of this crucial omission, see below, "Jonah?" in chapter 7.

[11] Even though other such prayers exist in Scripture. See Ps 9, which is both a psalm of thanks and petition for the future, and Ps 118:21–25; see Amos Ha-

sense the problem seem to hedge at this point, perhaps because they cling to the notion of a single prayer. We thus end up with equivocations such as the claim that it is a "psalm of thanksgiving for deliverance from drowning, which purports to be the prayer for deliverance uttered by Jonah when in the belly of the fish."[12] Such hedging is in fact a valuable hint as to what actually happens, since, to be sure, both are conceivable: Jonah asks to be saved and then says thanks. This would suggest, however, that there is more than one prayer, as a few critics have proposed.[13] But if Jonah did pray for his life, what happened that made him change his mind and refuse suicide? And wasn't that suicide, so ardently pursued, itself the object of prayer? That would add yet another prayer. Let's see how many of these can be located in this multilayered and sophisticated text.

The Preamble (2:1-2)

The text of Jonah's praying is preceded by a brief introduction whose two verses seem to consist of two distinct parts and purposes:

> Now the Lord appointed a large fish to swallow up Jonah. And Jonah was in the loins of the fish for three days and three nights. And Jonah prayed to the Lord his God from the loins of the fish. (2:1-2)

Now if, as some have argued, the prayer is not an organic part of the book, then the first verse would immediately be followed by v. 11, which resumes the action of restoring Jonah to the main plot, his mission to Nineveh:

---

cham, *Commentary to the Book of Psalms* [Hebrew] (2 vols.; Jerusalem: Mossad Harav Kook, n.d.), 1.40. Further examples include Hannah's prayer in 1 Sam 2:1-10; Ps 90; Hab 3.

[12] R. B. Y. Scott, "The Sign of Jonah," *Int* 19 (1965): 21.

[13] Landes ("The Kerygma," 15), for example, concludes as follows: "In the sequence of events following the prophet's ejection from the ship, we are also to understand that he prays, not just once, but twice. The text of the first prayer is not given, but it is explicitly referred to in vv. 2 and 7 of the psalm."

Now the Lord appointed a large fish to swallow up Jonah. And Jonah was in the loins of the fish for three days and three nights. Then God spoke to the fish, and he vomited Jonah upon dry land.

The problem with this tidy solution, of course, is that motivations— the main puzzles of the entire book—remain unexplained. For if God wants Jonah to resume his mission, why drag the matter out for three whole days and nights? And if Jonah refused his mission the first time around, would the double violence of being swallowed alive and then vomited out be seen as inducements?

So, as we are told by what we will later call a "mediating narrator,"[14] Jonah prayed, and this praying forms the sole transition to the suspended plot. The deceptive simplicity of this brief text actually projects those ambiguities that characterize Jonah's descent as worthy of that Being who both "kills and gives life" (1 Sam 2:6). For, when read together as forming a single unit, these two verses, as a good preamble should, forecast the main tensions of the prayers that follow. Stylistically, two figures carry this burden: repetition and ambivalence, both of which project the ambiguity of Jonah's situation.

The figure of "descent" or flight or escape studied above—of "leaving the world truly to itself"—is reinforced by another set of images, those of enclosure. These began with the sanctuary of the ship, especially its "belly," and progress to the belly of the big fish. Or perhaps, fishes, since the word occurs no less than three times in these two verses, once in the female gender. The rabbis explored this repetition in the form of a midrash:

> It was a male fish, and since its insides were quite spacious Jonah gave no thought to prayer. The Holy One Blessed-be-He gestured to the fish to vomit him into the mouth of a female fish which was heavily pregnant. Jonah was then uncomfortable and prayed. As it is said: "And Jonah prayed . . . from the loins of the fish" (*ha-dagah*, female gender, 2:2). (Rashi, citing the Midrash)[15]

---

[14] See below, "The Mediating Narrator," in chapter 10.

[15] This reading seems to take the preposition *min*, "from," as causative: "He prayed . . . *because of* [the narrowness of] the fish's loins." This causative

Whatever one thinks of the exegetical value of this midrash—it does, after all, provide at least some explanation for the variable gender of the fish—one can appreciate its sensitivity to Jonah's ambivalent or rather changing attitude towards his enclosures: from a desired security and protective shelter to growing isolation and suffocation.

The dual or reversable nature of Jonah's situation is also projected in the divine names. Whereas it is the Beneficent Lord (the tetragammaton) who first sends the huge fish, the vomiting is stated to come from the Lord-God (Yahweh-Elohim), the Beneficent One who is also Jonah's Judge.[16] To attribute the destructive swallowing to divine beneficence might seem ironic, until we understand that this reflects Jonah's suicidal perspective. However, beyond mediating Jonah's own point of view, the narrator also gives his own: this beneficence is also a negative judgment on the character (the Lord *his* Judge), one that Jonah will come to accept later in the praying when he acknowledges the "Lord *my* God" (2:7).

To carry out this double purpose, the fish (singular or plural) is/are endowed with opposing valences. Thus the swallowing—typically viewed only in its negative connotation—also occurs in a purely neutral context in the Hebrew Bible.[17] And the "loins" to which Jonah descends have, in addition to the negative reference to ingestion, the positive sense of procreation.[18] And, even more positively, "loins" in Scripture are also the locus of both tender parental feeling and erotic love:

> [God:] Is Ephraim My precious son? . . . My loins are moved towards him; I will surely have mercy on him. (Jer 31:19)

> My beloved put his hand by the latch of the door, and my loins are moved towards him. (Cant 5:4)

---

sense of the preposition seems preferable in the following verse as well, as Simon thinks, quoting Radak: "I called out *because of* my distress"; see below, n. 30. For an alternative midrashic reading, see below, Excursus 4: "Male and Female Fish."

[16] See the summary in James Limburg, *Jonah: A Commentary* (Louisville, KY: Westminster John Knox, 1993), 60, 45–46.

[17] See Simon, *Jonah*, 18; citing Isa 28:4.

[18] Sasson, *Jonah*, 152.

Since the loins are twice referred to in this preamble, it is possible that, like the duplicate divine names and fish, the repetition refers alternately to both aspects of Jonah's descent, the destructive and the salvational.

The Text of the Psalm

Here is the text of what is known as the Psalm or Canticle of Jonah. I translate according to the interpretation that follows, highlighting the verbs that express crucial points of transition and dividing the text into its several components:

Introductory Summation, or Table of Contents:

> ³I called out of my distress to the Lord,
> *and He responded to me*
> (From the belly of *She'ol* I cried out;
> You heard my voice).

The Final Descent to Death:

> ⁴*And You cast me out* into the depths,
> into the very heart of the sea:
> The current enfolded me;
> All Your breakers and Your waves
> passed over me.
> ⁵But as for me, though I had thought
> to be driven from Your Presence,
> Yet I continue to gaze
> towards the Temple of Your Holiness.
> ⁶The waters choked me to my very life,[19]
> Tehom enfolded me.
> Seaweeds closed upon my head.
> ⁷To the base of the mountains I descended,
> the underworld,
> its bars around me, forever.

---

[19] *nefesh*, literally "soul"; "neck" is also possible, as in the *Pirkei de-Rabbi Eliezer* quoted above, "Assisted Suicide," in chapter 1.

The Salvation from Death:

> *And You raised up* my life from destruction,
> O Lord my God.
> [8]As my life-force closed upon me,
> I remembered the Lord,
> and my prayer reached you,
> to the Temple of Your holiness.

The Moral and Thanksgiving:

> [9]Those who care for empty vanities
> Forsake their love.
> [10]But as for me, with a voice of thanksgiving
> I shall sacrifice unto You:
> What I vowed I shall pay.
>> Salvation is the Lord's.

> [11]And God spoke to the fish, and he vomited Jonah upon dry land. (Jonah 2:3–11; emphasis added)

The Table of Contents (2:3)

Let us access this narrative poem through an apparent textual difficulty. The opening verse gives us a carefully crafted outline of the prayer's topic or, rather, topics of the prayers:

> I called out of my distress to the Lord,
> and He responded to me
>> (From the belly of *She'ol* I cried out;
> You heard my voice). (2:3)

It has been noted that the logical order is inverted here, since one cannot expect God to "respond" until He has first "heard" my voice.[20] An even greater difficulty is the nature of God's response to the prayer:

---

[20]Sasson, *Jonah*, 1990, 168. See Ps 4:2: "Have mercy on me and hear my prayer," which may also mean simply: "Have mercy by hearing my prayer."

... He responded to me. . . .
You heard my voice,
and You cast me out into the depths. (vv. 3–4)

Is this how God responds to prayer?[21] Well, it depends on what
exactly the prayer was for in the first place. However, if this verse
is read as a complaint or a lament rather than a petition, then the
difficulty is compounded even further, since after all it was Jonah
who sought death and it was only on his own insistent request that
the sailors (not God) cast him into the sea!

These objections fall, however, when we look beyond a possible parallelism that collapses the two halves of v. 3—widely regarded as an "introduction to the whole poem"[22]—into a single
meaning, for denying such a parallelism enables us to see the
verse as describing not one but *two* levels of experience and *two*
corresponding prayers:

a) a great state of anguish, relieved or "answered" in response
   to an indirect petition "to the Lord" (in the third person);

b) death or, as the current phrase has it, a near-death experience, here represented by the belly of *She'ol*. That this
   latter experience is *near*-death rather than complete death
   is shown by Jonah's ability still to cry out; that it is death
   nevertheless is indicated not only by the figure of *She'ol*
   but also by his failure to direct his outcry (contrast: "to the
   Lord" in the first part of the verse). This generalized and
   visceral scream far exceeds the previous anguish of "calling
   out" in prayer; it is a more elemental or primal shriek that
   finds its fulfillment only in "salvation," as the rich parono-

---

[21] The difficulty can of course be obviated—or disregarded—by deleting the
waw-connective "*and* You cast me," as e.g., F. M. Cross, "Studies in the Structure of Hebrew Verse: The Prosody of the Psalm of Jonah," in *The Quest for the
Kingdom of God: Studies in Honor of George E. Mendenhall* (ed. H. B. Huffman,
F. A. Spina, and A. R. N. Green; Winona Lake, IN: Eisenbrauns, 1983), 161; Landes, "The Kerygma"; Simon, *Jonah*. However, this deletion conceals the causal
sequence that establishes God's response as the casting out itself.

[22] Jerome T. Walsh, "Jonah 2, 3–10: A Rhetorical Critical Study," *Biblica* 63
(1982): 225. Similarly, Limburg (*Jonah*, 66) senses that this verse "is a *brief summary* of the story told in the psalm," although his sense of the psalm's contents
is quite different.

masia and verbal echo of 2:3, 10 (*shiwa'ti / yeshu'atah*) will make perfectly clear.[23]

The verb tenses of the topic-verses (2:3, 4, 7, 8) support this analysis. The four *waw*-conversive imperfects (highlighted in our text) not only signal "either a major shift in Jonah's fortunes or an important change in action sequence";[24] they are in fact the key to the overall structure and four-part thematic development: God responded to his initial petition (to die) first by casting him out, then raising him up as Jonah's (second) prayer (for rescue) reached him. Since Jonah is narrating a past event, he begins in the perfect tense "I called out" (*qara'ti*) and then makes a normal switch to the imperfect or *waw*-conversive in order to continue the narration of successive past actions or events: "and He responded to me" (*wayya'aneni*). Since this is indeed a topic-verse, however, and before continuing the past narration, Jonah parenthetically reverts to the perfect tense in order to state the topic of his second prayer: "From the belly of *She'ol* I cried out, and You heard my voice." He then returns to his narrative of successive past events by describing God's answer to his first prayer: "and you cast me out . . ." [*watashlikeni*]. Thus the sequence of action is as follows:

Prayer one and God's response. Jonah asks God to die and is taken all the way down:

> I called out of my distress to the Lord,
> and He responded to me . . .
> And you cast me out into the depths, . . .
> the underworld,
> its bars around me forever. (2:3a, 4, 6, 7a)

Prayer two and God's salvation. Jonah, having changed his mind, screams for life and God "hears":

> From the belly of *She'ol* I cried out;
> You heard my voice. . . .
> And You raised up my life from destruction,
> O Lord my God.

---

[23] *Shw'* means "to utter a series of successive screams," *HALOT*, 1443.
[24] Sasson, *Jonah*, 170.

As my life-force closed upon me,
I remembered the Lord,
and my prayer reached you,
to the Temple of Your holiness. (2:3b, 7b, 8)

This helps us understand that Jonah's first of two prayers is but a piece with his suicide or ongoing wish to die. In his "trouble" with this life or with God or whatever, he asks to be relieved of living and God obliges by casting him further into the depths into which he had already asked the sailors to lower him. God calls his bluff (his supposed death wish) and takes him down to the very depths of nonexistence, here described as the "base of the mountains" (2:7), that point diametrically antithetical to the place where the psalmist (Ps 121:1) would look for divine help. But is it conceivable that Jonah actually prayed to die? Well, he did later:

And he prayed to the Lord . . . "Please, Lord, take my life." (4:2–3)

Let us now examine each prayer more closely.

Jonah's First Prayer: "Lord, Take My Life!" (2:3a–4, 6–7a)

A woodcutter, clad only with leafage,
Under the weight of wood as well as of years,
Trembling and bowed, walked along with heavy steps,
Trying to reach his smoke-filled cottage.
Finally, exhausted with effort and pain,
He puts down his wood and reflects upon his misery:
What enjoyment has he had since he has been in this world?
Is there anyone poorer on this round earth?
No bread at times and never any rest;
His wife, his children, soldiers, taxes,
The creditor, and forced labor
Make him the perfect model of a miserable man.
He calls upon Death. She comes without delay
And asks him what he would like.
"Well," said he, "I need help
Reloading this wood; please be quick about it."
Death cures all things;

But let's not budge from where we are.
better suffer than die,
That's the motto for humans.[25]

One intriguing stylistic feature in La Fontaine's treatment of what might be called a near-death experience is the plethora of details, on the one hand, and a complete reticence, on the other. In the first instance, the woodcutter's final decision to die is dramatized by the enumeration of specific items until the dam bursts, so to speak, and Death is beckoned. On the other hand, however, the woodcutter hedges completely on his motivation. Why in fact does he change his mind about dying? Is it the somewhat philosophical conclusion of the last lines, according to which things could always be worse and that it is thus better to stay where we are? Or is it rather, as it seems to us, the sheer terror of the face of Death as, say, Ingmar Bergman might portray it?

The parallels between La Fontaine's brief but intense allegorical drama and the first two chapters of the book of Jonah seem tempting. Both protagonists, because of their misery, "want to die." When confronted by the awe-full reality of death, however, each changes his mind. The main difference between the tales is also telling. Whereas the woodcutter's reasons for wanting death are clearly spelled out, Jonah's misery remains a mystery to be investigated.[26]

The parallel with La Fontaine also helps us understand the transition from prayer one to two. Previously, we noted that the prayer has very little petition or thanksgiving in it and is almost entirely a detailed narrative of a near-death experience. Notice the abundance of detail, especially in the description of Jonah's

---

[25] Jean de La Fontaine, "Death and the Woodcutter," *Fables choisies* (Mont-Royal, Québec: Modulo-Griffon, 2004), emphasis added.

[26] In his study of Jonah's psalm, Jerome Walsh gives an important clue: "His physical separation from Yahveh is a sign of the more poignant distress of apparently unwarranted moral separation. The focus of attention is backwards, towards Yahveh, and the psalmist's tragedy is abandonment." See his "Jonah 2, 3–10: A Rhetorical Critical Study," *Biblica* 63 (1982): 227. I would merely read "erotic" instead of "moral." For an account of the kind of misery involved here, see below, "Erotic Clues and Vocabulary," in chapter 5.

descent. Indeed, one cannot avoid the dramatic detailing of every step of the way down to death's very threshold, parallel to La Fontaine's itemized account of each specific cause of his pain. One could hardly find a more careful account of each successive stage of a near-death experience, of the progressive approach to that point of oblivion that appears final:

> I called out of my distress to the Lord,
> and He responded to me.
> And You cast me out into the depths,
> into the very heart of the sea:
> the current enfolded me;
> All Your breakers and Your waves
> passed me over. . . .
> The waters choked me to my very life,
> Tehom enfolded me.
> Seaweeds closed upon my head.
> To the bottom of the mountains I descended,
> the underworld,
> its bars around me, forever. (Jonah 2:3b–7)

With the exception of v. 5, which parenthetically addresses the state of Jonah's relationship with God, these three verses narrate a sequential or consecutive descent of three stages into the underworld;[27] or, put in less mythological terms, Jonah describes the ebbing of his consciousness, through drowning, into blackout. Analytically, the structure is as follows:

v. 4a: a general description of the process

v. 4b: Jonah sinks below the sea's surface

v. 6: Jonah sinks through Tehom, all the way to the bottom

v. 7: Jonah enters the underworld, or loss of consciousness

The abundance of detail allows a very close look not only at the physical actuality but also, mainly through wordplay and tone, at Jonah's emotional reactions and state.

---

[27] Jonathan Magonet, *Form and Meaning: Studies in Literary Techniques in the Book of Jonah* (Sheffield: Almond, 1983), 40.

Broadly put, Jonah's long descent marks his transition from the acceptance, even the desire for death, to a confrontation with its harsh reality. This means that God's initial action is *in response to* Jonah's prayerful request. And Jonah's descent into the fish, at least during the three days and nights, is received not as a punishment or even a torment but rather as a desired and comforting response to a pleading "come, sweet death!"—until the point at which Jonah, like La Fontaine's woodcutter, has a change of heart, when, according to the Midrash, he entered the second or pregnant fish.[28] Thus the stages of *yeridah*, or "descent"—into the ship and into the depths—plot a plunge from pure *comfort* to complete *torment*, and what is at first received with pleasure takes on darker overtones as the narrative advances. Let Ginzberg's compilation of the various midrashim state the initial phase:

> At the creation of the world, God made a fish intended to harbor Jonah. He was so large that the prophet was as comfortable inside of him as in a spacious synagogue. . . . Three days Jonah had spent in the belly of the fish, and he still felt so comfortable that he did not think of imploring God to change his condition.[29]

As the reality of death approaches, the literary figures, especially of descent and enclosure, take on a growing ambivalence. Stylistically, v. 3 is an important example of two larger tendencies in Jonah's prayer: intertextual borrowing and wordplay.

a) It shares the same opening words with Ps 120:1:

To the Lord in my distress I called
And He responded to me.

I called out of my distress to the Lord
And He responded to me. (Jonah 2:3)[30]

---

[28] See below, Excursus 4: "Male and Female Fish"; also above, n. 15.

[29] Louis Ginzberg, *The Legends of the Jews* (6 vols.; Philadelphia: Jewish Publication Society, 1968), 4:249.

[30] "*Out of* my distress" probably means "because of" here, as it does in the preceding verse (see above, n. 15). This marks a subtle difference with Ps 120:1, which uses the preposition *b*-, "in my distress," meaning either "*at the time of my distress*" or "*in the situation of.*" For other causal uses of min, *HALOT*, 675 lists Job 14:9; 7:14; Ezek 28:18.

Assuming the precedence of Ps 120, the inversion is particularly significant. Whereas in the psalm the focus of the prayer is on God and not, for example, on flesh and blood,[31] the Jonah text, by contrast, highlights the self-absorption of a suicidal state of mind.

b) "And He responded to me." Read also: "and he afflicted me."[32] This means that God sent him the comforting escape of the fish, but this refuge gradually became more painful; thus, combining the two, "He responded by afflicting me."

Further wordplay disrupts what has become our usual reading, preventing a rush to negativity. For example:

All Your breakers and Your waves
passed over me. (2:4)

When compared to the probable source, however, what appears as a complaint is actually a sigh of relief and quite possibly even an expression of trust and thanksgiving, as can be seen in the only exact duplicate to this expression in the Bible:

All Your breakers and Your waves
passed me over (i.e., passed me by). (Ps 42:8)

Again:

Seaweeds [*suf*] closed upon my head.[33] (Jonah 2:6)

Jonah's growing sense of unease is modified by an opposite valence:

The reeds comforted my head.[34] (v. 6)

Magonet finds the "downward direction" of these verses emphasized by the repetition of the verb *yesobebeni*, "to turn about, or

---

[31] Hacham, *Commentary*, 2:439.

[32] Duane L. Christensen, "The Song of Jonah: A Metrical Analysis, *JBL* 104 (1985): 229.

[33] One could imagine a midrashic reading of this verse on the basis of Qoh 3:11: *mero'sh ve'ad sof*, "from beginning to end." The meaning would be: "My end enclosed my beginning," meaning "I died."

[34] See the second definition of *hbsh* given in BDB, 290; also see Hos 6:1; Isa 61:1.

surround," first with reference to the *nahar* or "surface currents" (v. 4),[35] and then to the *tehom*, or deep (v. 6).[36] However, the resonances of this word are also ambivalent, for in addition to a gradual and choking closure there is a clinging sense of protective enclosure as well:

> He [God] found him in a desert region,
> In an empty howling waste.
> He engirded him [*yesobebenhu*], watched over him,
> Guarded him as the pupil of His eye. (Deut 32:10, NJPS)[37]

The verses of Jonah's first prayer are thus, in addition to being a prayer to die, also a narrative account of Jonah's near-death experience at God's hand. They are included, especially in such detail, because they record both a divine response to a petition and also Jonah's reaction to that response. They can thus also be conceived as part of a prayer of thanksgiving, even though, as the sequel shows, the gratitude is ironic—ironic from the reader's point of view but dead serious in Jonah's eyes—since Jonah ends up thanking God for *not* answering his prayer to die.

If we are willing to depart from ingrained readings, it is even possible to recover the text of Jonah's earlier prayer from his later one:

> Now Jonah prayed to the Lord and said: "Please, Lord, wasn't this my word while still in my land:
>
> [this is why (*'al ken*) I hastened to flee to Tarshish: because (*ki*) I knew that You are a compassionate and gracious God, slow to anger and abounding in kindness and repenting of evil].[38]
>
> 'Now, Lord, please take my life'?" (4:2–3)

---

[35] Conspicuously absent from Jonah's descent both into the fish and especially the underworld is its traditional darkness. One wonders whether these "surface currents," or *nahar*, do not also cast light, suggested by overtones of the Aramaic *nahara*, "light" (see Job 3:4).

[36] Magonet, "Form and Meaning," 40.

[37] See Ps 34:8, based on the same verbal root.

[38] The self-contained nature of this self-quotation is further stressed by the coordinated structure of causality *ki* / *'al ken*; see T. A. Perry, "The Coordination of *KY* / *'L KN* in Cant. 1:1–3 and Related Texts," *VT* 55 (2005): 528–41.

As Simon has pointed out, the long justification for his flight ("this is why . . . repenting of evil") is purely parenthetical to his present prayer,[39] which itself is stated to be a repetition (and thus a quotation) of his earlier prayer or "word while I was still in my land": "Now, Lord, 'please take my life.'" That is to say, Jonah in 4:2–3 is referring, through quotation, to his earlier prayer to die.

Jonah's Second Prayer: "Help!" (2:3b, 7b, 8)

Jonah *cries out* and God saves him:

"From the belly of *She'ol* I cried out;
You heard my voice. . . .
And You raised up my life from destruction,
O Lord my God.
As my life-force closed upon me,
I remembered the Lord,
and my prayer reached you,
to the Temple of Your holiness." (vv. 3b, 7b, 8)

The precise point at which Jonah notes his rescue is at the moment of the eternal closing of the gates:

Its bars [*berikhehah*] around me forever. (2:7a)

At the very moment of passing beyond, his exclusion from this world is finalized by the earth's "bars," an unusual word (the gates of the earth? the gates of *She'ol*?),[40] but one that evokes the very beginning of his rebellion, described as a fleeing [*libroakh*] (1:3). The point of this rather refined, even exquisite pun is to evoke the principle of measure for measure, something like: "I bolted [forth], I was bolted [in]."

The theme of the second prayer, that of salvation from extinction, is hinted at in the unusual way that *She'ol* is presented: the *belly* (*beten*) of *She'ol*. Dictionaries give the mean-

---

[39] Simon, *Jonah*, 38.
[40] This latter possibility is accentuated by *yaradeti*, "I descended," in the first part of the verse. See Simon, *Jonah*, ad loc.

ing of "within,"[41] as in Job 38:29. The two primary meanings of *beten* according to frequency of usage, however, are a) "belly, the place of ingestion and destruction (of food)," and b) "the mother's womb, the place of birth or rebirth." Thus, belly is a conceptual merism, a single word whose two opposite meanings form a whole: both death and birth, amounting to the equivalent of human existence. This ambivalence is carried over into *shiwa'ti* (Jonah 2:3), signifying the scream both of death and of rebirth.

Other such merisms reinforce this ambivalence:

metsula (Jonah 2:4): Whereas in Jonah it refers to the path leading to death, in other texts it points to salvation, either through the destruction of Israel's enemies (Exod 15:5; Neh 9:11) or the removal of sins (Mic 7:19). Its sound (*metsula*) of course also evokes the protective shade (*tsel*) of the succah (4:5), itself a wordplay with the *kikayon*'s salvational activity (*lehatsil*; Jonah 4:6).

lebab (Jonah 2:4), lit. the "hearts" of the seas. The famous Rabbinic reading of Deut 6:5 sees a reference to the two basic urges of the human being (towards good and evil). Here the figure seems to hint at the two functions of the sea and its large fish that correspond to God's own powers over death and life: "The Lord kills and gives life, brings down to *She'ol* and lifts up" (1 Sam 2:6).[42]

To understand how Jonah changes his mind about wanting to die and now seeks to return to life, we have posited an instinctive reaction to death's horror. However, some will find this hypothesis of limited value to explain a Jonah so much under the spell of *Liebestode*, and a comparison with other literary accounts of near-death experiences may be needed to round out the picture. Here then, to take a different example, is how the famous Renaissance philosopher Michel de Montaigne described his horse-riding accident:

---

[41] Abraham Even-Shoshan, *A New Concordance to the Torah, the Prophets, and the Writings* [Hebrew] (Jerusalem: Kiryat Sefer, 1992), 165.

[42] See also Deut 32:39; 2 Kgs 5:7; Ps 30:4.

> There lay the horse bowled over and stunned, and I ten or twelve paces beyond, *dead*, stretched on my back, my face all skinned and bruised, . . . having no more motion or feeling than a log. . . .

> After I had been taken for dead for more than two full hours, I began to move and breathe; for so great an abundance of blood had fallen into my stomach that *nature* had to revive my forces to discharge it.

> . . . It seemed to me that my life was hanging only by the tip of my lips; I closed my eyes in order, it seemed to me, to help push it out, and took pleasure in growing languid and letting myself go. It was an idea that was only floating on the surface of my soul, as delicate and feeble as all the rest, but in truth not only free from distress but mingled with that sweet feeling that people have who let themselves slide into sleep.[43]

This text reinforces the distinction at the center of La Fontaine's fable between wanting to die and dying itself, but it isolates the latter—easy enough to do, since Montaigne has no motive or wish to die—and thus brings the horror hypothesis into question. For what especially emerges from this account is that near-death for Montaigne was not horrible but sweet, thus comparable to Jonah's initial comfort within the fish. Indeed, Montaigne is here a mere bystander,[44] life returns from unconsciousness automatically, so to speak, the *natural* desire to live just "kicks in," and the holder of that life is a somewhat bemused spectator, slightly astonished that life is still made available and especially that it does not have the gruesome aspect fostered by some moral and religious traditions. If this reading seems closer to Jonah's suicide, then his return to life is easier to explain than his *desire* or *scream* to return.

In our search for imaginative parallels we might look at yet another literary example, Saint-Exupéry's moving account of Guillaumet's courageous survival in the Andes after a plane crash in dead winter:

---

[43] Michel de Montaigne, *The Complete Essays of Montaigne* (trans. Donald Frame; Stanford: Stanford University Press, 1976), 269–70.

[44] Montaigne's almost scientific indifference, as well as his project to experience the quality of death from the inside, so to speak, is analysed by Hugo Friedrich, *Montaigne* (Paris: Gallimard, 1968), 290.

After two, three, four days of walking you want only to go to sleep. . . . Remorse emerged from the depths of consciousness [conscience, which could also mean moral conscience]. Suddenly the dream mingled with precise details. I thought of my wife. My insurance policy would make her life easier. Yes, but the insurance. . . . In the case of a disappearance legal death is postponed for four years! This detail seemed astonishing. I thought: "If I get back up . . ." Once standing, I walked for two nights and three days. . . .

What I did, I swear, no animal could ever have done.
(*Terre des hommes*)[45]

Although not fleeing life—far from it—Guillaumet yields, as did Montaigne, to death's sweetness, until he is suddenly dissuaded by what might be called the ethical memory of a loved one. He suddenly remembers his wife and a rather concrete consequence of his death's finality: insurance cannot be collected!

With a similar stress on what seems almost random memory, Jonah quite mysteriously explains his return to life:

I remembered the Lord. (2:8)

This may of course mean, by noting a possible parallelism, that Jonah prayed:

And my prayer came before You. (v. 8)

Alternatively and as in Montaigne's return to consciousness, Nature just seems to kick in. Here "remembering God" would mean that God—*Deus sive Natura*—takes over and brings him back, in a pure act of mercy. Jonah does not have to wait until chapter 4 to discover this aspect of God; he learns it here:

For I have learned [i.e., *ki yada'ti*, "experienced,"] that you are a gracious God. (4:2)

Note the perfect tense: I experienced your love when you saved me.[46]

---

[45] Antoine de Saint-Exupéry, *Oeuvres* (Paris: Gallimard, 1959), 164–65, 161.

[46] In this interpretation Jonah does not ask to die in 4:2f. Rather: "Please, God, wasn't this what I said, that I *deserved* to die; therefore, since I deserve death, take my life (if You wish)."

It is possible, too, that the impetus of memory cannot be forced into an either/or explanation. Note that of the four structuring verbs of Jonah's "psalm," the first three have God as actor and only in v. 8 does the action finally pass to Jonah. Psalm 69, which is also about salvation from the "waters," also captures the reciprocity of prayer, which in Jonah's case is also that of memory:

> And I, my prayer, to you, Lord,
> in an acceptable time:
> God, in the abundance of Your love,
> answer me with the truth of Your salvation. (Ps 69:14)

I am my prayer, my prayer is me, I am revived and reconstituted as a person of prayer, in direct dialogue with God.

Or, as in Ps 42, the context of memory is exile from God's memory and Presence. And again the appeal is to *khesed*, God's "love." The word that snaps Jonah into recognition is "forever"; he finally realizes that the ultimate consequence for his longing for repose is not the simple removal of consciousness but loss of the possibility of God's love, as he immediately acknowledges in a maxim-like indirection that strikes to the core of his own desire:

> Those who care for empty vanities
> Forsake their love [*khesed*]. (2:9)[47]

Between the subjective genitive "my love for God" and the objective genitive "God's love for me," it seems impossible to decide, undoubtedly because both are intended.

Jonah's Third Prayer: "Thanks!" (2:10)

There is general agreement that, whatever else it is, Jonah's psalm includes thanksgiving:

> But as for me, with a voice of thanksgiving [*todah*][48] I shall sacrifice unto You:

---

[47] For this meaning of *khesed* see below, "Erotic Clues and Vocabulary," in chapter 5. The connection between vv. 8 and 9 may well be Ps 73:17, where it is the contact with the Sanctuary that evokes the downfall of the wicked.

[48] For another meaning of this word and thus a possibility of yet a fourth prayer, see below, "Thanksgiving or Confession?" in chapter 6.

"What I vowed I shall pay.
    Salvation is the Lord's." (2:9–10)

What we can now recognize is that there is not one but two levels of Jonah's gratitude: Thanks for saving me, and thanks too for *not* answering my first prayer!

Let us bring Part One to a close by considering an alternative scenario. What if the sailors hadn't thrown Jonah overboard (and we are quite convinced by this point that Jonah was about to take his own life)? Would the Judge of all the earth then judge the presumably righteous (sailors) along with the wicked (servant; see Gen 18:23) and send the entire ship to the bottom of the deep? If not, why then would God have put Himself in such a position? It may be that He was outmaneuvered by Jonah, and God's only (rather shabby) answer to His prophet, as delivered by the sequel of the story, would go something like this:

> [God to Jonah:] "First you sought death, then you withdrew under stress. You criticized the sailors for wanting to live; but when push came to shove, you cared for your own life also!"

We now have multiple reasons for God's appointing the fish: first to kill Jonah (to assist in his suicide?!), then to make him uncomfortable, then to save his life, and finally to get the sailors (and Himself!) off the hook for a murder rap. We now have yet another reason why the story at the start of chapter 3 has to revert to the beginning: not because God used a heavy hand—or fish—to forcibly bring Jonah back but rather because the match (shall we say the erotic duel?) between the two is still a draw.

Jonah even has grounds for thinking he has won the argument, since there is no way that Jonah can know that the sailors were *not* punished for their crime in throwing him overboard.[49] This may explain Josephus' curious placement of the sacrifice and vow scene (1:16b) before the casting of lots (1:7).[50] His intention seems to be to remove any mention of the sailors once they cast Jonah overboard because it is at that point that they vanish from

---

[49] As against Sasson (*Jonah*, 332): "Jonah . . . readily accepts his charge once mercy is shown the sailors."

[50] See Sasson, *Jonah*, 138, n. 13.

Jonah's perception. For, we must ask: How could Jonah know? He is already on his way to the bottom of the sea! Would we imagine that he dons a life-jacket long enough to see what happens to the sailors, perhaps even floating around long enough to witness their vows and sacrifices? The question is not rhetorical since, having delivered his message of doom to the Ninevites, he does, this time around, station himself on the sidelines in order to "see what will be." For, to be sure, Jonah is very much concerned with their fate, and God will later remind him of the outcome. But for the moment, Jonah disappears below the surface and is probably well on his way down when the fish gobbles him up. Incidentally, this also means that the sailors do not know that he has been saved, and this strengthens their psychological need to bring a sin sacrifice as well as a thanksgiving one.

To summarize from the point of view of the book's dialogic structure, then, we may say that at the end of Part One God tested Jonah and won. When pushed by God to the brink, Jonah backed down and refused death. But Jonah also tested God and also won: the Gentiles really did compromise their morality in order to save their own necks. Round one (Part One) is thus a draw and we are led back to square one so that the (still equal) debate can resume from where it left off. God may have given Jonah another chance, but Jonah has returned the favor.

PART TWO

THE DRY-LAND EXPERIMENTS
Jonah 3–4

> . . . and the dry land. . . .
>
> (Jonah 1:9)

> If I am only for myself, what am I?
>
> Mishnah *Abot* 1:14

> Any prospect of awakening or coming to life to a
> dead man makes indifferent all times and places.
>
> Thoreau, *Walden*, "Solitude"[1]

*Jonah has survived and is now back to square one, where the
action of plot can finally begin. Well not quite, since, in addition to
a renewed command to take up the burdens of his condition, his restored existence is now at the other side of death, so to speak, if only as
the memory of near-death. One compelling interpretation of Jonah's
situation at the start of chapter 3 is that of LaCocque and Lacocque:*

> *One very important aspect of the post-mortem life is that every-
> thing gets doubly precious, gets piercingly important. . . . If
> you're reconciled with death, . . . then every single moment of
> every single day is transformed because the pervasive undercur-
> rent—the fear of death—is removed.*[2]

---

[1] Henry David Thoreau, *The Portable Thoreau* (ed. Carl Bode; New York: Penguin Books, 1982), 385.

[2] André LaCocque and Pierre-Emmanuel Lacocque, *The Jonah Complex* (Atlanta: John Knox, 1981), 103.

There are two problems with such a reading, however. On the one hand, not until the very end of his descent did Jonah show the slightest fear of death; on the contrary, his progressive withdrawal from living, culminating in his deep and unperturbed sleep during a storm, was quite self-assured. And, on the other, when the face-to-face confrontation with death does occur, its power to jolt Jonah back into existence is such that one cannot imagine ever "going beyond" such a fear: death seems no longer an option for Jonah precisely because it is so frightful, and our prophet is so permanently fearful because so well informed.[3]

Surviving the death temptation or ordeal was difficult enough, but "as the sequel of the tale shows, 'the worst is not death but the rebirth itself. . . . It means for the first time to be subjected to the terrifying paradox of the human condition, since one must be born not as a god but as a man.'"[4] *Jonah is thus spewed back into existence, where the fear of death is not transcended but rather subordinate to an even greater fear, that of life itself.*[5]

The passage from Part One to Part Two of Jonah has been described mythologically and archetypically. For Jung, Jonah's "whale complex" involves a wish to regress to the womb in order to avoid the responsibilities imposed by the "father" and to disappear into the "ocean" of instinctual life.[6] *LaCocque and Lacocque develop these insights by relating Jonah's voyage to other ancient myths in which a hero descends into the netherworld in order to overcome the forces of chaos and return to that mysterious "primordial milieu where life begins."*[7] *Yet, from what we have seen it*

---

[3] See also below, "Fear-Prayer," in chapter 6.

[4] LaCocque and Lacocque, *The Jonah Complex*, 109, quoting Ernest Becker, *The Denial of Death* (New York: Free Press, 1973).

[5] In such works as *De L'Existence à l'existant* (2d ed.; Paris: Vrin, 1990) Emmanuel Lévinas raises the issue of an anxiety intrinsic to existence itself. As Catherine Chalier asks: "Isn't the fear of being, in effect, at least as primordial as the anguish over nothingness . . . ?" See her *Lévinas: L'Utopie de l'humain* (Paris: Albin Michel, 1993), 43.

[6] Harold Fisch, *A Remembered Future: A Study in Literary Mythology* (Bloomington: Indiana University Press, 1984), 133–34, quoting Carl G. Jung, *Symbols of Transformation* (trans. R. F. C. Hull; London: Routledge and Keegan Paul, 1956), 330–31, 408, 419–20.

[7] LaCocque and Lacocque, *The Jonah Complex*, 55. Jack M. Sasson (*Jonah: A New Translation with Introduction, Commentary, and Interpretation* [AB 42B;

is also clear that such a return "to the very source of his existence" is as much a death wish as a desired renewal. When Jonah does return— against his will, but also when his deepest will is seen to coincide with God's own—then the archetypal space changes radically from the oceanic abyss to dry land, signifying a progression from instinctual life to historical existence. Indeed, in Jonah's return to his original point of departure at the start of chapter 3, the ocean is left resolutely behind and Jonah's consciousness now has a different landscape entirely: that of the dry land composed of populations and large cities. On the open sea the sailors experienced the sway of "sauve qui peut," every man for himself! On dry land, however, the suspension of the ethical is impossible and Jonah too must try to live with others.

The real remaining question of the book, then, is not why Jonah wants to die but why he wants to live.[8] Two answers are sketched. The first is the one already mentioned, that there is in our innermost being a desire to live (the woodcutter). This desire is purely instinctual, automatic, one might say, asserted biologically and in spite of our duties towards others—the woodcutter does not have in mind the needs of his family as he returns to life. Quite the contrary, it is the hardship of family burdens that drives him to want death in the first place.

Having brought Jonah the man back to life, God still wishes the return of His servant; He still has a mission to be performed in this world, and beyond the biological motivation there is also the ethical one evoked by the Saint-Exupéry example. The parallel is imperfect, to be sure, since Guillaumet loved his wife whereas Jonah seems not to hold the Ninevites in particular esteem. In both cases, however, the desire to remain alive is linked to a duty or mission beyond the individual; survival is motivated by a concern for others. The problem, for Jonah, is that Nineveh seems at best a detour to reinstatement.

These observations are reinforced at the symbolic level. Harold Fisch concludes that in Western literature generally the function of ocean and desert is that of type and antitype, "really the spatial aspects of two opposing myths." Fisch then brings the topic home:

New York: Doubleday, 1990], 185) details the references to Jonah's sea as a reversion to "a primordial body of water."

    [8] That his desire to die returns in chapter 4 will be discussed below, "The Kiss of Death," in chapter 5.

There is one short book of the Bible, the book of Jonah, where in fact the two myths are set side by side, and the hero is, in a manner, required to choose between them.[9]

Jonah, who longs only to stay at home, the center of things, has become a long-distance voyager. First he puts out to sea and heads for outlying Tarshish; then he undertakes a land trek to the "great city of Nineveh." Each trip occupies an entire half of the book and has its own characteristic ambience. The first half takes place in a sea setting, spanning the vertical distance from the "mountain of the House" (Isa 2:2; Jer 26:18) in Jerusalem and continuing the downward spiral: to Jaffa, the ship, its bowels, the sea to its deepest abyss, and then back to dry land. By contrast, the entire second half is set in a horizontal voyage with two distinct environments: the great city of Nineveh and a spot "east of the city," actually a vantage point from which things in town can be seen, assessed, understood. If the sea setting focused on Jonah's instinctual and biological existence,[10] *his return to shore indicates a progression to what might be called the dry land of ethical relations. For, as the Mishnah asks, "if I am only for myself, what am I?"*

If Part One can be seen as a return to the original watery chaos of biological existence, which then yields to a salvation narrative, in a parallel way the dry land of Part Two has two landscapes: the special disintegration of Nineveh, on the one hand, and the desert haven where God sends His prophet a protective canopy, on the other. These then become the settings of two further salvations: God's rescue of Nineveh through Jonah, and Jonah's attempt, under the kikayon *east of the city, to salvage his intimacy with God. From this latter perspective, which is Jonah's overriding concern from start to finish, both the ocean and city settings represent the chaos of a loveless relationship, and seeming type and antitype both must yield to yet another dominant element in Jonah's prayers: the references to God's Temple of Holiness (2:5, 8).*

---

[9] Fisch, *A Remembered Future*, 133–34.

[10] More precisely, the dominant biological metaphors, not surprisingly, refer to digestion/nutrition (the *belly* of the ship and of *She'ol*) and to their *me'ayim*, or "loins" (of reproduction).

CHAPTER THREE

The Ninevites: Jonah 3

Back to Square One?

It would seem, from the book's structure as established from the almost verbatim repetition of God's command in 3:1, that Jonah is simply back to square one. But if that is indeed the case and things remain exactly the same, then we must expect another refusal and a repetition of Jonah's flight. Since Jonah, this second time, does react differently—his acceptance of the Nineveh mission in fact indicates a complete about-face—we must seek to understand his change of attitude.

The slight changes of language offer important hints. Let us again recall the remarkable repetition that structures the book's two parts:

> *The word of the Lord came to Jonah* son of Amittai: "*Go to Nineveh, that great city, and proclaim . . .*" (1:1; emphasis added)

> *The word of the Lord came to Jonah* a second time: "*Go to Nineveh, that great city, and proclaim . . .*"(3:1; emphasis added)

The point of adding *shenit*, "a second time," seems an important reminder of one of the book's major themes, that of repentance: God does give a second chance. Indeed, the theme stresses once again that repentance is grounded in God's generosity. But it also adds, if we follow the rabbis here, that God does give a second chance, *but* perhaps not a third. This is thus both a concession to

Jonah concerning the Ninevites but also a warning to the prophet himself: this is the last time I order you to go!

The deletion of "son of Amittai" seems to point in the same direction. At the start of the Abraham story God makes the following declaration:

> Get yourself[1] from your land and from your extended family and *from your father's house.* . . .
>
> And I will make you into a great people, and I will bless you, and I will *make your name great.* (Gen 12:1–2; emphasis added)

It would seem that, as a condition of having a great name, separation from the father is required (note the parallelistic placement of both members, each occupying the third position of a triad). A parallel case would be Saul's evolving independence as reflected by the first two versions of the popular proverb:

> "What is all this with the *son of Kish*? Is Saul too among the prophets?"
>
> And a man from there spoke up and said: "And who is *their* father?"
>
> Wherefore the proverb arose: "Is *Saul* too among the prophets?" (1 Sam 10:11–12; emphasis added)

Saul is henceforth to be regarded no longer merely as the son-of-someone-else but rather as the son of his own actions.[2] There is thus, again, a further implied warning in that second calling, for from now on Jonah is being judged solely by his own actions and no longer assisted by any merits that may accrue from his father. Thus the limitation may apply: a second time He will speak, but not a third.

Whether Jonah's motive is now one of repentance must be questioned, however, since Jonah's prayers in chapter 2 make not

---

[1] Rashi interprets the unusual "go to yourself" (*lek leka*) as "for your own benefit."

[2] See my forthcoming study, "On Proverb Formation: 'Is Saul too among the prophets?'"

the slightest move in that direction: "no admission of remorse nor vow of obedience," in the words of one commentator.[3] Nor is it in the least clear from those same prayers that Jonah is now "ready to accept his mission."[4] Rather, God's word must come to Jonah a second time precisely because His prophet still shows no such readiness. In fact, when Jonah is unceremoniously deposited back on dry land, he has every reason to believe that God has relented and agreed to his reinstatement.

A possible motive may be found in what is perceived as a defect in God's first command. Let us notice yet again the resumptive repetition that starts both major halves of our story:

Go to Nineveh, that great city, and proclaim . . . (1:2)

Go to Nineveh, that great city, and proclaim . . . (3:2)

Here the second text adds to the first as follows:

Go to Nineveh, that great city, and proclaim *against her, for their evil has come up before Me.* (1:2; emphasis added)

Go to Nineveh, that great city, and proclaim *to her the cry that I am speaking to you.* (3:2; emphasis added)

The content of that cry is then specified, but only in the second text:

And he called and said: "*In another forty days Nineveh will be overturned.*" (v. 4; emphasis added)

It is generally assumed, perhaps because of the partial repetition of the introductory formula, that the second prophecy is a mere duplicate of the first, a simple repetition of the original terms of the command: "In forty days," etc. According to this understanding, the addition "the cry that I shall speak to you" could only, at best, note God's desire "to ensure Jonah's punctilious

---

[3] Rudolph, cited in Jonathan Magonet, *Form and Meaning: Studies in Literary Techniques in the Book of Jonah* (Sheffield: Almond, 1983), 131, n. 60. Similarly, George M. Landes had expected in Jonah's prayer "a confession of sinful disobedience embodying penitence." See his "The Kerygma of the Book of Jonah: The Contextual Interpretation of the Jonah Psalm," *Int* 21 (1967): 4.

[4] Magonet, *Form and Meaning*, 52.

observance."[5] It seems more likely, however, that *as a condition of his return* Jonah has now negotiated more precise terms, and less for himself than for the Ninevites:[6]

In forty days [and no longer!] Nineveh will be overturned.

This more explicit version would reflect God's concession to Jonah, who perhaps felt that the original mission was poorly defined and left too much leeway to the wicked Ninevites. This is why God, the second time around, specifies "the command *that I am speaking to you now* (and not the one I gave to you previously)."[7] An alternative, and to my mind more congenial, perspective would read:

In forty days and no less.

The difference between "proclaim *against*" and "proclaim *to*" is enormous: the first projects impending destruction,[8] whereas the second can mean even "*beg them* to repent" (Jonah 1:6, 14; 2:3; 1 Kgs 8:52). Jonah's initial refusal, therefore, would be out of pity and hope for the Ninevites rather than hatred.[9]

---

[5] Jeffrey H. Tigay, "The Book of Jonah and the Days of Awe," *Conservative Judaism* 38 (1985/86): 68.

[6] Alternatively, Ben Zvi suggests the following scenario: "If YHWH is imagined as not knowing whether punishment will be executed or not at the time narrated in Jonah 1:2, such characterization might be affected by the change of language in Jonah 3:2. Was YHWH construed as intentionally removing a strong negative connotation and choosing a more neutral one?" See *Signs of Jonah: Reading and Rereading in Ancient Yehud* (JSOTSup 367; Sheffield: JSOT Press, 2003), 37. My suggestion is that God was out-maneuvered or persuaded—willingly—by Jonah.

[7] God uses the participle to indicate a present rather than a past action, as Marvin A. Sweeney points out in *The Twelve Prophets* (2 vols.; Collegeville, MN: Liturgical, 2000), 324.

[8] Uriel Simon, *Jonah: The Traditional Hebrew Text with the New JPS Translation* (trans. Lenn J. Schramm; JPS Torah Commentary; Philadelphia: Jewish Publication Society, 1999), 4.

[9] See below, "Jonah's Knowledge of God," in chapter 8, and especially n. 20. Of course, Jonah's detractors cannot allow such positive motivation: "it was the belief that the Ninevites would repent that prevented him [Jonah] from going to Nineveh in the first place"; John Day, "Problems in the Interpretation of the Book of Jonah," in *Quest of the Past: Studies on Israelite Religion, Literature, and Prophetism* (ed. A. S. van der Woude; OTS; Leiden: Brill, 1990), 45.

At any rate, now the terms of reprieve are known and there will be an end to it all, both to his mission and to the Ninevites' evil. Since the whole affair is now defined with clear limits, Jonah can go to Nineveh, brush through the city while delivering his sermon, and await the outcome. This gives further motivation to the careful notation of his positioning himself:

> Now Jonah went out of the city and sat to the east of the city, ... until he should see what will be with the city. (Jonah 4:5)

Jonah's prayer in 4:2–4 in fact addresses this very issue, as we shall see below.[10]

The Ninevites and Their Animals

The comparison of humans to animals rarely redounds to the credit of either. Let Qohelet's contempt epitomize this view:

> Man has no superiority over the beast. (Qoh 3:19)

While Qohelet sees the defect less in the status of animals than of creation itself ("for all is but vanity"), the blanket judgment—that humans are no better than animals—hardly represents a positive view of either:

> For they [humans] are like beasts to one another. (v. 18)[11]

Thus when the Ninevites, confronted with the prediction of doom, come up with the original idea of having even the animals fast and dress in mourning, the idea seems comical to us, for how could such lowly creatures effect the slightest improvement in the Ninevites' lot?

The Ninevites are neither so ridiculous or bizarre[12] as may appear, however (whether they will later revert to their wickedness is

---

[10] See below, "The Purported Displacement of 4:5," in chapter 6.

[11] Michel de Montaigne began his classic discussion with the thesis that humans are no better than animals and went on to show the latter's superiority. See his "Apology for Raymond Sebond" in *The Complete Essays of Montaigne* (trans. Donald Frame; Stanford: Stanford University Press, 1976), 330–58.

[12] Despite Jack M. Sasson, *Jonah: A New Translation with Introduction, Commentary, and Interpretation* (AB 42B; New York: Doubleday, 1990), 257.

another question altogether). In his description of the locust plague the prophet Joel views the cattle's suffering as a form of prayer:

> How the beasts moan,
> the herds weep,
> for lack of fodder. . . .
> Even beasts in the field
> complain to you. (Joel 1:18, 20)[13]

Lest the comparison be regarded as purely metaphorical, the psalmist projects God's reaction as inclusive:

> Man and beast do you save, Lord. (Ps 36:6)[14]

The solidarity of humans and animals, according to Zornberg, begins at the beginning:

> Adam . . . proclaims a common identity with the animals as created beings who owe adoration to an invisible Creator. And he does this in no obsequious humility but in a paradoxical perception that "to stand in the presence of God" is precisely to achieve full "majesty and strength." He makes common cause with the animals.[15]

And just as animals are, as it were, capable of petition and worthy of rescue, so too can they join the universal chorus of thanksgiving:

> Let every thing that has breath praise the Lord. (Ps 150:6; see Ps 148:10, 13)

The idea of linking human guilt to that of animals in the Bible begins with the story of the flood. For, puzzled by why the animals have to perish because of human evil, the rabbis

---

[13] James L. Crenshaw, *Joel: A New Translation with Introduction and Commentary* (AB 24C; Garden City: Doubleday, 1995), 84, 109.

[14] See also Gen 8:1; 9:15; Ps 147:9. Hosea 4:3 stresses how closely animal welfare is tied up with human behavior. In the return of the ark scene in 1 Sam 6:7, the Philistines' elaborate ritual includes the use of milch cows who will be forcibly separated from their nursing young. Presumably, animal suffering will awaken God's compassion.

[15] Aviva Zornberg, *Genesis: The Beginning of Desire* (Philadelphia: Jewish Publication Society, 1995), 23.

speculated that the animals too must have sinned,[16] for surely God could have used more selective methods of extinction, perhaps the tried and true fire and brimstone used at Sodom and Gomorrah. The underlying assumptions to this midrash are three: that God would not have punished *innocent* animals, that animals too—under human influence?—have some kind of free will, and that the normal state of animals is one of innocence. Surely, this is the point of God's closing question to Jonah, used to justify divine pardon: that the Ninevites in turn must strive to regain or participate in an animal-like innocence. As for Nineveh's possession of *many* animals, the text may wish to remind us both of the solidarity (Limburg) between humans and animals,[17] and also of their natural fertility:

I will make them teem with humans like flocks. (Ezek 36:37)[18]

But, again, the crucial *moral* point here is one of innocence: if animals (at least domesticated ones) do not typically[19] engage in acts of violence towards humans, shouldn't humans also refrain from violence? Or indeed—continuing the *a fortiori* argumentation—if animals can be brought to restrict even their normal pleasures (through fasting and "repentance"), then can't humans also!? The very notion of vicarious animal sacrifice—common both to the Bible and the ancient world in general—confirms the validity of the Ninevites' tactic. Indeed, if animals can atone for human misdeed,[20] then the surprise is not that the Ninevites caused their animals to fast but rather that they did not consider the substitution as sufficient atonement!

If the Ninevites have quite correctly appealed to the principle of solidarity between humans and animals, however, their general

---

[16] Perhaps by mixing their seed; see Rashi on Gen 6:12, quoting *b. Sanhedrin* 108a.

[17] James Limburg, *Jonah: A Commentary* (Louisville, KY: Westminster John Knox, 1993), 82.

[18] Abarbanel comments that "it is in the nature of animals to multiply greatly."

[19] The exception is the *shor mu'ad*, the ox who is accustomed to gore; see Mishnah *Baba Qamma*, chapter 4.

[20] Or, more grimly, if humans can be fit sacrifices precisely because they are like animals, as Ezek 36:37 (just quoted) clearly implies.

imposition of penance upon the entire general populace, "from great to small" (Jonah 3:5), has a sinister side. For one might ask: even if the general public is guilty of "evil," what about the innocent? What about children, who have not reached the age of responsibility, and animals, who may not be even capable of evil? From this point of view, Nineveh's inclusion of innocents has the aspect of hostage taking. It may further be seen as a desire to give God a taste of His own medicine, as if to say: "This, the suffering of innocent children and animals, is what Your global retribution would produce!" One might even venture the impression that, just as the beasts take on the penitential deportment of humans, humans in turn, in donning their hairshirts, disguise themselves as animals. The effect is one of high masquerade.[21]

The Reprieve

Let us also notice that God's second command not only specifies the terms of reprieve, as noted above, but also hints at the method of punishment.

> And he called and said: "In another forty days Nineveh *will be overturned.*" (Jonah 3:4; emphasis added)

Since this language of utter extermination is used repeatedly in the Sodom and Gomorrah episode (Gen 19:25, 29; Deut 29:22; Amos 4:11), the suggestion seems inescapable: Like Sodom and Gomorrah, Nineveh will also be reduced to ashes.

This strong verbal affinity invites further comparison between Abraham's and Jonah's negotiations with God, both of which are about saving a wicked city.[22] Abraham can win acquittal if a

---

[21] "Why do we dress in sackcloth [when we fast]? Abba bar Hiyya said: 'Because we regard our selves as animals'" (*b. Ta'anit* 16a). Rashi surmises that this is because sackcloth is made from the hair of animals.

[22] Abraham's question and God's answer share a common assumption, namely, that the few can atone for the many, that moral merit can be transmitted and vicariously enjoyed. Their only bone of contention is not the principle itself but merely the number or quota necessary to render the principle operative. Both stories accept the principle of the destruction of the wicked (if unrepentant).

minimum number of righteous people can be found, since it is unthinkable that the Judge of the entire earth will not act justly. Though not recorded, Jonah's argument may be reconstructed from God's peculiar insistence on Nineveh's size:

Nineveh *that large city*. (1:2; 3:2; emphasis added)

Nineveh *that large city*, which has many more than one hundred and twenty thousand humans. (4:1; emphasis added)

Such single focus on Nineveh's mere numbers strikes the reader as naive, albeit part and parcel of a more general interest in size in the book.[23] God's point, however, may well be Abraham's at the gates of Sodom and Gomorrah: in such a large city, it is inconceivable that there not be some righteous people, and will God sweep up the righteous with the wicked? In other words, God's insistence on their number seems an open invitation to Jonah to plea-bargain their acquittal.[24]

But what are the terms of that acquittal to be? Presumably Nineveh does not have a minimum number, and God is yet willing to give them a chance! Yes, God projects, if the Ninevites repent. That this possibility was not made available to the Sodomites seems to presume that it was known that they would not repent. But how do you know that beforehand?

In the face of the widespread destruction of Sodom and Gomorrah, Abraham had asked whether God would treat the righteous as the wicked. This astonished, even indignant query is revised in Jonah, and in two related but distinct ways. First of all, instead of focusing on the *righteous*, the book asks: will you treat the *innocent* as the guilty? This was Voltaire's issue with Providence at such moments as the Lisbon earthquake, underlining the principle that children and domesticated animals depend for their very survival on adults. Secondly, in the book of Jonah God seems willing to equate sinlessness—the removal of sin—with innocence.

---

[23] See below, "The Mediating Narrator," in chapter 10.

[24] Simon, *Jonah*, 4, reads the opposite message: "as is the size of the city, so is the magnitude of its wickedness."

Jonah and the Ninevites: A Tale of Two Cities

Given the pervasive presence of Assyria in the Hebrew Bible and especially its largely negative relations with ancient Israel, scholars have diligently pursued possible historical connections with the book of Jonah. Except for the single detail of Nineveh's wickedness, however, such an inquiry seems a mere distraction from the generic suggestions of the book itself, which projects a *story* rather than a *history*.[25] Indeed, it has seemed to many that the book of Jonah sees Nineveh as a figure for humanity itself, and that such an extreme case (the city's current wickedness) simply offers the exception that tests the rule through *a fortiori* reasoning: if such is the case for wicked Nineveh, that they can repent and thus be forgiven, then all the more so for other cities.

What is abundantly clear is that Nineveh occupies our concern from start to finish. From the opening "get yourself to Nineveh" to the repeated command at midpoint and throughout the entire second half, everyone's sights are set on the Assyrian capitol. Of preeminent interest is Jonah's own shifting perspectives, as the city becomes in turn the object of flight, then of directed prophecy and concern, then of perplexing curiosity (4:5), and finally of intense debate. What matters most from Jonah's theological point of view, however, may be clarified by Calvino's suggestion that such a city is not one but in fact two, depending on one's point of departure and approach:

> The city displays one face to the traveler arriving overland and a different one to him who arrives by sea. . . . Each city receives its form from the desert it opposes; and so do the camel driver and the sailor see Despina, a border city between two deserts.[26]

---

[25] See Simon, *Jonah*, Introduction, xv–xxi; Thomas M. Bolin, "'Should I Not Also Pity Nineveh?' Divine Freedom in the Book of Jonah," *JSOT* 67 (1995): 109–20. Marc Zvi Brettler sees a similar generic method in Judges 19: "Jonah is much more ambiguous in terms of its lesson than Judges 19, perhaps because Jonah is so theological, whereas Judges 19 is more political. But they both use the garb of history to teach," *The Book of Judges* (London: Routledge, 2002), 91.

[26] Italo Calvino, *Invisible Cities* (trans. William Weaver; New York: Harcourt Brace, 1974), 15–16.

This poetic insight enables us to characterize Jonah's attitudes towards the Assyrian capitol not as foregone conclusions (e.g., Jonah hates Nineveh) but rather as multiple possibilities. Thus the sea traveler who has escaped drowning may be more sensitized to the Ninevites' imminent peril and need to exist. Once the human contact has been made, the prophecy delivered and the people saved from destruction, however, then Jonah's view of them from the east raises entirely different expectations. For, seen from the sea, Nineveh's citizens must urgently earn the right even to exist, to again merit the life that they have forfeited through their evil behavior. Seen from the opposite desert "east of the city" and having indeed achieved existence, however, they may now also be capable of responding to a different prophetic call. We shall explore this expanded possibility in chapter 8, in the difference between God's concession (of mere existence) and Jonah's goal (of true love).

CHAPTER FOUR

East of the City: Jonah 4

In the desert I am worth what my gods are worth.

Saint-Exupéry, *Lettre à un otage*[1]

Oh that I had wings like Jonah! Then I
would fly away and be at rest.
Lo I would then wander far off and
would lodge in the wilderness!

(Ps 55:7–8)

Calvino proposed viewing the city of Despina (our Nineveh) as located between two deserts, the real one and the sea. Considering both of the dominant and successive settings of the book of Jonah—the sea and the dry land—as deserts raises the issue of their relationship, whether, as some have argued (see above), the settings are antagonistic, or, as now implied, they have a shared essence. We must now ask, if the sea-desert raises the very question of survival and existence itself, what does the desert east of Nineveh represent, what prophetic concerns does it project?

Jonah's Joy, or Surviving Betrayal

Jonah ben Amittai is quite possibly the most persistently and intensely dejected character in literature. We have seen how he

---

[1] "Je vaux, dans le désert, ce que valent mes divinités," Antoine de Saint-Exupéry, *Oeuvres* (Paris: Gallimard, 1959), 395.

flees from his prophetic mission, thus showing little apparent concern over the lives of sailors brought to the point of death through his own initiative, indeed over the lives of an entire great city that could be saved through his prophetic intervention. From the very start his dominant emotion is one of upset, to the point of wanting first to flee, then to sleep it all off, and then, insistently, to vanish into the depths. Despite his biological reaction and his salvation from the abyss, in Part Two his escapist desires not only return but become more explicit:

> "Now, Lord, please take my life, for I would rather die than live." (4:3)

> And he asked to die, saying: "Better die than stay alive." (v. 8)

> And he said: "I am upset unto death!" (v. 9)

At the risk of succumbing to the current critical fashion of transforming a tragic character into a comic (or at least an all-too-human, pathetic) one, we could plausibly speak of Jonah's almost clinical depression. This would at least coincide with the Lord's own disbelief: "Are you really so upset, Jonah?" (4:3, also v. 9).

Our story presents one notable variant to this rather drab portrait. The case involves the *kikayon* plant and goes as follows:

> Now the Lord God appointed a *kikayon* plant, which rose up over Jonah to act as a shade over his head, to save him from his distress, *and Jonah was joyful over this* kikayon *with a great joy*. (4:6; emphasis added)

His happiness is so unexpected and exaggerated that we are tempted in turn to ask: "Are you really *so* happy, Jonah?" For on the face of it, the reaction is absurd: Jonah, the chronically depressed who can take pleasure in nothing, not even in his divine mission, suddenly goes overboard over a plant! Commentators either pass over this absurdity[2] or explain it inadequately. For example, Ben-Menahem: "because it protected him from the heat of the sun," forgetting the verse immediately preceding, which

---

[2] Jack M. Sasson, *Jonah: A New Translation with Introduction, Commentary, and Interpretation* (AB 42B; New York: Doubleday, 1990), ad loc.

specified that "Jonah made himself a booth and sat there in the shade." No, rather than argue the pressing physical need,[3] we must look elsewhere to understand the Lord's subtle trick in converting Jonah's excessive "distress" into "great joy." One solution, I shall suggest, lies in the dialectical opposition—actually a complementarity—between Jonah's *two* shade options: the succah booth and the *kikayon*.

The Succah that Jonah Built: The Merit System

> But the hater of gifts will live. (Prov 15:27)

> The height, the deity of man is to be self-sustained, to need no gift. (Emerson, "The Transcendentalist")[4]

> And he [Jonah] requested his soul, that it should die. (Jonah 4:8)

> The reward is according to the effort. (Mishnah *Abot* 5:23)

One of the more curious hypotheses used to explain Jonah's refusal to preach to the Ninevites is that, should his prophecy of destruction not come about, his professional standing would be compromised. But with whom? Surely not the Ninevites, now able to hope, as the result of his warning, for a reversal of the divine decree and for continued life! The text is silent about Jonah's circumstances in Nineveh and in particular his relations with the Ninevites. In view of a receptivity that reached up to the king's very throne, however, one must imagine that the city's prophet of salvation was offered highest honors, including, one would expect, at least suitable dwelling and compensation.

---

[3] To confine our understanding to the physical level is to authenticate John Day's puzzlement: "What, one cannot help asking, has happened to the booth that he now needed a castor-oil plant to shelter him?" See "Problems in the Interpretation of the Book of Jonah," in *Quest of the Past: Studies on Israelite Religion, Literature, and Prophetism* (ed. A. S. van der Woude; OTS 26; Leiden: Brill, 1990), 42. One might prefer to attend to the narrator's irresistible pun between the previous "shade" [*tsel*] that protected Jonah in his booth (4:6) and the Lord's present wish to "save" [*lehatsil*] Jonah.

[4] Ralph Waldo Emerson, *The Portable Emerson* (ed. Carl Bode; rev. ed.; The Viking Portable Library; New York: Penguin Books, 1981), 95.

Instead, Jonah both withdraws from the city and sets up residence in a makeshift shelter:

And Jonah made himself a booth. (4:5)

Two distinct models can be proposed to explain Jonah's strongly independent attitude. The first is Abraham in his rejection of any booty from the rescue of Lot and the war with the four kings:

So that you should not claim: "It is I who made Abraham wealthy." (Gen 14:23)

According to this understanding, Jonah's decision to build a shelter is a principled rejection of a more sumptuous one available from the Ninevites, and building himself a succah is not only sequential with his withdrawal from the city but also part of the same motivation: to refuse any help *from the (wicked) Ninevites*, or, at a different level, to pretend that he needs no help from the One who rejected him.

A second model, even more philosophical in nature, extends the refusal of gifts to include all sources whatever. Students of Renaissance literature recall the radical distinction between nature and art, the former designating the given and the latter, what humans add to the given by way of effort. Closer to the wisdom books of the Bible, the Greek Stoic philosopher Epictetus makes a parallel distinction, reducing the entire creation to two complementary categories: "what comes *from me* and what comes *from without*."[5] Notice how the Jonah text makes a special effort to delineate and distinguish these two points of view:

And Jonah *made for himself* a booth. (4:5)

By opposition,

---

[5] Epictetus, *Enchiridion*, in *The Discourse Manual* (trans. W. A. Oldfather; 2 vols.; Cambridge, MA: Harvard University Press, 1966), 2:483. As useful background to this debate one might wish to consult Michel de Montaigne's finely nuanced distinction between Cato and Socrates on virtue and goodness, art and nature, effort and the "given" in "Of Cruelty"; *The Complete Essays of Montaigne* (trans. Donald Frame; Stanford: Stanford University Press, 1976), 306–18.

> Now *God provided a kikayon* plant, which rose up over Jonah
> to act as a shade over his head, to save him from his distress.
> (v. 6; emphasis added)

If Jonah (or the reader) still does not get the point, God goes on
to make it perfectly clear:

> "You cared about the *kikayon* plant, *which you did not work for
> or grow.*" (v. 6; emphasis added)

In short, Jonah's hut, made by his own hands and effort, is
the symbol of his newly acquired (and also faked?) independence.
From whom or what? From God, who seems to have deserted
him. Jonah makes this point one final time when, instead of again
asking God to take his life, he—in dramatic contrast—now seeks
permission only from himself:

> And he [Jonah] requested his soul, that it should die. (4:8)

We shall later describe the wonderful symbolism of the *kikayon*/
succah in Jonah's Bible, that of an enclosure signifying God's protective love. For the moment, we may already discern in Jonah's
project of independence a dual amorous twist. We recall that part
of Jonah's argument is that the Ninevites may not fully deserve
God's love. From this perspective, Jonah's self-constructed succah
is a bitter reminder of his bridal canopy with God.

God's *Kikayon* Trick: The Gift System

> One takes a vow of poverty but not of wealth.
>   (Midrash de Rab Mattityah)[6]

> In the wilderness, I find something more dear and connate
> than in streets or villages . . . an occult relation between man
> and the vegetable. (Emerson, "Nature")[7]

---

[6] In today's world one would have thought exactly the opposite: everyone
says, "I am going to get rich"; few say, "I am going to strive to be poor." Nowadays
even the project to be "poor in spirit" gets short shrift.

[7] Emerson, *The Portable Emerson*, 11.

Only God can make a tree. (Joyce Kilmer)[8]

Jonah's speedy exit from Nineveh and withdrawal to a make-shift dwelling is highly perplexing and, once again, raises the issue of the prophet's motivation. For, since his message was incredibly well received, then surely the prophet would receive honorable hospitality. However, if Jonah will not take from the Ninevites, he will take from God, at least under certain conditions.

The opening of the book of Qohelet engages a debate on the value of human labor:

What profit does a human derive from all the labor ['amalo] that he labors under the sun? (Qoh 1:3)

Using the same term, 'amal, God takes note that Jonah's claim to the kikayon is limited by the fact that he did not labor in its production or maintenance (4:10). In both cases and speaking more generally, the debate raises the question of whether humans can take legitimate pleasure only from what comes from their own effort or also from God's gifts, parallel to the Renaissance "given" and to Epictetus' "what comes from without." And, coincident with Qohelet's own terminology, Jonah's happiness over the kikayon plant is also termed a simkhah.[9]

The kikayon thus becomes the instrument of God's connivance, for God has indeed tricked Jonah into enjoying or feeling contentment for something that he hasn't worked for and thus doesn't deserve. What's more, God has brought Jonah to care for that thing—something he refused to do (according to some readings) in the case of the Ninevites. Now the stubborn prophet himself, not through words but through his instinctive reaction,[10] has admitted that merit is not the only criterion to judge a life, that, theologically put, Mercy (khesed) also has its place in the order

---

[8] Joyce Kilmer, "Trees," in Trees and Other Poems: Candles that Burn, by Joyce Kilmer and Aline M. Kilmer (Atlanta: Cherokee, 1994), 19.

[9] See T. A. Perry, Dialogues with Kohelet (University Park, PA: Penn State University Press, 1993), 31.

[10] Once again God has reached Jonah at the instinctual level. For just as Jonah in the belly of the fish is returned to life through a visceral scream, here too the reaction is deep and pre-reflective, part of the natural apparatus, so to speak, that Jonah (and everyone?) is given: as a gift!

of things and is indeed sometimes to be preferred to the merit system of strict deserving and Justice. Jonah's distress thus arises not from the sun's heat but rather from the problem he had from the start, the nature of God who gives according to criteria other than exact merit and thus deprives humans of the full possibility of making their own happiness and being totally responsible for their own actions.

At this point God's argument would sound like this:

> [God to Jonah:] "You stand on behavior and effort. I like this argument and even use it myself. Note the terms of my forgiving the Ninevites: 'And God saw their *deeds*' (3:10). But I have other criteria as well. I noticed that the *kikayon* sprang up without effort and you still liked it."

One may wonder, though, how Jonah was so easily tricked. We recall the progression of prayers in chapter 2 of Jonah, where the prophet came to know his own mind by petitioning God's reversal of his plan to die. Here again the text chronicles Jonah's unsuccessful assertion of his independence. But what is behind it?

The *Kikayon* Episode in the Context of Elijah's Epiphany

Whatever the *kikayon* is, its general characteristics enable us to understand its function: it provides shade and, through an exquisite paronomasia, salvation. But from what? From the sun's heat, to be sure, although this answer is hardly sufficient because Jonah had already provided for that need by building himself a succah. What then is the needed additional salvation? Here we must attend most carefully to the text's insistence on two of the plant's further characteristics. First of all, its elevation, expressed through a lengthy wordplay on *'al*.[11] Recall that God's first appointment, the fish, connected Jonah with the sea and the underworld, placing him once again at the roots of his physical existence.[12] Similarly but in the opposite direction, the

---

[11] It is totally consistent, therefore, that the agent of its destruction is, continuing the pun, a worm, a *tola'at*, the reversal of ascension. See also nn. 43 below and 34 in chapter 8.

[12] There may be also a pun here on "he appointed," *wayeman*, and *man*, "manna," since the manna of the desert is proof of God's loving care.

plant is a symbol of elevation, of reconnection between Jonah and his divine roots.[13] Stated differently, both the fish and the *kikayon* are allegories of transcendence, but in opposite directions, and both have to be laid aside: by spitting Jonah out, and by drying him out further. Thus the succah and *kikayon* are not to be seen in opposition but rather in cooperation, both as kinds of enclosure, something like the Cloud of Glory resting upon the Temple.

Jonah, renewing his quest for quiet enclosures, again withdraws from the crowd and settles down[14] east of the city, in a desert hut of his own manufacture. Whereas the hollows of the boat to Tarshish had been surrounded by bustling sailors, now he is at last totally alone. Perhaps some sources of Jonah's uncharacteristic and overwhelming joy have now been sketched out: he is happy with the rediscovery of an independence based on his own effort. He is happy that he was able to separate himself from Nineveh's enticing wealth and find contentment in a simple hut, since "the wealthy person is one who is happy [*sameakh*] with what he has."[15] But the deepest level has not been reached. Maimonides provides an enticing clue:

> Prophecy does not come to rest [upon a prophet] while he is in a state of stupor or a state of melancholy but only in a state of joy.[16]

At some unspecified point the *kikayon* appears, and its mystery is compounded by the larger context in which it is carefully set. This larger series, comprising four distinct elements, is of particular importance since it alone bears the burden of explaining Jonah's rollercoaster passage from distress to great joy and back again to apparent despair.

Here is the text:

---

[13] "One of the common sites of divine revelation . . . is in the shade of a tree," observes Alexander Rofé (*The Prophetical Stories* [Jerusalem: Magnes, 1998], 177, n. 112). He lists a number of examples (e.g., the Man of God in 1 Kgs 13) but neglects the possibility of the Jonah *kikayon*.

[14] For this lengthening of Jonah's stay, see below, "Pastoral Pedagogy" in chapter 9 and n. 11.

[15] Mishnah *Abot* 3:1.

[16] Maimonides (1968, 51, referring to *b. Pesahim* 117a).

Now the Lord God appointed a *kikayon* plant, which rose up over Jonah to act as a shade over his head, to save him from his distress, and Jonah was joyful over this *kikayon* with a great joy.

But then God appointed a worm at the rising of the dawn on the morrow, which struck the *kikayon* so that it dried out.

And it was that, when the sun rose, God appointed a silent east wind.

And the sun struck upon Jonah's head, and he swooned, and he requested his soul, to die. (4:6–8)

First, the plant is destroyed by a worm, transforming God's benign trick into a dirty one. Two further elements now appear, constituting a group of four:

a) *kikayon*

b) worm

c) silent east wind

d) sun

These four elements are integrated in a carefully delineated temporal sequence. First, the *kikayon* is appointed at night and perishes at night, most likely the same night, given the stress God puts on the brevity of its existence (4:10). The worm is appointed "at dawn *on the next day*" (4:7).[17] Indeed, the *kikayon* is entirely a creature of the night, able to thrive, like the divine being that appears to Jacob (Gen 32:23–33), only until the break of dawn. This may explain why, although the direct cause of the *kikayon*'s demise is the worm, it is noted that this occurs precisely at the break of dawn. The introduction of the second of two elements takes note of the sun's rising, which, again coin-

---

[17] The Targum attributes a somewhat greater longevity to the *kikayon*, "That this night was and another night had perished," but the MT seems to imply the very next night, as Uriel Simon observes; see *Jonah: The Traditional Hebrew Text with the New JPS Translation* (trans. Lenn J. Schramm; JPS Torah Commentary; Philadelphia: Jewish Publication Society, 1999), 45.

cidentally, marks the arrival of the east wind. This unity of time sketches a precise chronological development, as night yields to dawn, then the rising of the sun, then the full sun of day. It may be the case that this chronology is even more compressed, since the *kikayon* could have arisen at any point during the night, close to dawn perhaps; and, at the opposite extreme, the sun that beats down on Jonah's head could have struck shortly after dawn, which would be the case if Jonah is lying down rather than in a vertical position.[18] The shortest possible time for the complete series would therefore be less than two hours. What an exemplary setting for the perfectly classical tragedy *à la française*: absolute unity of place, extreme concentration of time, and a series of actions unified by the strangest coincidences!

The arrival of the east wind is particularly puzzling, for what indeed is it doing there? This wind just floats, to no apparent purpose, in the middle of two distinct operations: that of the worm that kills the *kikayon*, and that of the sun that, as is usually thought, causes Jonah to "swoon." In consequence, critics are wont to attach the wind either to the preceding or to the following. Most (e.g., the Septuagint), with no textual grounding, assume that it is a *hot* wind, thus one that assists—and perhaps needs help from—the sun.[19] Not differently, Simon imagines that it reduces the prophet's ability to withstand the sun's heat—thus, again, a hot wind. At the opposite extreme, Ibn Janah[20] assumes, with no more textual support but also with no less, that this is a cold wind but also a *dry* one, thus seconding the work of the sun but also of the worm, which, we recall, was sent to dry out the *kikayon* and Jonah along with it.[21] All agree, however, that the east wind's impact on our prophet is destructive.

---

[18] It was noted that, in the succah of his own making, Jonah *sat* (4:5). Since the *kikayon* lives only by night, however, it is quite possible that Jonah was *lying* down under it and asleep, or indeed that the whole thing was a prophetic dream.

[19] Elyakim Ben-Menahem, "Sefer Yona," in *Sefer Tere'asar: im perush "Da'at Mikra"* [The Minor Prophets] (Jerusalem: Mossad Harav Kook, 1974–1976), 18.

[20] Quoted in Ben-Menahem, "Sefer Yona," 18.

[21] See below, *wet and dry*. For the drying effect of the east wind, see Ezek 19:12; Hos 13:15. Ezek 17:9–10 presents two causes of withering, the second of which is the east wind. Moshe Greenberg notes that, of the two, the second "describes the destruction of the vine through a more 'spiritual' instrumentality,"

A counter-analysis might begin by noting that the *kikayon*, entirely beneficent, is destroyed by the worm, thus creating a merism expressing the rise and fall of the *kikayon*:

kikayon (+) / worm (-)

In the next series, the valuation is unclear:

east wind (?) / sun (-)

We notice that both the worm and the sun bring their miniseries to an end by the same action: *tak*, "to strike," a parallelism suggesting a similar structure to both. Thus, in the second merism, just as the sun's action mimics the worm's in its destructive effect, the east wind would have a *positive* value parallel to that of the *kikayon*:

east wind (+) / sun (-)

Before these suggestions are tested by metaphorical analysis, we must raise a major question: are God's dramatic manipulations essentially meteorological, simple object-lessons intended to teach Jonah a lesson, or do they refer to other levels of experience altogether, perhaps even different manifestations of the divine?[22]

There is a scholarly consensus on the unusual verbal similarities between Jonah's *kikayon* experience and Elijah's epiphany, but the full implications remain to be described.[23] To stress his

---

an observation that could be applied to the progressive intensification and "spiritualization" of dryness that occurs in Jonah from the worm to the east wind to the sun. See *Ezekiel 1–20: A New Translation with Introduction and Commentary* (AB 22; Garden City: Doubleday, 1983), 313–14.

[22] This latter hypothesis receives support from the different names of God attached to each revelation:

the *kikayon*: YHWH-Elohim
the worm: ha-Elohim
the wind: Elohim
the sun: no name (see below)

[23] See Sasson, *Jonah*, 284–86, 305; Simon, *Jonah*, 38, 44. Sasson, *Jonah*, 298, senses the importance of this comparison, since it could as easily be applied to Jonah. After rejecting—perhaps hastily, in view of its importance for Jonah as developed below—the importance of the broom tree (1 Kgs 19:4–5), he continues: "Far closer to the *kikayon*, as a manifestation of God's grace and as a

solitude, it is carefully noted that Elijah leaves his servant behind
and takes refuge under a bush:

> He came to Beer-sheba, which is in Judah, and left his servant
> there; but he himself went a day's journey into the desert. He
> came to a broom bush and sat down under it, and prayed
> that he might die.

> He lay down and fell asleep under a broom bush. Suddenly an
> angel touched him. (1 Kgs 19:3–5)

These verses serve as a prelude to God's revelation to Elijah on
Mount Horeb:

> And behold the Lord passed by. And there was a great and
> mighty wind, splitting mountains and shattering rocks before
> the Lord. But the Lord was not in the wind.

> And after the wind, an earthquake. But the Lord was not in
> the earthquake.

> And after the earthquake, fire. But the Lord was not in the
> fire.

> And after the fire, a thin, silent voice.

> And when Elijah heard, he wrapped his face in his mantle and
> went out and stood at the entrance of the cave. (vv. 11–13)

The detail of the prophet's solitude is crucial, as Michel Masson
explains:

> . . . the narrator can only transmit the recollections of a per-
> son who is alone. This implies that the statement "There was
> a storm, etc." can only mean: "Elijah had the impression that
> there was a storm, etc." From the start, the text is thus entirely
> situated in subjectivity.[24]

---

symbol of reconciliation, is Elijah's encounter with God at Horeb, coming as it
does immediately after he bitterly protests being abandoned (1 Kgs 19:9–18)."
[24]Michel Masson, "L'Expérience mystique du Prophète Elie: 'Qol Demama
Daqqa,'" *RHR* 208/3 (1991), 258–59.

This situation creates a level of uncertainty regarding not only the "thin, silent voice" experience but also the meteorological phenomena that lead up to it: "They can be considered as real but . . . just as easily as imaginary," "internal" just as easily as "external." We would like to explore the "internal" possibility that, like Elijah's, Jonah's solitary experience under the bush is the "narrative of an exstasis that involves four stages, expressed metaphorically."[25] Several of the stages in the experiences of Elijah and Jonah are remarkably parallel.

Silent/Still East Wind

When the sailors in Part One pray that the sea's rampage become quiet, their wish is that the wind entirely cease (Jonah 1:11). As the psalm puts it:

> He made the storm a calm, so that their waves were quieted. (Ps 107:29)

Yet, the arrival at Jonah's desert doorstep of the east wind—known in Scripture for its tumultuous violence[26]—presents the paradox of a still or even silent (*kharishit*) wind, as in the Targum. The paradox is not removed but rather intensified by the overtones of the alternate rendering of the Hebrew as a wind "that makes furrows like a plow," which may conceivably remove some of the sound of the east wind but retain its violence. No, the wind is still tremulously agitated and yet calm and even silent!

It should have been easy for critics to imagine the paradox of a noisy silence or a silent sound. Who has not experienced the sea's tranquil uproar[27] or a mountain peak's deafening hush, or, in a negative sense, the incessant silent buzz evoked by Lévinas' "strange obsession that one holds over from childhood and which resurfaces in insomnia, when the silence resonates and the emp-

---

[25] Masson, "L'Expérience," 260.

[26] Exod 14:21; Ezek 27:26; Ps 48:8. On the east wind, see Nahum Sarna, *Songs of the Heart: An Introduction to the Book of Psalms* (New York: Schocken, 1993), 161.

[27] Recall the title of Vercors' novel *Le Silence de la mer* (Paris: Club des Libraries de France, 1964).

tiness remains full."[28] In the Hebrew Bible the silence of words/ speech characterizes nature's praise of the Creator and, by extension, the words of Torah: "Their voice cannot be heard" (Ps 19:4). In wisdom literature this paradox distinguishes Eliphaz's recollection of his prophetic dream:

"I heard a silent voice." (Job 4:16)[29]

Thus, when Elijah's epiphany culminates in the "still, silent voice," we clearly see the possibility that Jonah's *kharishit* east wind might share in the tradition of the divine revelation as a silent sound.

As to the *easterly* origin of the wind, an unusual expression is inserted to describe Jonah's flight:

I hastened [*qidamti*] to flee. (4:2)

The verb is based on the root *qdm*, literally: "I eastened [*sic*] to flee." The locution acquires special interest from its contextual use: Jonah is reminding God of something important, of what he did, of his motivation perhaps, as a reaction to God's own action. The metaphorical sense is given additional stress by the fact that Jonah's literal flight was anything but in an easterly direction. Although traveling in an opposite direction, he was nevertheless traveling "east."

The next related use of *qdm* (4:5) defines the place from which Jonah can see what is happening in Nineveh. What he sees, however, is less what is happening *in* Nineveh than what will happen *to* Nineveh, in other words, what God intends concerning the city. Thus, again, the focus is on Jonah's relationship with God, less on what happens *in* the city than what God will reveal to Jonah *east* of the city. In short, *east* is the place where God will reveal Himself to Jonah.

Sun

There is also the issue of the sun, related to both the wind's easterly origin and to the careful alternation of night and day

---

[28] Emmanuel Lévinas, *De L'Existence à l'existant* (2d ed.; Paris: Vrin, 1990), preface.

[29] Lit. "I heard a silence and a voice," a hendiadys.

that characterizes Jonah's epiphany. Its main importance is said to be its ability to cause Jonah to "swoon." But did he in fact lose consciousness from the sun's heat, as commentators generally believe, or, rather, did he in fact "disguise or cover himself," as the alternate meaning of the Hebrew would suggest? The ongoing parallel with Elijah is again decisive:

> . . . and after the fire a still small voice. And when Elijah heard, he covered his face with his mantle. (1 Kgs 19:12–13)

Similarly:

> And the sun struck upon Jonah's head. And he covered over his face[30] and requested his soul, to die. (Jonah 4:8)

Such a covering over of the face and especially the eyes in the presence of the Almighty is well known in the Bible (Exod 3:6; 33:20–22). In such cases it expresses the conviction of death's proximity due to the overwhelming divine Presence. Thus in the presence of the Sun, both literally and figuratively, Jonah covers his eyes. What distinguishes Jonah from the other cases is his acceptance of his seeming fate, since, he goes on to explain, "my death would be better than my life" (4:8).

Dramatic Progression: x, x+1

The use of numerical structures based on incremental numbers as principles of rhetorical organization is well established in the Bible.[31] Let one text exemplify their most important characteristics:

> There are six things that the Lord hates, and seven which are an abomination to Him. . . . (Prov 6:16–19)

---

[30] The usual renderings "swooned" and "fainted" are guesses, although this may in fact have occurred. The root *'lp* in the Hitpael conjugation means "covered over" (Cant 5:14), and it is specifically applied to concealing the face in Gen 38:14–15.

[31] For a discussion and full bibliography see Shalom Paul, *A Commentary on the Book of Amos* (Minneapolis: Fortress, 1991), 13–14, 27–30; also Yair Zakovitch, "The Pattern of the Numerical Sequence Three-Four in the Hebrew Bible" (PhD diss., The Hebrew University, 1978).

Here the numbers are explicitly stated in order to stress the principle of climactic enumeration. The use of two different numbers expresses the idea of both similarity and difference or contrast: the first six share common characteristics, but the seventh, while still retaining similarity, belongs to another (perhaps qualitative) category altogether. Thus, the six are hateful but the seventh is so hateful as to be abominable.

This principle of similarity/difference is also in evidence in those structures based on the incremental numbers three/four. For example, in Prov 30:29–31 the group of four shares a "lordly stride" but the first three, drawn from the animal world, are contrasted with the culminating human fourth, the "king against whom there is no rising up." In the same chapter of Proverbs (30:11–14), the number four is not explicitly stated but remains the organizing principle as the word "generation" occurs before each of the four examples, and the incremental principle seems also to be implied by the qualitative difference between the first three and the fourth.[32]

Such three/four structures are very much active in Elijah's epiphany, all the more so for being implicit. And, in turn, the entire Elijah episode is a striking illustration of how such structures function. Like Jonah's, Elijah's epiphany has a series of four components:

---

[32] On Prov 30:15–33 see R. N. Whybray, *Proverbs* (NCB; London: Marshall Pickering, 1995), 91–98. For Prov 30:18–19, see below. Although these structures have a particular affinity for proverbs, other examples occur as well, most notably in the long series at the start of Amos:

For three transgressions of Damascus,
And for four, I will not turn away its punishment.
(Amos 1:3; see also 1:4–2:8)

The usual rendering begs the question as to whether God will turn away punishment for four, since He will not do so even for three! If the principle of similarity/difference is again applied, however, then a clear meaning emerges, as Harold Fisch (*A Remembered Future: A Study in Literary Mythology* [Bloomington: Indiana University Press, 1984], 687–88), translates:

For three transgressions of Damascus I will turn away its punishment,
But for the fourth I will not turn away its punishment.

For a satiric use of the three/four structure, see Jotham's fable in Judg 9:8–15, where the first three examples occupy the high ground and the fourth and culminating example turns to parody.

	Elijah	Jonah
1	wind	*kikayon*
2	earthquake	worm
3	fire	silent east wind
4	thin, silent voice/sound	sun

In both epiphanies the number four indicates a negative progression, a destruction that is actually an elevation, a gradual removal of the necessary preliminaries resulting in a growing disclosure of their Sponsor, the One who has "appointed" them. That is to say, the progression from start to finish is propelled by the supposition that, in each case, the entire four-part revelation is indeed divine—thus all components or stages are similar. Yet, the rumpus of each of the first three is successively disqualified, despite their place of eminence in the Sinai epiphany, and dismissed: No, God is not in the wind/earthquake/fire, i.e., not where you would expect Him to be.

Jonah has come to the desert in search of God. He has accommodated God's wishes; can he now hope for reinstatement? Again, the Elijah comparison may be helpful, since he too underwent three progressive apparitions, all of which, through their *negative* disclosures (i.e., "But the Lord was *not* in the wind, earthquake, fire"), prepare the final, direct revelation. Jonah too has an awareness that, while God is not in them, all three agents are sent or "appointed" by God, an awareness undoubtedly shared by Elijah as well. In the fourth and climactic apparition, however, expectations are upset in both texts. In Elijah's case, the three gradual disclosures-through-denial should have been followed by something like, "But God was indeed in the still small voice."[33] For Jonah too, the divine messenger sent to deliver the final blow

---

[33] Michel Masson's interesting explanation deserves careful study: "Now this amputation in such an important passage can only be deliberate and meaningful: the indication that God is not in the wind or the earthquake or the fire implied . . . a form of vigilance, that is to say, a residue of discriminative consciousness. The notice that God is in the fourth phenomenon would also have suggested such a residue. By contrast, the absence of any indication whatsoever expresses in the most skillful way the removal of any discriminative consciousness and by that very fact the total fusion of the human in the divine, resulting from a concentration carried to its highest level," "L'Expérience," 264.

should also have been perceived as such: "Then God appointed the sun." Instead, in the quadripartite configuration of the *kikayon* episode, the sequence leads from the apogee of Jonah's beatitude to his total surrender. What is often thought to be a studied diminuendo from the point of view of Jonah's happiness, however, is in fact a highly controlled experiment conducted by God as a crescendo, the full dramatic effect of which will only be grasped (by Jonah) at the end. And here is the surprise: Whereas the first three elements (*kikayon*, worm, east wind) are all deliberately introduced by the identical narrative formula ("Now God appointed x"), the fourth and climactic event simply happens: first as an almost casual indication of time and weather ("And when the sun rose"), then—but without the expected formula—as the concluding divine emissary, as it were: "The sun beat down upon Jonah's head." Surely this Sun—the second one—has an importance for Jonah far beyond the environmental!

Thus, following the possible parallel with Elijah as understood by Masson, Jonah had progressed from his earlier, preparatory experience:

> God appointed a *kikayon*,
> But God was not in the *kikayon* (since it withered).[34]

With the arrival of the wind, again:

> But God was not in the wind (since it too was merely an "appointee").

Yet, rather than reading the wind's arrival as following the sun's, it seems more likely that the two occurred at the same time, the wind being merely the one who precedes and announces the sun's arrival, just as in Gen 3:8 the wind signifies God's arrival.

An erotic reading of this episode would notice that the *kikayon* bush/tree, the divinely appointed *khuppah* or "bridal canopy," that is superimposed on Jonah's own succah, yields to the Sun in its full strength:

---

[34] He was, at best, *behind it*, which would be rather different, however, since in this case God's purpose would be pedagogical rather than mystical, intending to teach Jonah a lesson rather than reveal Himself to His prophet.

> And He (the sun/God) is like the groom who comes forth
> from His bridal canopy. (Ps 19:6)

Retrospectively, the sun's erotic implications seem mirrored in the possible parallel between Jonah's *kikayon*/worm/wind/sun epiphany and the "too wonderful" disclosure riddle of Prov 30:18–19:

> Three things are too wonderful for me,
> Four that I cannot fathom:
> The path of the eagle on the heavens,
> The path of a snake upon the rock,
> The path of a ship upon the high seas,
> And the path of a man upon a woman.[35]

The correspondences with Jonah are quite suggestive. First, like the *kikayon*/succah, the eagle merely seems suspended from the sky with no visible support. Second, the two creeping creatures—the snake and the worm—just seem to appear out of nowhere. Third, the ship is propelled by an invisible wind. Just as they are all just short of miraculous, the mystery of their appearance in Jonah can only be pointed at by the declaration that they come from God.[36] The most remarkable parallel—given our erotic reading of Jonah—is the fourth, the "path" or, better, "manner" in which lovers relate, far beyond the poet's power to fathom or "know"—a deliberate pun, pointing to the underlying paradox on erotic "knowing."

Wet and Dry

The dominant metaphorical cluster describing Jonah's epiphany unites the last three degrees of revelation: worm/wind/sun.

---

[35] The first three domains (air, earth, sea) are again contrasted with the nobler category, presumably representing the element of fire.

[36] Whybray comments: "It is no doubt to be inferred that all these things are part of the mysterious action of God," *Proverbs*, 416. More specifically, and with Menahem Ha-Meiri, the four wondrous activities are similar in that "they pass without leaving a trace of their passing," pointing to the basic paradox of four paths that are pathless, *Perush 'al Sefer Mishlei* [Commentary on the Book of Proverbs] (ed. Menachem Mendel Zahav; Jerusalem: Otsar ha-Poskim, 1969), 285.

We have seen how each of the book's two parts are defined geographically: the sea and Nineveh/desert. With a slight adaptation à la Claude Lévy-Strauss, we might now propose that the book's two dominant and antithetical modes are the wet and the dry,[37] with Jonah's unceremonious dumping, at the exact midpoint of the narrative, as the moment of transition between the one and the other:

> The Lord commanded the fish and it spewed Jonah out upon *dry land*. (2:11)

From this point on, Jonah's journey takes him ever more distant from the waters until, like the *kikayon* above his head, he too is dried out. From this perspective, we see the wind as operative midway between the worm and the sun, thus also involved in the drying out of the *kikayon* and, symbolically, Jonah himself and his hopes for happiness. Spatially viewed, just as the worm cuts off the ground supply of moisture and the sun strikes Jonah's head from above, the wind's horizontal sweep closes off any remaining source of humidity.

Now it is clear that dryness in the Hebrew Bible often has negative connotations, referring to the Lord's rebuke and destruction (Nah 1:4, 10), loss of hope (Ezek 37:11),[38] and ravenous craving from being deprived of delicacies (Num 11:6). However, Jonah's *kikayon* experience points in more positive directions. With the tripartite drying out east of Nineveh, Jonah has reached the point diametrically opposite his liquid descent into the depths of non-existence. Once this opposition is perceived, we understand that Jonah's experience under the *kikayon* is part and parcel of a vertical matrix represented not only by the tree itself, but even by the creature, the *tola'at*, or "worm," appointed to dry it out through a paradoxical etymology of motion upward.[39] We now see that, just as Part One tested Jonah's instinct to survive the depths, Part Two enjoins his desire for elevation.

---

[37] See the inclusive merism in Ezek 21:3, also Num 6:3.

[38] There are moist bones, signifying high spirits, as well as dry bones; see Moshe Greenberg, *Ezekiel 21–37: A New Translation with Introduction and Commentary* (AB 22A; New York: Doubleday, 1997), 745.

[39] See n. 34 in chapter 8.

Literary comparisons suggest various directions for interpretation. At an almost literal level, dryness can refer to the lack of desire (and bodily fluids!) following amorous coupling.[40] In Jonah's case, this would add emphasis to his precipitous fall following the delight of the *kikayon* experience. Another possibility—this one also both erotic and mystical—would not be sequential with the *kikayon* experience but rather coincidental with it. Here dryness refers to that state of restraint described by Chandidas as the secret of love that leads to salvation:

> Make your body *dry as a stick*. For He that pervades the universe seen of none, can only be found by one who knows the secret of love.[41]

This approach, anchored in the physical—Jonah's body, subject to the weather conditions—is also a sign of spiritual liberation. Finally, the prophet Joel relates the condition of dryness to a more general absence or removal of happiness,

> . . . for happiness has dried up from human beings. (Joel 1:12; see vv. 11–12)[42]

This would signify, for Jonah, either a loss of that happiness symbolized by the *kikayon*, or a desire to pass beyond happiness, as expressed by his final request to die.

In both cases, of course, the end points meet: both polar opposites express Jonah's need to overcome the death wish. In Part One he succeeds; in Part Two he does not. Thus the otherwise incomprehensible 4:8: "I would rather die than live." Either Jonah has learned nothing from his first near-death experience, or he

---

[40] The sixteenth-century poet Gilles Corrozet, writing about the mating of nightingales: "Quand prend fin la volupté charnelle,/Tombent soubdain dessus le rameau sec" (*Le Compte du rossignol* [ed. Ferdinand Gohin; Paris: Garnier, 1924], 44). Thus the eunuch complains that "I am just a dry tree" (Isa 56:3).

[41] See Ananda Coomaraswamy, *The Dance of Shiva* (New York: Noonday, 1957), 128. Maurice Scève states that the soul "de son corps en fin se desherite, . . . Plus desseché qu'en terre de Lemnos." The latter reference is to a kind of red chalk. See poem 353 in Scève, *La Délie* (ed. I. D. McFarlane; Cambridge: Cambridge University Press, 1966).

[42] This complex passage is based on the wordplay between *yabesh*, "dry," and *bush*, "embarrassment," that arises from lack of pleasure. See below.

has moved to a point beyond that where he now rejects the possibility of resurrection of the dead. Why this is the case would be a matter of considerable speculation. Here are two, and our conclusion below presents yet others:

1) The Sun of full revelation is too strong: take my life.[43]

2) But if Jonah now accepts death, why would he cover his face, assuming that viewing the Sun would in fact achieve his wish? Two solutions may be proposed:

   a) because his decision to die is only a conclusion of his own reasoning, as indicated by his use of the wisdom argumentative structure of better-than;[44]

   b) covering his face is in fact a disguise, an attempt to conceal his identity from God.

Why would this be? Embarrassment perhaps. A midrash explains:

> When the righteous wish to sit at ease in this world, the satan comes forward and disputes with them: "Is it not enough for them that it is laid up in the world to come that they wish to live at ease in this world also?"[45]

By accepting death Jonah avoids the charge. But in so doing he acknowledges placing his own needs above those of his Beloved's.

---

[43] God's reply to Jonah might well take the following reading of the book's final question: "You were content with a lesser revelation (the *kikayon*). Can I not take satisfaction in lower levels of spirituality as well?"

[44] See Excursus 2, "Better Than."

[45] *Gen Rabba* 84:3, cited by Rashi on Gen 37:1, who relates this speech to God Himself. For Satan as God's alter ego for expressing His own doubts, see Meir Weiss, *The Story of Job's Beginnings: Job 1–2, a Literary Analysis* (Jerusalem: Magnes, 1983), 41.

PART THREE

THE THEOLOGY OF THE BOOK OF JONAH

Many waters cannot quench love,
nor can rivers drown it.

Cant 8:7

"I have loved you" said the Lord. And you
have asked: "How have You loved us?"

Mal 1:2

The close parallel between Jonah and Elijah may have seemed to the rabbis as an open invitation to read into the book of Jonah the national situations and aspirations of the Jewish people. That the Israelites do not appear even once in the book may not constitute an insurmountable obstacle, however, if the matter is understood theologically. In such a reading, the desire of both prophets to die has a dual focus: the drama of personal failure, and the sense that the grand prophetic relationship, launched by God to the Israelites—and through them to the entire human race, at least in Jonah's understanding—has been stalled, perhaps irretrievably. At its deepest level, the book of Jonah is a theological elaboration of these intertwined crises.

The book of Jonah is in reality many books: of love, of prayer, of repentance, and of prophecy. The tendency to overstress the repentance aspect, undoubtedly influenced by its liturgical use on the Jewish Day of Atonement, has come at the expense of the other three, so that even its prophetical perspective has been co-opted by the repentance plot. My argument for a more inclusive understanding of prophecy, one that stresses Jonah's love as well as God's, allows the human-divine relationship to be viewed as a prophetic dialogue of love based on prayer and repentance. This means, among other things, that all these aspects or "books" of Jonah are to be conceptualized as, rather than different paths *to God, different modes of an ongoing and two-way conversation and argument.*

CHAPTER FIVE

THE BOOK OF LOVE

> *Ha-tsaddik ka-rasha'*, "Do we all
> get the same treatment?!"
>
> (Gen 18:25; free translation)

> I hate them that regard vain idols;
> But I trust in the Lord, I will be glad
> and rejoice in Your love [*khesed*].
>
> (Ps 31:7–8)

East of the City: *le désert d'amour*

As a prelude to his love negotiations with the flirtatious so-
cialite Célimène, her jealous lover Alceste declares his despairing
intention "to flee to a desert far from any human access." His
desire, of course, is not only to avoid the competition—all judged
by him to be wicked—but also and especially to have his beloved
all to himself. The familiar topos of the desert as a place of reconciliation and amorous encounter in the Hebrew Bible affords us
a convenient transition to the erotic theme of Jonah. For the dry
land setting of Part Two has not one but two components. The first
is the one intended by God—Nineveh—which Jonah traverses
at breakneck speed.[1] The second is Jonah's Walden, his place of

---

[1] See, however, Uriel Simon's attractive conjecture that Jonah's walk of three
days' duration in Nineveh refers not to the time "required to cross the city in a
straight line but to the period needed to traverse its streets and byways so that all
the inhabitants can hear his proclamation," *Jonah: The Traditional Hebrew Text
with the New JPS Translation* (trans. Lenn J. Schramm; JPS Torah Commentary;
Philadelphia: Jewish Publication Society, 1999), 28.

solitude and refuge—that spot "east of the city"—which can only be the desert.

Now the *midbar,* or "desert," has a special place in the love relationship between God and His people, first as a place of love and seduction:

> I am going to entice her
> and lead her towards the wilderness
> and speak intimately with her. . . .
> And she will respond there as in the time of her youth,
> as on the day she came up from the land of Egypt.
> (Hos 2:16–17)[2]

Simply reverse the gender of the pronouns and we have the subplot of Jonah's withdrawal to the desert:

> I, Jonah, am going to entice Him.[3]
> May He respond . . . as on the day He brought us up from the land of Egypt.

Hosea 2:16 also points to a second and related sense of desert:

> I am going to entice her.
> I will lead her towards the wilderness [*midbar*]
> and speak [*wedibarti*] intimately with her.

The wordplay on the root *dbr* also evokes the place where one speaks.[4]

Indeed, readers have been sensitive to the sharp verbal exchanges between God and Jonah. Haim Lewis speaks of a running debate between the two.[5] One wonders, though, about the tone of these exchanges, whether these are appropriate to debate or to something else:

---

[2] See also 13:5: "I knew you in the desert"; Cant 3:6; 8:5; Jer 2:2 (see below).

[3] The Jonah/dove seducer is a possible reading of Hos 7:11: "Ephraim is like a seducing dove," interpreting the root *pth* in the sense it has in the Piel, as Rashi does in Prov 20:19.

[4] "And your speech [*midbarek;* alt. "mouth"] is comely" (Cant 4:3). See Harold Fisch, *A Remembered Future: A Study in Literary Mythology* (Bloomington: Indiana University Press, 1984), 133.

[5] Haim Lewis, "Jonah—A Parable for Our Time, *Judaism* 21 (1972): 159–63.

Jonah: "I want to die!"

God: "Are you so upset?"

Well, Jonah was indeed so upset that he broke off conversation without a word and fled! If God's tone is teasing, it is in the manner of Emerson's put-down that combines superiority with loving concern, an effort to put Jonah's pain into a perspective of reconciliation:

"So hot? my little Sir."[6]

Here we need the help of new literary parallels because the usual ones do not serve. No prophet behaves so irrationally (flight, endless brooding), and with none does God show such playful irony—in fact, God doesn't blow His stack even once with Jonah, though in other contexts He needs far less provocation. To find a parallel to God and Jonah's peculiar relation, one thinks not only of the Song of Songs[7] but also of the exchanges between Alceste and Célimène in Molière's *The Misanthrope*, for Jonah from the start sounds like a misanthrope in love, and his exchanges with God take on the tones of a lovers' quarrel. We should consider, in short, whether Jonah's persona as runaway prophet/servant is not doubled by that of a rejected lover, yielding the unusual combination of the irrationality of a lovers' spat, on the one hand, and what Dennis Taylor called "the delicacy of a spiritual conversation" on the other.[8]

Jonah's initial waywardness is of course startling, that God commands him to go to Nineveh and His chosen one takes just the opposite course: he goes . . . to Tarshish. This pattern is repeated yet more subtly in the very next expression: God said: "Call upon Nineveh" (1:2) and, instead, Jonah called upon . . . Him (2:3)! In time, God does deliver Jonah, after a manner of

---

[6] Ralph Waldo Emerson, *The Portable Emerson* (ed. Carl Bode; rev. ed.; The Viking Portable Library; New York: Penguin Books, 1981), 190.

[7] E.g., the cat-and-mouse game of pursuit in Cant 3:1–5, and especially the premature departure of the lover in 5:6: He is miffed because she didn't open the door to him in time!

[8] Dennis Taylor, "The Need for a Religious Literary Criticism," *RelArts* (1996): 124–50.

speaking. But He does not simply deposit him on dry land, He has the fish *vomit* him. The lovers' reconciliation is in progress but is far from complete.

The Opening Scene

In our attempt to solve the haunting issue of Jonah's motives in fleeing from God, it is crucial to expand our analysis of a number of opening clues that, taken together, can shed light on the book's covert erotic situation. Quite frankly, such an exercise can appear either tedious or at least overly inventive. Taken collectively, however, these examples can generate a much needed refocus:

The Word of the Lord unto Jonah (Beloved)

How can we avoid the overtones of Beloved in Jonah's very name? Recall that as a term of endearment the Hebrew word *yonah* (Eng. Jonah), "dove," has few parallels in the Hebrew Bible's vocabulary of personal love.[9] Listen to how the Bride is addressed in the Song of Songs:

> My dove is in the clefts of the rock. (Cant 2:14)

> Open to me, my sister, my love, my dove, my blameless one! (Cant 5:2)

> Unique is my dove, my pure one. (Cant 6:9; also 1:15, 4:1, 5:12)

Now repeat the verses as they sound in Hebrew and pretend that your name is Jonah, with its richly erotic overtones of "Beloved":

> My Jonah is in the cleft of the rock.

---

[9] This point—the erotic sound and use of Jonah's name—avoids any attempt to discover an allegorical meaning ("dove, son of fidelity") that Joseph Blenkinsopp rightly finds forced; cf. *A History of Prophecy in Israel* (rev. and enl. ed.; Louisville, KY: Westminster John Knox, 1996), 241. See, however, my concluding midrashic readings below, where the attempt is no longer resisted.

Open to me, my sister, my love, my Jonah, my blameless one!

Unique is my Jonah, my pure one.

The opening words now sound quite different:

The word of the Lord unto Dove, His Beloved.

"And It Was," wayehi

The book of Jonah opens with a well-known formula: "And it was . . .":

And it was, the word of the Lord unto Beloved. (Jonah 1:1)

Limburg points out that many narratives begin in the same way (Joshua, Judges, 1 and 2 Samuel, Esther, Ezekiel), but by narrative he means story. Sasson cautions that such a view can lead to a modern misapprehension that what follows is fiction, perhaps even of the time "Once in a time," whereas all of the above mentioned works "were considered by the Hebrew to have been 'historical.'"[10] The rabbis heard different, more wrenching tones as well.

Wherever in the Bible we find this expression, "And it was in the days of," the approach of suffering [*tsa'r*] is indicated.[11]

Thus, they continue, the opening of Esther intones the arrival of Haman; the book of Judges forecasts a famine, as does Ruth. Would this opening in Jonah project the dramatic intensity of our erotic theme of divorcement?

"Go!" lek *(Jonah 1:2)*

God's command recalls the start of that first and greatest of love stories, that of God and Abraham:

---

[10] See James Limburg, *Jonah: A Commentary* (Louisville, KY: Westminster John Knox, 1993), 37. See also Jack M. Sasson, *Ruth: A New Translation with a Philological Commentary and a Formalist-Folklorist Interpretation* (2d ed.; Sheffield: Sheffield Academic Press, 1989), 14–15.

[11] See *b. Megillah* 10b.

And God said to Abram: "Go . . ." (Gen 12:1)[12]

The parallel is important in several regards. First of all, it is now clear that Jonah "flees" because God first told him to go away, thus in some way he is provoked by a command. Secondly, although in the Jonah text what he is called upon to leave behind is not specified, from the comparison with Gen 12 ("from your land, etc.") its weight is palpable. From Jonah's later complaint that he was "exiled" (*nigrashti*, 2:5), his natural reaction was to "go," as in "And he exiled him, and he went" (Ps 34:1).

"Get Up/Stand Up (and Get Moving)," qum

The Lord's very charge to "Get up!" does not arise out of the blue; the word itself says pages about the ambient and previous situation, indicating "a significantly new development, especially a discontinuous one,"[13] and, one might add, a negative one as well (Num 32:14; Deut 13:2). The primary meaning is one of incitement,[14] best construed here, as often, as a helping verb: "get moving to go!" The previous point is hereby accentuated by the strong language of incitement: *qum lek*, "get up and go, get moving," as if Jonah did not want to move or go anywhere. This sense, however, hardly excludes the more concrete meaning: "*Stand up and go*," suggesting that Jonah had been sitting. Where? Undoubtedly in his house, where one both sits and dwells (Deut 6:7; 11:19). However, from his flight "from *before* the Lord" (see below) we infer that he had been enjoying the divine Presence; indeed, his repeated "going down" indicates that he had been living in the Temple precinct in Jerusalem, the highest point in the city. And here the literal and metaphorical senses become fused:

---

[12] Literally "go for yourself" ("for your benefit," Rashi) or, literally "to yourself," typically rendered as "get yourself going." Or, vocalized differently: "Go, go!"

[13] Nahum Sarna, *Exodus: The Traditional Hebrew Text with the New JPS Translation* (JPS Torah Commentary; Philadelphia: Jewish Publication Society, 1991), 239, n. 9.

[14] *lashon zeruz*; see Elyakim Ben-Menahem, "Sefer Yona," in *Sefer Tere'asar: im perush "Da'at Mikra"* [The Minor Prophets] (Jersualem: Mossad Harav Kook, 1974–1976), 1.

Happy are those who sit/dwell in Your house. (Ps 84:5)

He who sits/dwells in the secret place of the Most High. (Ps 91:1)

And such "sitting" becomes the focus of intense and exclusive love:

> One thing alone have I asked of the Lord,
> That alone do I seek:
> To *dwell* in the house of the Lord all the days of my life.
> (Ps 27:4)

From such a perspective, the sudden call to "get up and go" signals a transition from a situation of shared delight to one of separation and exile, perhaps, too, from contemplation to action.

To Nineveh

The strangeness of the command to go to Nineveh—already declared repulsive by the Lord (1:3)—is compounded by the fact that only Jonah and Elijah are sent on prophetic missions out of the land. When Jonah does finally get around to his mission, an interesting word is used:

> Now Jonah began (*wayyakhel*) to go into the city . . . (3:4)

This typical translation captures the usual understanding, but the same verb (*khll*) may convey quite a different sense:

> The people *profaned themselves* (*wayyakhel*). (Num 25:1)

Some conflate the two meanings, for example the Targum: "They began to commit harlotry." More likely, however, the initial meaning "to begin" also evokes the ambience in Num 25:1, where harlotry is linked with idolatry. We thus have yet another reason for Jonah's reluctance to travel to Nineveh: not only that he had to leave the Temple, but also that he had to travel to an impure land, one associated with a *rejection* of God.

To Flee

According to the normative conventions of Western love, it is the beloved who flees or leaves or is absent. In Jonah, especially chapters 1–2, we have a variant situation in which it is the lover who flees. In both cases, perhaps (surely in the latter), an erotic dialectic is engaged whereby absence contrives precisely the opposite, since it is intended to arouse desire.[15] As Terry Eagleton has put it, Jonah wants to force God to save him.[16]

To Tarshish

When commanded to go preach repentance to the Ninevites, Jonah flees to Tarshish from the Lord's Presence/service. It is commonly supposed that Tarshish, wherever it was, was in the opposite direction from Nineveh. This view is compelling, however, only if Jonah is fleeing from Nineveh, his original point of destination. What is more probable is that the (ideological) direction of Tarshish was opposite not to Nineveh (with which it had everything in common), but, like Nineveh itself, to Jerusalem, for what Jonah especially wanted was to escape from his point of origin, the place of God's Presence. This point is reinforced by his decision, after preaching to the Ninevites, to station himself *east* of the city, again in order to distance himself further from Jerusalem. From an erotic point of view, therefore, Tarshish is Jonah's parody of Nineveh, or, more precisely, of God's command to go there. For, more generally speaking and as we have seen, Tarshish is less a particular place than a figure for the sea itself, and this provides yet another clue to Jonah's motivations. The crucial text here is Isaiah's oracle against none other than Assyria:

> Ah, the uproar of many peoples that roar as the roaring of the seas. (Isa 17:12)

---

[15] Quoting Wallace Steven's "not to have is the beginning of desire" ("Notes towards a Supreme Fiction"), Aviva Zornberg made this notion the leitmotif of her *Genesis: The Beginning of Desire* (Philadelphia: Jewish Publication Society, 1995). The notion is of course an erotic commonplace. Leone Ebreo (sixteenth century), for example, declared desire to be based on absence as well as knowledge. See T. A. Perry, *Erotic Spirituality: The Integrative Tradition from Leone Ebreo to John Donne* (University: University of Alabama Press, 1980), 10.

[16] Terry Eagleton, "J. L. Austin and the Book of Jonah," in *The Book and the Text* (ed. Regina Schwartz; Cambridge, MA: Basil Blackwell, 1990), 232.

The waters are a figure for the enemies of God, in this case precisely the ones on whose behalf Jonah was exiled from God's Presence. Jonah's message to God seems to be:

> You object to my flight amidst the waters, yet You Yourself cast me out among the "waters."

Alternatively, Jonah wants to leave. But he could have committed suicide in Jerusalem! Say, then, that he wanted to leave the land of prophecy, so as not to hear the divine word any longer. But he could have left by land! Why precisely by sea? In order to drown out the sorrows of his love. But this experiment fails, since,

> Many waters cannot quench love, nor can rivers drown it. (Cant 8:7)

According to this reading, Jonah's parody turns against himself.

From the Lord's Presence

With Jonah's determination not only to drop out or "flee" but also "from the Lord's Presence"—spoken not once but twice in the same verse (1:3)—we now return to the central question of the book, for Jonah is not only sick of life, he is upset with God; indeed, this is precisely why he wants to die. Whether the most appropriate term for his flight is rebellion[17] must now be considered. This exercise in rereading will require that we suspend our usual (generic and theological) preconceptions and listen to yet other rhythms in the text. Then we shall consider in greater detail the meaning of standing "in the divine Presence."[18]

Erotic Clues and Vocabulary

In searching for a credible interpretative model, our focus here will be on words and metaphors that occur in both non-erotic and erotic contexts in the Hebrew Bible. Convinced by habits of reading

---

[17] Simon, *Jonah*, 3.
[18] See below, "Life at the Center: Love's Canopies."

Jonah, critics typically disregard these clues. Their frequency and importance, however, should give us pause.

"Flight," libroakh

It is often claimed, for example, that Jonah heads for Tarshish in order to flee from God's Presence—that is in fact what the text seems to say! In fact, however, Jonah will be leaving the divine Presence even if he goes to Nineveh, as will be the case in chapter 3. The problem may be in the usual understanding of *libroakh*, "to flee," i.e., to depart out of fear from a threatening situation. Such meanings are reinforced by the idea of haste, as when the rabbis speculate that Jonah, in his rush to escape, bought up all places on the ship. Ibn Ezra was the first to point out, however, that the verb carries this meaning only when followed by the preposition *mipne*.[19] Our preposition *milipne*, however, means simply to depart from someone's presence, as Jacob from Pharaoh's (Gen 47:10). Or, once the conversation is over, Cain leaves the place in which God appeared to him (Gen 4:16). Moreover, the verb itself has erotic connotations that have been ignored in the discussion: "Flee, my Beloved" (*berakh dodi*), the concluding verse of the Song of Songs, 8:14, which repeats 2:17, except that *berakh* replaces *sob*, "to turn around and away," thus a synonym. Other uses do not at all stress haste but rather "movement towards a destination without ever losing sight of the place that one is leaving."[20]

"Distress," tsar, tsarah

Important to our inquiry is the glossary of Jonah's psalm. Let us again remind ourselves that the plot itself can be reduced to one fourth of the book (the third chapter), while the entire remainder deals with an issue quite unusual in prophetic literature:

---

[19] Numbers 10:35 gives the perfect example of *mipne* (here used with another verb to flee: *yanusu*, carrying overtones both of haste and fear. The text carefully uses *mipne* rather than *milipne*, since God-haters cannot be imagined as having been in God's Presence.

[20] André Robert, Raymond Tournay, and André Feuillet, *Le Cantique des cantiques: Traduction et Commentaire* (Paris: Gabalda, 1963), 327.

the psychological problems that God and prophet are having with one another. From such a perspective, the prayer could deliver up, in its very selection and slight adaptations of traditional formulas, crucial information on Jonah's mental state. Those readers who detect a tone and meter of lament (*qinah*) in this text are not wrong, but the motivation needs to be clarified. As seen above, Jonah does not lament his approaching death; he prays for it and welcomes it. Nor does he lament his return to life, once he has seen death's true nature. Why then is he so sad? Over his amorous separation from God. Again, it is the overtone that discloses:

> I called out of my distress (*mitsarah li*) to the Lord. (2:3)

It is the very word that David uses in a poignant lament of love after death's final separation:

> "I am distressed (*tsar-li 'aleka 'akhi*), Jonathan . . .
> Wonderful was your love to me." (2 Sam 1:26)[21]

It is the word that describes the state of being abandoned by God in Deut 4:30.[22]

"Banishment," grsh

Further into the prayer, Jonah complains as follows:

> "But as for me, though I had thought
> to be driven (*nigrashti*) from Your presence,
> Yet I continue to gaze
> towards the Temple of Your holiness." (2:5)

If we persist in seeing Jonah's departure as a flight on his own initiative, then the complaint to be driven away (i.e., by someone else) makes no sense. A second issue is one of language and tone. A parallel text offers the variant (*nigrazti*, Ps 31:23), "I am cut off from Your sight," and some critics have proposed emendation of our text on the strength of that parallel. The language of our text is no accident, however. In the Hebrew Bible the root *grsh*, "to be

---

[21] Note the dative *li* in both cases.
[22] See above, "Jonah's First Prayer," in chapter 2.

exiled," occurs in two highly relevant contexts: marital divorce,[23] and God's driving away Israel's enemies.[24] Jonah's message to God now seems more directed: "I feel 'driven away' from Your sight like a divorcée or a foreign enemy." Hosea (9:15) captures God's usage perfectly, bringing it even closer to Jonah's personal situation: "I will drive them from my house."

The two first and thus paradigmatic instances of exile in the Bible give an even stronger coloration: the first man's banishment from paradise and his firstborn's loss of the divine Presence:

> So the Lord God banished him from the garden of Eden . . . He drove the man out (*wayegaresh*). (Gen 3:23–24)

> "Since you have banished (*gerashta*) me this day from the soil and I must avoid your presence . . ." (Gen 4:14)

Particularly the scene depicted in Gen 3:24 expands the interpretative possibilities of Jonah's decision to station himself east of the city, for to the east is the entrance to the Garden of Eden and the angels with the "overturning swords" (described using the same word that depicts Nineveh's destruction or "overturning"). The journey east thus summarizes in a single emblem Jonah's desire both to reenter the paradise of the divine Presence and also to threaten vengeance upon the Ninevites.[25]

"From Your Sight," mineged 'eyneka

This expression literally means "from the presence of your eyes," again further stressing Jonah's separation from the divine Presence. From the expression in Joel 1:16, we might translate: "from before Your very eyes."

Two erotic connections should be pondered. The first use of the preposition *neged* is used to describe Eve's relation with Adam: "a helper in his presence" (Gen 2:18, also 2:20). What-

---

[23] Lev 21:7; Ezek 44:22. The passive form *gerushah* is used only of a divorced woman.

[24] Exod 21:31; 33:2; 1 Chr 17:21.

[25] This latter point is based on the pun of the sword that overturns (*mithhapekhet*) and Jonah's threat that Nineveh will be overturned (*nehepakhet*; Jonah 3:4). God's threats are carried out by similar maneuvers in both cases.

ever the term means, it is clear that the erotic presence of the spouses to one another is strongly hinted. The second aspect, that of living "in the eyes" of the beloved, is an erotic commonplace, expressed, for example, even in Cressida's rather pathetic:

> "I could live and die in the eyes of Troilus."
> (*Troilus and Cressida*, 1.2.242)

It conveys the sense of basking in the warmth of someone's esteem ("eyes"), and its active coordinate is captured in the English tune: "I only have eyes for you." Both active and passive senses of "seeing" receive extraordinary emphasis in describing the mutual relations between God and Israel. On the one hand, God is one who delights in both seeing and being seen. Reciprocally, Israelites come to the Temple to be seen and also to see. It does not seem much of a stretch to consider the desire to "be seen" by someone as synonymous with the desire "to be loved" by that person.[26]

"Casting Out," wa-tashlikheni

Further and in the same vein, Jonah's prayer is framed by the following notation:

> And You *cast me out* into the depths,
> into the very heart of the sea. (2:4)

In addition to again accusing God of something Jonah himself asked the sailors to do (to throw him into the sea), the language of "casting out or down" is a bit harsh—why not use the gentler "lower me down" (1:12, 15)? Why portray God as so angry as to use a word that to Hebrew readers conveys such abandonment? There is again the image of casting out the enemies of Israel:

> Their pursuers You cast into the depths. (Neh 9:11)

---

[26] For its more literal reference to the Temple, see below, "Life at the Center: Love's Canopies."

The phrase sticks in the memory because both the verb and its complement are repeated, and because the reference is to the major events of Israelite salvation from Egypt. Further and even more crucial is the resonance of total dereliction:

Do not cast me out from Your presence! (Ps 51:13)

Do not cast me out at the time of my old age. (Ps 71:9)

It is interesting that Jonah's charge "and You cast me out" is leveled ambiguously, thus giving Jonah an escape. For the Hebrew can be read either as

and You cast me out . . .

and also

and the deep cast me out . . .

Although God is thus, as least grammatically, off the hook, Jonah's horrible insinuations hover over the text: God has rejected him either as an enemy or as a former wife who had enjoyed His continued intimacy.

"Love," khesed

Jonah's deepest motivations are further hinted in what seems a throw-away verse in the prayer—one that of course cannot even be considered by those who excise the prayer from the text:

Those who care for empty vanities forfeit their mercy [khesed]. (2:9)

The usual reading of this verse involves two problems: the generality and the reference. Why would Jonah suddenly interrupt the personal and intimate tone of his prayers—he immediately takes it up again—merely to take a poke at idolaters? What these people forfeit may not be exactly mercy, however, since one of the meanings of khesed in the Hebrew Bible is "love," as in the following crucial passage:

I remember the *khesed* of your youth, your love as a bride. (Jer 2:2; also 31:2)[27]

I will betroth you unto me with *khesed*. (Hos 2:21; also 6:4, 6.)

In the Hosea texts this *khesed*, or "love," leads to *da'at* (Ps 36:11), a love whose flowering is intimate "knowing" of the Other.[28]

This reading greatly expands our understanding of Jonah's later complaint, where he belatedly explains his upset and which again turns on the key word *khesed*:

"For I know that You are a gracious and merciful God, long suffering and full of *khesed*." (4:2)

The expression "full of *khesed*" may in fact imply not only "full of love" but even "*too* full of love."[29] For although Jonah surely cannot object that God has love, isn't such abundant love a bit much, if it implies not only mercy for the wicked (the usual reading) but especially disregard for true love? Doesn't Jonah complain that God has *too much* love for the unworthy, and thus not enough for a righteous beloved? Of course, Jonah has concerns for justice, that God will not punish the wicked according to their deserts.[30]

---

[27] Yvonne Sherwood (*A Biblical Text and Its Afterlives: The Survival of Jonah in Western Culture* [Cambridge: Cambridge University Press, 2000], 261) explores the much neglected parallels between Jonah and Jeremiah. See, for example, the erotic implications of Jer 20:7–8: "O Lord, You have seduced me and I was seduced; you have overcome me and you have prevailed."

[28] Henri Meschonnic (*Jona et le signifiant errant* [Paris: Gallimard, 1981], 75) gives the fullest understanding of *khesed*: "Il désigne le rapport réciproque de la divinité à l'homme et de l'homme à la divinité, un rapport d'amour." See also "In Your love [*bkhsdka*] you have led forth the people whom You have redeemed" (Exod 15:13). The term figures importantly in characterizing David and Jonathan's bond: 1 Sam 20:8, 14, 15; see Limburg, *Jonah*, 70, 91, for further examples.

[29] See Num 16:3, 7, where *rab lakem* means "you have gone *too* far." In Exod 1:9, NJPS renders *rab we'atsum* as "much *too* numerous."

[30] This accounts for the astonishing omission or even deletion of "truth," i.e., justice, in Jonah's quotation of Exod 34:6–7 on the divine attributes, and who is more qualified than "Jonah son of truth" to make such an assessment! Also Ps 86:15. It is true that while Num 14:18 also omits "truth," some MSS include it nevertheless; see Jacob Milgrom, *Numbers: The Traditional Hebrew Text with the New JPS Translation* (JPS Torah Commentary; Philadelphia: Jewish Publication Society, 1990), 111.

But there is further upset concerning love: Jonah is tormented because God's love for others means less love for himself. Jonah has the jealousy of a jilted lover.

Such a view would suggest yet other translations of 2:9:

a) Those [the sailors and the Ninevites] who worship worthless idols abandon the One who loves them.[31] I would even suggest that here the language of indirection has reached further into the dangerous area of veiled accusation (the method of concealment is to use a plural for a singular and also to invent a new verb form, a kind of *tikkun soferim* or Massoretic "correction"), yielding a masterpiece of double entendre:

b) Those [i.e., like God in this case] who protect worthless idol-worshipers abandon the ones [like Jonah] who love them.[32]

A compromise of these two positions is also conceivable:

c) Those who worship idols thereby lose their ability to love God.

The prophet Hosea, followed by Jeremiah and Ezekiel and the Song of Songs, projected the analogy of divine love as a human marriage: God's relation with His people can be understood according to the model of husband and wife. Briefly to review some characteristics of that relationship:

a) it is unique and mutual and exclusive. Thus the erotic version in the Song of Songs: "I am my beloved's and my beloved is mine" (Cant 6:3) is parallel to "I will be your God and you will be my people" (Lev 26:12);

b) God is a jealous lover;

---

[31] Thus, for example, Limburg, *Jonah*, 72: "Those who rely on worthless idols abandon the one who loves them." "Abandon" continues the ambience of marital divorce (Prov 2:17).

[32] Jack M. Sasson thinks that the word for love here (*khesed*) denotes a situation in which "a person in a higher position . . . acts favorably to another person or entity in a lower position" (*Jonah: A New Translation with Introduction, Commentary, and Interpretation* [AB 42B; New York: Doubleday, 1990], 198).

c) deviation from this close and unique bond is termed "whoring." Hosea and Jeremiah thus provide God's perspective: God is the jealous, injured husband and Israel, the unfaithful wife who has gone a'whoring after strange gods.

The book of Jonah, in retaining all these premises, dares to ask whether God is the only partner entitled to be jealous.[33] For our book inverts the perspective by describing a situation in which it is the wife (Jonah) who is cast aside and the husband (God) who seems to favor other consorts. Transformed from the favored wife to the hated wife,[34] Jonah is cast out among the wicked and impure, wanting to die but nevertheless continuing to gaze towards the place of bliss. Thus to God's command "thou shall have no other lovers before Me" (Exod 20:2–3), Jonah asks:

"And shall *Thou* have other beloveds before *me*?"[35]

For if the essence of an erotic relationship is its equality or at least mutuality, and if jealousy is a dominant prerogative, then it is truly Jonah who is godlike—a "lover transformed into the beloved," as the courtly theoreticians liked to put it. And if this is indeed the case, then Jonah asks what we are to think of God's promiscuity.

We imagine explanations—often theologically motivated—that mislead, such as universalism versus particularism. Imagine what it would feel like, however, if your spouse announced that he/she was bringing home another spouse but "not to worry" because you will still be loved as much. The real-life situation is to feel displaced, betrayed by the one you love most and who should have loved you most as well. From the point of view of love theory at least, the real opposition to universalism (= polygamy) is eroticism, one's clinging to the unique other. And in its essence

---

[33] At best, one could imagine a scenario restating the one in Hosea. By sending Jonah out among idol worshippers, maybe God wishes to give Israelites yet another object lesson similar to the one foisted upon poor Hosea: "Go out and take a whore so that you can understand *My* predicament!"

[34] Deut 21:15; Isa 60:15.

[35] Limburg, *Jonah*, 72: "like a child forsaking a loving parent, *or a husband or wife abandoning a loving spouse*" (emphasis added).

erotic theory cannot resolve the dilemma, since, as the old courtly theoreticians declared, "No heart can be in two places at the same time." Blenkinsopp has proposed a plausible real-life situation against which Jonah reacts: "The point is that they [the Gentiles] are to embrace the religion of Israel when it is preached to them, which is in fact what happens to the pagans in the book of Jonah (1:16; 3:5) and what no doubt was actually happening in various parts of the Near East and the Levant at the time of writing."[36] Blenkinsopp continues: "If we must find a target for the writer's criticism, it would not be Ezra and Nehemiah but the kind of prophetic threat represented by the author of the so-called Isaian apocalypse . . . 'This is a people without discernment' (Isa 27:11)." In fact, that is what God admits about the Ninevites in his parting question to Jonah: "they do not know their right hand from their left" (4:11).

Life at the Center: Love's Canopies

> O God, we ponder your love
> In the midst of Your Temple. (Ps 48:10)

> Time can never mar a lover's vows
> Under that woven changeless roof of boughs.[37]

To many readers Jonah seems to fall from the heavens, to appear out of nowhere. His suppressed history (2 Kgs 14:25) resumes or arises abruptly and magically out of the opening divine command: "The word of the Lord unto Jonah." Yet the sparse setting, in Eric Auerbach's words "fraught with background,"[38] delivers up essential clues, and even the opening scene just studied has a prehistory. One crucial notation is Jonah's physical location

---

[36] Blenkinsopp, *A History*, 243–44.

[37] W. B. Yeats, "The Man who dreamed of Faeryland," in *The Collected Works of W. B. Yeats: Volume I, The Poems* (ed. Richard J. Finneran; rev. 2d ed.; New York: Scribner, 1996), 43–44. Yeats has squared the circle, integrated natural abundance (boughs) with human artifact (*woven* roof) to produce the perfect lovers' refuge.

[38] Eric Auerbach, *Mimesis: The Representation of Reality in Western Literature* (trans. Willard Trask; Garden City: Doubleday, 1957), 9.

at the start: Where indeed was Jonah when the Lord issued His command? He was "before the Lord," since that is the place from which he fled (Jonah 1:3, 10). In his subsequent prayers (Jonah 2) this location is twice specified. It is the place to which Jonah continually directs both his gaze and his prayer: "the Temple of Your Holiness" (2:5, 8). In the Hebrew Bible the reference of being "before the Lord" can be as concrete as the Temple gate (1 Sam 21:8; Lev 1:3, 5), although the sense is often enriched by further dimensions:

a) divine service;[39]

b) the spirit of prophecy (1 Kgs 17:1).

Taken together, all of these create a full picture that moves from concrete physical location (the Holy Temple, especially its entrance) to the commitment of divine service, and finally to the intimacy of total attachment. As mentioned previously, it is from this central and supreme vantage point that the book's "real" geographical polar opposites—Tarshish and Nineveh—are aligned, both being places of exile over which death itself seems preferable. The Temple, both in Jonah's past and projected future, occupies center stage, with both Tarshish and Nineveh at the peripheries that ideologically touch one another, with the boat/fish and succah/*kikayon* complexes as the points of transfer in either direction. Thus,

Tarshish   boat-fish   //Temple//   succah-*kikayon*   Nineveh.[40]

Some supporters of a comic view of Jonah have read him as misanthropic, meaning as simply having an unusually developed

---

[39] Deut 10:8; 18:7; 1 Sam 6:20; 16:21, 22; 1 Kgs 8:11; Ezek 44:15.
[40] Alternatively,

Temple   boat-fish   ocean // Nineveh   hut-*kikayon*   wilderness.

In both parts the function of God's agents (the wind/fish, the worm/wind) is to bring Jonah within a hair's breath of death, to induce what we have called near-death experiences. This model is circular rather than linear in that the extremities—each only barely hinted—meet: both the Temple and the Wilderness (Jer 2) are places of intimate encounter between God and His prophet.

taste for privacy. A variant of this view senses Jonah's withdrawal as that of a contradiction between personal and public interests, that the prophet opts out of public service.[41] I argue that Jonah's private interests are amorous rather than halachic or legal in nature, stemming from his concept of God's love as a *unique* and essentially private relationship; and I would like to note, at the metaphoric level, that Jonah's taste for privacy is strongly expressed by his love for enclosures. He begins by leaving the Temple in Jerusalem, descending into a boat, then into its innermost parts, from there to the sea, then the fish. Returning to dry land, he rushes through the city and retires to a succah and the shade of a *kikayon* plant. If at first the enclosures provide a hiding place (the bellies of the boat and the fish), these then come to be seen as enclosures of love: Jonah is happy in his succah and even more so under the shelter of the *kikayon*. For whatever kind of a plant it is, the important thing is that it is *a replacement for the* succah and thus a love canopy (God-style) in its own right.[42]

The Hebrew Bible presents two related options for interpreting the succah/*kikayon* complex. According to the first, the succah was a symbol of the Holy Temple,[43] and no song would be more appropriate to the enamored Jonah than Ps 27:4–5:

> One thing do I ask of the Lord,
> that alone do I seek:
> to sit in the house of the Lord
> all the days of my life;
> to gaze (*lakhazot*) upon the pleasantness of the Lord,
> and to frequent His Temple.[44]
> Indeed, he will conceal me in His succah. (also Ps 84:3)

---

[41] See Ze'ev Haim Lifshitz, *The Paradox of Human Existence: A Commentary on the Book of Jonah* (Northvale, N.J.: Jason Aronson, 1994), xxiv, who cites *y. Berakot* 5:1.

[42] Gerda Elata-Alster and Rachel Salmon ("The Deconstruction of Genre in the Book of Jonah: Towards a Theological Discourse," *Journal of Literature and Theology* 3 [1989]: 51) note the parallel between Jonah's boat and succah but view both negatively: "While Jonah originally employed the boat in his attempt to countermand the story commanded by God, he now builds a booth for the same purpose."

[43] See Meir Weiss, "Psalm 27" [Hebrew], *Tarbiz* 64 (1995): 323–30.

[44] *hekal*, as in Jonah 2:5, 8.

Could this in fact even have been his vow,[45] which he now hopes to complete (after the fish interruption): like Samuel's, staying always within the Temple's precincts, constantly and uninterrupt-edly attached to God's Presence?

Jonah's concluding vows point in the same direction:

What I have vowed I shall pay. (2:10)

I will repay my vows to the Lord in the presence of *all His people*. (Ps 116:14, 18, emphasis added)

The prophet has thus come full circle, since, in Jonah's own words:

And my prayer came to You, to the Temple of Your holiness. (2:8)

All readers correctly understand this reference literally, yet the same readers avoid a similar reading in the related passage:

But as for me, though I thought
to have been driven [like a divorcée] from Your presence,
Yet I continue to gaze
towards the Temple of Your holiness. (2:5)

Although, to be sure, "Your presence" (lit. "before Your eyes"), like the opening "Your presence" (lit. "before You"; 1:3) can carry heavy metaphorical loads, the text also cannot be forced out of its literal reference to the Temple[46] except by wrongly construing the perfect tense ("Though I thought to have been driven") as a present tense, so that the context becomes the actual drowning instead of the location of the original decree of divorcement and separation.

---

[45] See Sasson, *Jonah*, 201.

[46] E.g., Simon (*Jonah*, 21) reads it as the Lord's providence. However, Mar-vin A. Sweeney notes the contrast between Jonah's successive descents (*yarad*, see above, "Jonah's Suicide," in chapter 1) and "the verb *'lh*, 'to go up,' which is normally employed for travel to Jerusalem and the Temple so that one may en-counter the presence of YHWH." See *The Twelve Prophets* (2 vols.; Collegeville, MN: Liturgical, 2000), 311.

There is a second stage of metaphoric transformation. It is said of the *kikayon* that it was intended "to form a shadow [*tsel*] over his head to save [*hatsil*] him from his evil" (4:6). Again, there is abundant use of this *tsel* in the Hebrew Bible's religious vocabulary to symbolize God's protection.[47] But the Song of Songs adds an important erotic dimension:

In his shade I delighted to sit [i.e., dwell]. (Cant 2:3)[48]

This usage completes the transformation of the succah of peace into a canopy of love.[49] Life in the succah looks forward once again to Lear's and Cordelia's "we two alone": The Dove is in the cage (or the enclosed garden), awaiting the Lover. We thus interpret Jonah's building a succah as a bold lover's gesture, and God completes the structure by adding the protective roof. In this view, Jonah's succah and God's *kikayon* roof are not oppositional but rather complementary. Continuing along this line of poetic conjecture, one notices a parallel between Jonah's enclosures and those ark/enclosures modeled by the Hebrew Bible at two crucial junctures. The purpose of the first ark, Noah's, was to secure physical survival; the second, the ark of the covenant, was to ensure spiritual survival. Similarly, the ship/fish enclosure was to rescue Jonah from physical death; the second, the succah/*kikayon*, was meant to reinstate his relationship with God.

Jonah's Trances: Provoking Divine Responsiveness

To view Jonah's succah in Part Two as a makeshift Temple of Meeting allows us to return to Part One with a deeper sense of the parallel between the parts, a simplified sketch of which was provided by Bickerman:

---

[47] Ps 17:8; 36:8; 57:2; 63:8; Isa 49:2; 51:16; etc.

[48] See André LaCocque, *Romance She Wrote: A Hermeneutical Essay on Song of Songs* (Harrisburg, PA: Trinity Press International, 1998), 84.

[49] Perhaps Lam 4:20 also be read from this erotic perspective: "Under His shadow we shall live among the nations." Here the nations are precisely those who unjustly and without merit—so Jonah might think—lay claim to God's love.

. . . two extraordinary miracles . . . are the hinges on which the whole narrative turns. Ancient readers understood the composition of the book. On Christian sarcophagi the story of Jonah is represented in two tableaux: left, the sea dragon which first gulps and then disgorges Jonah; right, Jonah reclining under the gourd.[50]

In our preliminary analysis we saw how Jonah's successive "descents" (*yarad*) were symbolic forms of suicide. Yet, when Jonah was swallowed up by the fish, the initial experience was pleasant. How this is possible may hinge on the semantics of the final stage of his descent, described as *yeradam*, he "fell asleep." When the frantic captain finds him, however, Jonah does not give the impression of someone merely sacking out:

"What's with you being in a trance [*nirdam*]?"

Or, even better:

"What's with you, entranced man?"[51]

Scholars have long recognized that the word *rdm* and its noun *tardemah* not only indicate a deep sleep but especially a "divinely induced, i.e., involuntary sleep, often associated with revelation."[52] What this means is that Jonah's situation in the deep enclosure of the ship is similar to his retreat to his succah (the boat and the succah being both human-made enclosures), and each illuminates the other. That is to say, both are simulations of the Temple experience in which God can join again with His prophet. And in both cases the human-made refuge is replaced by God's own version: In Part One the belly of the ship "that Jonah bought" is replaced by the great fish that God

---

[50] Elias Bickerman, *Four Strange Books of the Bible: Jonah, Daniel, Qohelet, Esther* (New York: Schocken, 1967), 14.

[51] This is Sasson's serendipitous translation, although no explanation for "trance" rather than "sleep" is provided; see *Jonah*, 103.

[52] T. H. McAlpine, *Sleep, Divine and Human* (Sheffield: JSOT Press, 1987), 59. Similarly, Sasson, *Jonah*, 102: "Prophets come to be *nirdamim* when, upon recognizing signs of God's presence, they make themselves ready to receive the divine message." By contrast, Blenkinsopp (*A History*, 245), wrongly, in my view, opts for a "sleep of imperception and spiritual dullness," citing Isa 29:10.

appointed; in Part Two, Jonah's homemade succah yields to, or is completed by, God's *kikayon*.[53]

In sum, the unusual word for sleeping, *rdm*, evokes a situation in which the sleep or trance comes from God rather than Jonah. What our narrative adds to this scenario is that the preparation for God's response is provoked by a series of Jonah's own actions, as the elaborate wordplay establishes. The fact that events eventually take another bad turn only emphasizes the parallel with the *kikayon* incident. There too Jonah laid the careful groundwork by building the succah, thus provoking or at least inviting a divine response. And there too God's *kikayon*—a second example of God's one-upmanship—completed the process, only to be destroyed. Moreover, in both the trance and the *kikayon* incidents, God's response is initially viewed by the prophet as conciliatory and benign. At this point Jonah has reestablished positive contact with God and can now calmly anticipate even such events as being swallowed alive as positive, salvational experiences.

The Kiss of Death

Jonah's spiraling descent was interpreted in chapter 1 as a suicide, and various hypotheses were put forward to explain his motivations: to bring charges against the sailors, to provoke God to save him, etc. Jonah really prayed to die, until push came to shove and, following La Fontaine's parable, he looked death in the face. His return to life and to his prophetic mission, therefore, also signifies his rejection of suicide. How then are we to understand his renewed and repeated death wish in chapter 4?

Now, Lord, take my life, for I would rather die than live. (4:3)

He begged for death, saying: "I would rather die than live." (v. 8)

---

[53] This reciprocity or interaction is modeled by the Temple sacrifice, in which the smoke of the sacrifice that ascends is greeted by the consuming fire that descends. Thus God's reception is provoked by human initiative. See Perry, "Metaphors of Sacrifice in the Zohar," *SCR* 16 (1986): 188–97.

I am upset unto death [I am so upset I want to die]. (v. 9)

For, as Sasson asks, "does Jonah really expect God to bring him death when the Ninevites, wickedest of men, have just experienced divine mercy? Has Jonah so easily forgotten what it was like to taste death?"[54] This puzzle has been discussed but not satisfactorily applied to Jonah.[55]

When Jonah returns to his desire to die, his language has a peculiar resonance:

Please, Lord, *take my life*, for I would rather die than live. (4:3)

Elijah's request is expressed in similar language:

Take [*qakh*] my life, for I am no better than my fathers. (1 Kgs 19:4)

The same verb is used of Enoch's demise:

Enoch walked with God and then was no more, for God took [*laqakh*] him. (Gen 5:24)[56]

In the Hebrew Bible the verb "to take" (*laqakh*) is the most frequent way of expressing marriage: "Do you *take* this person to be your lawfully wedded spouse?" Thus,

Miriam and Aaron spoke against Moses because of the Cushite woman he had married [*laqakh*]: "He married [*laqakh*] a Cushite woman!" (Num 12:1)

What all three cases have in common (Jonah, Elijah, Enoch) is that legends exist according to which all three did not suffer

---

[54] Sasson, *Jonah*, 283.

[55] See Sasson, *Jonah*, 284–86, for a discussion and several suggestions. Carl A. Keller makes the interesting comparison of Jonah to a new Jeremiah in his cursing the days of his birth (Jer 15:10f.; 20:14–18). See "Jonas," in *Osée, Joël, Abdias, Jonas, Amos* (eds. Edmond Jacob, Carl-A. Keller, and Samuel Amsler; CAT XIA; Genève: Labor et Fides, 1992), 288. However, this would imply, recalling Job and perhaps Qohelet, a negation of an entire life, a total rejection of living.

[56] See Ibn Ezra ad loc., where he refers also to Ezek 24:16, 18: take = kill. He also quotes Ps 73:23 and 49:16 to the same effect.

death.[57] The confluence, through the verb "take," of death and
marriage recalls the erotic legends of the deaths of both Moses
and Aaron, said to have died "by the kiss of God."[58] Could the
peculiarly worded petition of Jonah—"Please Lord, *take* my life"—
be the very basis of the legend that God had indeed acceded to
Jonah's prayer and "took" his life, paradoxically, without death
intervening?

Fear and Love

> But as for me, in my abundant love for You [*khasdeka*][59] I
> come into Your house, I bow down to the temple of Your
> holiness in fear of You. (Ps 5:8)

In the book of Jonah the concept of fear [*yr'*] appears in four
different verses, all occurring in the first chapter:

1) And the sailors feared . . . (1:5)

2) "And the Lord, God of the heavens, I fear . . ." (v. 9)

3) And the sailors feared a great fear . . . (v. 10)

4) And the sailors feared the Lord a great fear . . . (v. 16)

Three of these references concern the sailors' fear (1, 3, 4) and
the remaining one is Jonah's (2). The most obvious effect, rendered palpable through their concentration in a single chapter,
is one of contrast between the sailors and Jonah, for whereas the
former—in the grips of a horrific storm at sea—fear for their
very lives, Jonah has given up on his and even gone to sleep.

---

[57] In 2 Kgs 2 Elijah is taken to heaven without dying. For Enoch see Louis
Ginzberg, *The Legends of the Jews* (6 vols.; Philadelphia: Jewish Publication Society, 1968), 5.96. For Jonah see ibid., 6.351.

[58] *b. Baba Batra* 17a; Ginzberg, *Legends* (1968: 3.326–30, 473; 5.257;
6.112–13).

[59] I view the genitive as objective: "my love for You," continuing the first
person subject ("I . . . come into Your house") and anticipating the similar genitive at the end of the sentence: "in my fear of You." This seems superior to the
usual interpretation of a subjective genetive: "Your love for me" (e.g., "through
the abundance of Thy steadfast love," RSV, NJPS, etc.). According to my reading,
a love and fear of God such as Jonah's are synonymous.

At least from the point of view of the sailors' driving motivation to save their own lives, therefore, Jonah's attitude appears withdrawn and disinterested. Let us look more closely at each of these fears, focusing both on the studied contrast between Jonah and the sailors, on the one hand, and the finely graded dialogic structure, on the other.

With regards to the sailors' first expression of fear, their strong emotion of terror is anything but passive; it leads both to prayer and to practical remedies, in that order:[60]

> Now the sailors feared and they cried out, each to his own god, and they cast overboard the goods in the boat in order to make it lighter. (Jonah 1:5)

This juxtaposition of terror and prayer allows us to retrieve a major sense of the term in Scripture, the fear of God.[61] It is probably the case that the sailors' initial appeal to divinity is due more to natural piety (as well as self-interest) than to an abiding sense of awe, since at this point it is unclear whether each sailor thinks that his god has actually caused the storm.[62] It is quite clear, however, that each sailor certainly hopes that his god may be willing to save them.

The ensuing dialogue is provoked by the sailors' sense that the individual god of each of them is, well, not exactly responsive. No longer knowing to which saint to turn (as the French expression would have it), their four questions to the entranced prophet have been seen as helter-skelter, probably due to the storm conditions, and seem to be only partially answered by the prophet:

> "What is your occupation and where are you coming from; what is your land and what people are you from?"

---

[60] By contrast, Jacob's fear for his life at the hands of Esau leads first to practical response (he divides into two camps, Gen 32:8–9) and only then to prayer (Gen 32:10–13).

[61] See Josh 4:24. Especially in wisdom texts, the term is generally understood as a "sense of religion," a "feeling of the religious experience"; Meir Weiss, *The Story of Job's Beginnings: Job 1–2, a Literary Analysis* (Jerusalem: Magnes, 1983), 25.

[62] The point depends on whether we translate 1:6 as "God will change His mind"—thus He is also the cause—or simply as "God will turn His thought to us to save us."

And he said to them: "I am a Hebrew and I worship [*yare'*] God, the Lord of the heavens, who made the sea and the dry land." (1:8–9)

A closer look, however, will reveal remarkable coherence, at least in Jonah's interpretation of the sailors' questions and his response. First of all, and as suggested by the lack of connective between questions two and three, Jonah understands the four questions to be only a pair, each forming a single inquiry:

a) "What is your occupation and where are you coming from?"

b) "What is your land and what people are you from?"

Beginning with the last question first, Jonah's rejoinder ("I am a Hebrew") addresses both aspects, not only peoplehood but also the land that this people inhabits. Similarly, his response combines both his occupation and its locale, since "I worship *the Lord*" could only be, in his present understanding, the ultimate place of service and clinging, the Holy Temple itself.

When Jonah is called forward to account for his indifference, he makes the following declaration—this is the first time he opens his mouth in the book:

"I am a Hebrew, and the Lord God of the heavens I fear, who made the sea and the dry land." (1:9)

Whereas the sailors' fear is always expressed indirectly, through the narrative voice, it is Jonah himself who declares his fear. The term "declaration" is precisely meant, since here Jonah is attempting a definition both of self and especially of his relation to God and to the sailors.[63] This latter point is brought to our attention by the fact that, whereas the sailors directly address their gods, Jonah speaks only to the sailors. The point is a subtle one, understandably lost on most readers since the sailors themselves, as

---

[63] In what follows I take my distances from Phyllis Trible's wish to see Jonah's fear as yet another proof of his sin: "Tucked between cosmic descriptions of Yhwh, the report 'I (am) fearing' obscured Jonah's culpability," *Rhetorical Criticism: Context, Method, and the Book of Jonah* (Minneapolis: Fortress, 1994), 141.

seen in their reaction, miss the point, despite its great importance for Jonah's argument with God. Just as in Rabbinic theology the concept of fear is related especially to the *negative* commandments, to what is to be avoided, so already in Job: "He feared God and shunned evil" (1:1). Jonah's innuendo to the sailors would thus go like this: "*I*, at least, shun evil." From the sequel and the sailors' vowed sacrifice of atonement, it seems that Jonah, at least prophetically, was right.[64]

The next instance of the sailors' fears seems repetitive, a mere intensification of the first:

> *And the men feared a great fear* and they said to him: "What is this that you have done?" For the men knew that he was fleeing from the Lord's presence, for thus he had told them. (Jonah 1:10; emphasis added)

In a dialogic context, however, the sailors' fears are compounded by not one but two of Jonah's statements. First of all, and as already explained, he suggests that, as opposed to the diffused inefficacy of their multiple gods, his alone is God. His second statement is not recorded, despite impressions to the contrary, since the word "thus" in the usual translations ("for *thus* he had told them") does not occur in the Hebrew text. A more accurate translation would be:

> For the men knew that he was fleeing from the Lord's presence. For he had told [*higid*] them. (1:10)

Jonah does not tell them explicitly that he is fleeing (they inferred it for themselves); rather he conveys that he fears the Lord.[65] The word used for this telling gives a particular tonality and further defines Jonah's particular relationship to the sailors. Likewise, the psalmist:

> To declare [*lehagid*] your love each morning and your faithfulness at evening. (Ps 92:3)

---

[64] See above, "Assisted Suicide," in chapter 2.

[65] See Metsudah [eighteenth century], in M. Zlotowitz, *Jonah: A New Translation with a Commentary Anthologized from Midrashic and Rabbinic Sources* (Brooklyn: Mesorah, 1980), 96.

As well as Ibn Ezra: "*to declare*: to teach others of your love and to broadcast it to them." In other words, when Jonah declares to the Gentile sailors that he fears the Lord, he is what we today would call preaching, but with an Israelite twist: a preaching that is a teaching.[66]

There is yet another tonality to Jonah's declaration that he fears the Lord, one that looks beyond himself and the sailors and towards an attempt to comprehend his relationship with God. There is a Rabbinic dictum according to which "everything is in the hands of Heaven except the fear of Heaven."[67] According to this possibility, isn't Jonah now also looking back over his shoulder, reminding the Lord that he is doing all he possibly can?

The sailors' final fear has great stylistic interest:

> And they threw Jonah into the sea. And when the sea quieted from its anger, *the men feared a great fear, the Lord*; and they offered sacrifice to the Lord and made vows.

> Now the Lord appointed a great fish to swallow Jonah. (1:15–2:1; emphasis added)

The verbatim repetition of "the men feared a great fear" in vv. 10 and 16 is usually overlooked by critics, and its meaning thus passes unnoticed: that of forming an *inclusio*. For the text has interrupted itself for six full verses in order to present the evolution[68] of the sailors' fear from pure self-interest to a deepened sense of personal destiny brought on by moral reflection.[69] Their

---

[66] Consonant with the opinion of some that the sailors converted to monotheism, Jonah would thus be seen as proselytizing. This would be consistent with his efforts in Nineveh; see below, chapter 8; see also *b. Ta'anit* 16a, where Moriah means Torah or "instruction" for Jews, and *mora'*, "fear, respect" for Gentiles.

[67] *b. Berakot* 33b; the saying is ascribed to Rab Chanina.

[68] Sasson (*Jonah*, 138) finely observes the contrast between the positioning of God's name in Jonah's declaration (1:9), where it occurs at the head of the clause to give it special attention, and the sailors, who until now have "not seemed totally convinced by Jonah's words. . . . By shaping the clause this time to end in 'et-YHWH, the narrator is finally granting the sailors their own recognition of God's greatness."

[69] Trible (*Rhetorical Criticism*, 151) describes the sailors' latter fear in 1:16 as representing a change "from a negative emotion to a positive affirmation, from fright to worship of YHWH, . . . from ignorance to knowledge."

present terror certainly continues their previous fear for their lives, but in adding a few words the text adds a crucial element. God's fearful power arises in the final instance not from the ability to take life but rather to save it. This point is forcefully expressed by the synonymy conveyed by the unusual double accusative:

a great fear, the Lord.

What was first known as a great fear is now acknowledged to be none other than the Lord, the one who "kills and [then] gives life, brings down to *She'ol* and brings up again"[70] (1 Sam 2:6).

A final and crucial point of Jonah's "declaration" has to do with his different concept of serving God. Whereas the sailors' prayers and sacrifices relate to fear for their lives, Jonah, as we have observed, is disinterested in this respect. Or, if you will, Jonah does not fear for himself, feels no fear of self-interest of the common sort: pain or loss of money or power or even life itself. Rather, in an amazing semantic reversal, Jonah "fears" precisely the opposite. The Job text offers an important extension of the term, one that is not generally perceived. For the satan grants the point that Job is a "god-fearing person" but questions the motivation: "Is it *for nought* that Job is God-fearing?" (Job 1:9; emphasis added). What this means, in terms of ancient Hebrew usage, is that one could be God-fearing less out of fear of punishment than out of what later theologians would call "love without cause." "Fear," or worship of God, in short, can be understood, alternately, as either fear or love. This is the further sense of his astounding self-declaration; according to which, to fear God means to serve *out of love*, from no personal motives, for its own sake. But Jonah's understanding is even more literal and precise: for *his* own sake, God's, and the stress is not on service but rather on *love*.

Of course, the book of Jonah will go on to argue that, no less than serving out of fear (Ps 2:11), serving out of love has its own inherent dangers or limitations. For it is basically out of (jealous)

---

[70] For God-the-fearful-one see Gen 20:11 (where it is conspicuously absent), and Exod 20:17. See also the expression "the fear (*pakhad*) of the Lord" in 1 Sam 11:7.

love that Jonah wants the competition removed; out of love that he leaves God's innermost and intimate Temple precincts in order to escape a love he can no longer understand or control. He comes to realize that God does indeed desire that he live, but the love relationship still has to be clarified, or perhaps renegotiated. Jonah, at any rate, discovers that the lowest degree of *self*-interest is precisely the desire to live, but this desire is, at best, at the outer limit of selfishness, at the point at which my desire merges with God's desire for my life, since He created me! In other words, my desire to live ("If I am not for myself . . .") is part and parcel with the Creator's desire that I live. This, in sum, is the theological argument of Part One.

CHAPTER SIX

THE BOOK OF PRAYER

J onah's mutism has been contrasted with the volubility both of other reluctant prophets in the Hebrew Bible and of the other characters in the book: the sailors, the Ninevites, and God.[1] One must admit, however, that if the stunning silence of his opening rebellion seems to place him in a special category, it also sets up a dramatic contrast to the extended praying of chapter 2. When Jonah finally does open his mouth to God (before that point he does speak with the sailors), we can all the more appreciate both the volume and the complexity of his outpourings. Several types and motivations can be distinguished.

Fear-Prayer

Continuing our meditation on fear, let us say, then, that prayer and "fear" are intimately connected. For the sailors, it is fear *for their very lives*, in the face of threatened extinction, that leads the way. This is upgraded by a more complex fear that includes a positive, active relation to God: both respect for God's saving powers and fright of punishment for their possible guilt:[2]

---

[1] Carl-A. Keller, "Jonas," in *Osée, Joël, Abdias, Jonas, Amos* (eds. Edmond Jacob, Carl-A. Keller, and Samuel Amsler; CAT XIA; Genève: Labor et Fides, 1992), 266.

[2] This latter fear, while still centered on personal concerns, still reaches towards a God of salvation. By contrast, Jonah's declaration of fear focuses on the God of creation.

Serve the Lord with fear. (Ps 2:11)

The ambivalence in the Hebrew preposition *b-*, "with, by, in, at," allows an important distinction that expresses both dimensions of the sailors' fear. On the one hand and at the most basic level, one prays *in* fear; fear is an appropriate motivation and setting, as it were, of prayer. On the other, one can pray *through* fear; the emotion itself is a form of prayer, indeed the horrendously unspeakable is of prayer's very essence.[3]

In Part One Jonah has lost his fear and regains it only at the bottom of the mountains, where, in the words of the psalmist (136:6), the earth is "suspended on the waters," hovering in fear of the deep.[4] This allows a deeper sense of Jonah's final descent:

To the base of the mountains I descended . . .
When my life was ebbing away, I remembered the Lord
and my prayer came before You. (2:7–8)

As Simon notes, "the actual prayer is not mentioned in this verse," unless we conclude that the terror of final extinction is itself a form of prayer.[5]

Jonah's Psalms: Prayer Collage

What happens to prayer's creation and continuity in a highly developed literary and theological environment such as the Hebrew Bible? Although the words and formulas preexist, like flowers from a garden they are cut from their natural context and rearranged according to the present emotion. Or, to use a slightly different image, the formulas become elements in a new collage, now organized by the worshiper's dominant mood or passion or need. To dismiss prayer because its constituent parts

---

[3] As Michal Govrin argues in her novel *The Name* (trans. Barbara Harshav; New York: Riverhead, 1998).

[4] As per Ps 24:2.

[5] Uriel Simon, *Jonah: The Traditional Hebrew Text with the New JPS Translation* (trans. Lenn J. Schramm; JPS Torah Commentary; Philadelphia: Jewish Publication Society, 1999), 23.

preexisted would then be tantamount to rejecting a bouquet because the materials are not "original," in which case we would be dealing with a pastiche rather than a collage. Again and as was argued above, only the current context can decide such issues: in Jonah's case, how the prayer reflects and responds to his existential dilemma. To note parallels, as most critics have done, is not only an important exercise in reading but also a reminder of prayer's commonality, of its easy passage from the most intimate "I" to a public "you" or "we."[6] To restrict our study to the mere observation of formulaic repetitions, however, would be, by rejecting the possibility of an addressee, to deny the existential force and dialogic desire that is prayer's very soul. Further, the use of formulas developed and repeated over and over in communal settings transmutes even the most intimate and private prayers into public events, equally and paradoxically intimate. In this regard, prayer—the human voice reaching towards God— and prophecy—God's voice reaching down to humans—share a common focus.

Assisted Suicide, Again!

Not all of Jonah's praying occurs in the psalm of chapter 2. When he resumes his verbal dialogue with God in chapter 4, the same word for praying is used (2:2; 4:2), and this passage in fact, through its allusion to Jonah's opening flight to Tarshish, unifies the entire book under the sign of prayer:

But it displeased Jonah exceedingly, and he was angry.

And he prayed (*yitpalel*) to God, saying:

"(Please, Lord, was this not my thought when I was upon my own land? This is why I preempted and fled to Tarshish. For I have experienced that You are a gracious and merciful

---

[6] In the words of the Ari (Isaac Luria, sixteenth century), "everything said under divine inspiration relates both to the individual and to the congregation"; quoted by Yehudah Keil, *1 Samuel* [Hebrew] (Jerusalem: Mossad Harav Kook, 1981), 15, n. 11.

God, long-suffering and full of love and who repents of wrongdoing.)

"Now, Lord, please take my life from me, for my death would be better than my life."   S[7]

And the Lord said: "Are you really so angry?"
Then Jonah left the city and sat to the east of the city and made a booth there and sat under it in the shade, until he should see what will be concerning the city. (4:1–5)

That this prayer is a petition cannot be doubted, but its complex structure is unusual due to the long parenthesis that postpones the petition ("Now, Lord, please . . .") until the next verse. The content of this parenthesis is widely assumed to be twofold:

- a) Jonah protests bitterly over God's mercy. This explanation is highly suspicious, however, since, *as part of a prayer in progress*, Jonah's petition would presumably be granted out of the same storehouse of mercy.

- b) Jonah's protest-flight is due to God's projected mercy for the Ninevites.

Now the theory that this prayer concerns the Ninevites, despite its popularity, depends on editorial suppositions, as we shall see below.[8] It seems to me that the repetition of the word for prayer points in another direction, by suggesting that Jonah may be renewing the same petition to die—this is in fact what he is explicitly saying! If so, then Jonah, now that his mission is accomplished, reverts to his initial suicide, which, now with God's help, he wishes to pursue:

But it displeased Jonah exceedingly, and he was angry [that he was *still* needing to die].

And he prayed to God, saying:

---

[7] MT has a *setumah* here, indicating closure of the section that opened in 2:11. For further discussion see Jack M. Sasson, *Jonah: A New Translation with Introduction, Commentary, and Interpretation* (AB 42B; New York: Doubleday, 1990), 270–71, and below, "Jonah's Knowledge of God," in chapter 8.

[8] See also the previous note.

—Please, Lord, was this not my thought when I was upon my own land, [that I wanted to die], and this in fact is why I preempted and fled to Tarshish (truly, I know that you will grant my prayer again because You are a gracious and merciful God, long-suffering and full of love and who repents of wrongdoing)—:

"Now, Lord, please take my life from me." (4:1–2)

This text brings us back to an additional—perhaps even the original—sense of the Hebrew root [pll]. Consider the well-known proverb in 1 Sam 2:25:

If a person sins against another person, a judge can judge [pilel] him; but if he sins against God, who will judge [yitpalel] him?

The Jewish exegete Radak explains the meaning of the latter term as follows: "Who will enter into judgment on his behalf with the Holy One Blessed-Be-He?" One now wonders whether, considering Jonah's ongoing debate with God, this meaning of "entering into judgment," of "bringing a legal complaint" against God, can also be applied to Jonah's first prayer as well.[9]

The Purported Displacement of Jonah 4:5

Should one still wish to read this passage as referring to the Ninevites, however, then we should take another look at the alleged displacement of Jonah 4:5, which, in conformity with strict chronological requirements of the plot, seems to some to fit better after 3:4.[10] Such a proposed emendation would read as follows:

---

[9] This important Jewish tradition—a *Din-Torah* or lawsuit with God in Rabbi Levy Yitzhak of Berditchev's language—is studied by Anson Laytner, *Arguing with God: A Jewish Tradition* (Northvale, NJ: Jason Aronson, 1990), especially 179–89.

[10] See Sasson, *Jonah*, 287–90; for Jewish exegetes such as Rashi and Ibn Ezra, see Gerda Elata-Alster and Rachel Salmon, "The Deconstruction of Genre in the Book of Jonah: Towards a Theological Discourse," *Journal of Literature and Theology* 3 (1989): 45. These scholars also examine the "possibilities in meaning

Jonah began to go into the city, a walk of one day, and he cried: "Forty days more, and Nineveh shall be overturned." Then Jonah left the city and sat to the east of the city. (3:4; 4:5)

A much simpler explanation recommends itself, however, if one imagines the context of the verse to be less strict chronology than Jonah's ongoing dialogue or argument with God. The order of events would then be as follows:

a) Jonah's prophetic utterance (3:4), which conceivably—even most likely—takes the entire forty days. For why is it typically assumed that the prophecy was instantaneously received, especially in a such a large city?[11] A remote but viable possibility is to understand "day" as "year," although that usage is usually restricted to the plural *yamim*. In any event, as Moberly points out, "in Hebrew idiom 'forty days' (or 'forty years,' depending on context) is the idiom for an indefinite long period of time."[12]

b) Nineveh's repentance (3:5–9)

c) Nineveh's pardon (3:10). God "changed His mind concerning the evil which he said He would do, and He did not do it." This takes place after the stated reprieve (forty days). This could mean merely that God does not do the evil *then*.

d) Jonah now prays and talks with God (4:2–4). He is angry and wants to know two things: Is their repentance sincere?[13] Is there no retribution for wrongdoing?

---

which are lost through such an emendation" (44). For my arguments against the transfer, see below, "The Structure of Chapter 4," in chapter 8.

[11] E.g., Simon, *Jonah*, 28.

[12] R. W. Moberly, "Preaching for a Response? Jonah's Message to the Ninevites Reconsidered," *VT* 53 (2003): 159.

[13] This possibility becomes a likelihood in the Jerusalem Talmud and the Targum (see Eytan Levine, *The Aramaic Version of Jonah* (Jerusalem: Jerusalem Academic Press, 1978), 94. See Sherwood (*A Biblical Text and Its Afterlives: The Survival of Jonah in Western Culture* [Cambridge: Cambridge University Press, 2000], 107) for bibliography and discussion.

e) Then Jonah left the city and settled to the east of the city and made a booth there and sat under it in the shade, until he should see what will be concerning the city. (4:5)[14]

In the context of Jonah's *prayer*, this can only mean "to see what God's response to his prayer will be."

f) God's answer is forthcoming, not in words but in deeds in the form of an object lesson: the *kikayon*.

What d), e), and f) document is that prayer is not always a simple petition/response structure but an ongoing dialogue. For the response itself must be monitored, appreciated, or rejected, at least reacted to in some way.

Thanksgiving or Confession?

The status of Jonah's prayer as (at least) one of thanksgiving seems beyond doubt:

But as for me, . . . with a voice of thanksgiving [*todah*] I shall sacrifice to You.

What I vowed I shall pay. (2:10)

This view must be questioned, however, or at least expanded by wider considerations.

The first is how gratitude is itself valued. It is well known that the rabbis generally regarded praise/thankfulness as the highest form of prayer. Somewhat differently but with the same emphasis, Qohelet argues that we should love life and enjoy it because it is a gift, and he motivates this, in part, by the epicurean argument that gratitude is a large part of enjoyment. But what if someone does not like gifts, does not wish to feel indebted, wants to make her own life? What about Jonah's profound desire, whatever his underlying motivations, to go it alone, to withdraw to a hut of his

---

[14]For "settled" see below, "Pastoral Pedagogy," in chapter 9. Note that, according to this reading, the preposition "*in* the city" (*ba'ir*) is taken not as indicator of location—what the Ninevites will do *in* the city (see below, n. 70 in chapter 8)—but rather what God will do *concerning* the city.

own manufacture? God's ending answer in the book of Jonah is that everyone likes gifts but everyone does not know that and, like Jonah, must be tricked into recognition, just as Jonah also had to be tricked into loving life itself, first through the great fish and then through the *kikayon*. Jonah would of course have reason to express gratitude, but his attitude seems to avoid piety and veer towards Rabelais' Panurge in *Le tiers Livre*,[15] who "thanked" his master's heartfelt but easy beneficence with high irony. Transposed to our text, we would have the following highly charged dialogic conclusion for Part One:

> [God to Jonah:] "You wanted to die and I obliged. You wanted to live and I obliged."
>
> [Jonah to God:] "Thanks, Boss!"
>
> And the Lord spoke to the fish and it vomited out Jonah onto dry land. . . .
>
> And Jonah got up and went to Nineveh.

Later on, and dialogically, the matter of gratitude can be raised regarding God as well as Jonah. Imagine the following scenario, this time in Part Two:

> [Jonah to God:] "You wanted a prophet and I obliged."
>
> [God to Jonah:] "Do I need to say thanks?"[16]
>
> Now the Lord God appointed a *kikayon* plant.

But if Jonah's gratitude either does not exist or is ironic, how then do we understand his promise at the end of his psalm:

> But as for me, . . . with a voice of thanksgiving [*todah*] I shall sacrifice to You.
> What I vowed I shall pay. (2:10)

A possible answer relates to a further meaning of the biblical Hebrew *todah*:

---

[15] François Rabelais, *Le tiers livre* (Genève: Droz, 1964).

[16] Such a question did not seem outrageous to Jane Harrison, who "grew up with a country father who intrepidly, for grace before meals, said, 'For what we are about to receive, may the Lord be truly thankful.'" Guy Davenport in Anne Carson, *Glass, Irony, and God* (New York: New Directions, 1995), viii.

[Joshua to Achan:] "My son, glorify Yahweh, God of Israel, and give praise to him [*todah*]. (Josh 7:19)[17]

In view of the context, however, the NJPS translation is preferable:

"My son, pay honor to the Lord, the God of Israel, and *make confession to him.* Tell me what you have done; do not hold anything back from me."

Achan answered Joshua,

"It is true, *I have sinned* against the Lord, the God of Israel. This is what I did . . ." (v. 19; emphasis added)

Thus, in assessing Jonah's spiritual states, we must recall that *todah* is also the language of confession and remorse.[18]

In sum, and whether or not one holds to the theory that Jonah does feel remorse for his flight from God, Jonah's extensive praying relates to a major theme of the book.[19] Jews, it is well known, recite the book of Jonah on Yom Kippur, the Day of Repentance, as we shall presently discuss. If one consults the liturgy of that day, however, then repentance is named as but one of the powers capable of "removing the evil decree" of punishment, the other two being prayer and charity. Indeed, from the pervasiveness of prayer in Jonah, we have uncovered another source of Jonah's reconciliation with the Almighty, since the gates of prayer, like the gates of repentance, are never, ever closed.[20] Certainly, as Jonah's mutism is unblocked, his lengthy prayers can be considered a "therapy of the word,"[21] an attempt both to understand his perplexing behavior and to return to the source of his ultimate bliss.

---

[17] This translation is from Robert G. Bowling and G. Ernest Wright, *Joshua: A New Translation with Notes and Commentary* (AB 6; Garden City: Doubleday, 1982), 217.

[18] Cf. also 1 Kgs 8:33; Ezra 10:11; Mishnah *Sanhedrin* 6:2. On Jonah's remorse, see below, "Jonah's Knowledge of God," in chapter 8.

[19] Sasson, *Jonah,* 19, notes, as one of the signs of the book's unity, the allocation of prayers at "each major change of setting: the sailors' in 1, Jonah's in 2, the Ninevites' in 3, and a series of miracles in 4."

[20] *Devarim Rabbah* 2.

[21] This is the felicitous title of Laín Entralgo's *The Therapy of the Word in Classical Antiquity* (New Haven: Yale University Press, 1970).

The Place of Prayer

Some have argued that Jonah's prayer(s) in chapter 2 are clearly transplanted from other soil because of their cultic language and ambiance, since Jonah's actual return, presumably to Jerusalem, occurs only *after* he is spewed back onto dry land by the fish.[22] Further, if Jonah's prayers are recited in the Temple itself, then his remark that he "continues to gaze towards the Temple" (Jonah 2:5) would make no sense. Sweeney therefore refocuses the matter as follows:

> The situation of the psalm differs from that of the narrative in that Jonah is now in the Temple and not in the belly of the fish.[23]

The issue of the prayers' ambiance or situation has a parallel in Jonah's other lengthy prayer (4:1–3), where the petitioner's actual physical location has also seemed a matter of confusion. For, again according to the strict advance of the narrative, Jonah offers his prayer from Nineveh, where he remains until his removal east of the city (4:5).

I would like to suggest that the sense of dislocation, felt by all readers of the text, does not point to a narrative problem but rather suggests a removal from narrative reality to a realm peculiar to prayer. Many have taken note of the change of stylistic level of both passages: the cultic one of chapter 2 and the Toranic one of 4:1–3. What both have in common is a quotational mode, a turn to voices characteristic of the highest spirituality.

A parallel may be helpful. When Abraham is recovering from his circumcision, he is visited by three men (i.e., angels) in need of hospitality. Abraham speaks:

> My Lord, if I have now found favor in your sight, please do not pass from your servant. (Gen 18:3)

---

[22] This is based on the progression of the narrative line, which, in order to disrupt, one would have to resort to the Rabbinic tag according to which "there is no before and after in biblical narrative."

[23] Marvin A. Sweeney, *The Twelve Prophets* (2 vols.; Collegeville, MN: Liturgical, 2000), 317.

The use of the singular "Lord" requires comment. According to one suggestion, Abraham is here addressing the leader of the three. A second opinion is brought down by Rashi:

> The reference is to the Holy: he was asking the Holy One Blessed-be-He to wait for him while he runs out and greets his guests.

According to this reading, Abraham is in a state of prayer or contemplation, from which he absents himself momentarily in order to rejoin human society, as it were. The question of where Abraham actually is praying is irrelevant; presumably he is lying in bed, but the first notation of place is evoked only when he must run out towards his guests.

Where then is Jonah when he prays? Surely in the belly of the fish (Jonah 2) and in Nineveh (4:1–3). However, the matter is, like Abraham's bed, irrelevant. What matters is that the narrative disconnect that readers feel coincides with a spiritual removal, to a place of prayer. In Jewish spirituality this was the Holy Temple— but where is the Place of His Glory?—the true locus of his praying, the Place through which and to which all prayer travels. In this sense and despite his exile, when Jonah prays he never leaves the Temple precincts. This may be an explanation of what some have identified as Jonah's cultic mentality.

At another level of explanation, humans do not pray in a place; rather, the Place is where they pray. Of course, physical conditions do matter. But the direction of prayer, for example, is east, and that is because of Jerusalem and the Temple, which is where prayer ascends on high. If none of the physicals are available, they are only aids to prayer anyhow, since the essential is *sheyekawwen 'et libo lashamayim*, "that the heart be fixated upon Heaven." At the highest level the true, the only "place of prayer" is *hammaqom*, God, *the Place*.[24]

---

[24] "Why is God called 'place'? Because He is the Place of the world, and His world is not His place" (*Bereshit Rabba* 68).

CHAPTER SEVEN

The Book of Repentance

For Jews, the book of Jonah is primarily the book of repentance.[1] Recited at the most dramatic moment of the
yearly liturgy—as the gates of divine judgment are about
to close at the end of Yom Kippur, deciding who will live and
who will die—the book serves as a reminder that if God can
forgive even the wicked Ninevites, how much more so the average Joe! However true, such a reading, with its unique focus on
Jonah 3, inhibits the book's much broader perspective. Indeed,
the theme of repentance traverses the book of Jonah from start
to finish, characterizing to varying degrees the behavior of all of
the protagonists.

The Sailors and the Ninevites

While the Ninevites do in fact exemplify repentance, their
path of return to God is paved by that other group of Gentiles,
the sailors. We have seen both their reluctance to throw Jonah
overboard and especially, after the fact, their regret and vows to
offer sacrifices of atonement. Of great interest is the language in
which their concept of God is expressed:

> The captain approached him and said to him: "How can you
> be so entranced? Arise and cry out to your god! *Perhaps*

---

[1] See above, "Repentance or Punishment," in the Introduction.

['*ulay*] the god will give us a thought and we will not perish."[2] (Jonah 1:6; emphasis added)

The concept will not be lost on the Ninevites, moved to correct their ways by the same possibility:

> Perhaps [*mi yodea*] God may turn and repent and turn back from His wrath, so that we do not perish. (3:9; emphasis added)[3]

There are, of course, different levels of "perhaps." The "who knows" of the Ninevites focuses less on God than on human limitation,[4] while keeping open the possibility that, indeed, God's prophet *may* know something that they don't. And, as suggested above, Jonah's doomsday threat is only a threat, one that could not conceivably have been effective had it not aroused strong reactions of conscience among the populace of Nineveh. By contrast, the sailors' danger is extreme and imminent, and all human efforts have proved ineffective. Their "perhaps," grounded in terror, is the last straw: they do not know whether God will or will not save them, but they do know that otherwise they are doomed. For when ultimate danger is near and until it is past, most humans subscribe to Pascal's wager: why not believe in God; what do we have to lose?

When psychology passes into theology, however, more flattering motives may be proposed for the sailors. For example, according to Simon, the "perhaps" strategy can indicate "comprehension

---

[2] Kyle P. McCarter notes an interesting nuance to this term: "Biblical Hebrew *'ulay* is somewhat stronger than English 'perhaps.' It implies an expectation of the desired (or feared) result (Gen 16:2; Num 22:11; etc.) and so stands somewhere between 'perhaps' and 'surely'"; see *1 Samuel: A New Translation with Introduction, Notes, and Commentary* (AB 8; New York: Doubleday, 1980), 134, on 1 Sam 6:5.

[3] "Perhaps" is James L. Crenshaw's translation of "who knows" in Joel 2:14: "Perhaps He will turn and relent," *Joel: A New Translation with Introduction and Commentary* (AB 24C; Garden City: Doubleday, 1995), 138; cf. James L. Crenshaw, "The Expression *mi yodea'* in the Hebrew Bible," *VT* 36 (1986): 274–88.

[4] Although, as is well known, skepticism does have strong, if not necessary, ties to radical fideism. Michel de Montaigne's "Apologie de Raymond Sebond" is an extensive discourse on the subject; see *The Complete Essays of Montaigne* (trans. Donald Frame; Stanford: Stanford University Press, 1976).

of the nature of true prayer, which never presumes to impose itself magically on God."[5] Such is the approach and language of Moses after the grave sin of the golden calf in the desert:

> The next day Moses said to the people: "You have sinned a great sin. Yet I will now go up to the Lord. *Perhaps* [*'ulay*] I may win forgiveness for your sin." (Exod 32:30; emphasis added)[6]

Here too the only key available is prayer, predicated on the possibility that God can and may change His mind.

The God of Perhaps

But who is God that He should change His mind? Did God then make a mistake, or did the Omniscient not know what was coming down the pike? Or, constrained by His own Justice, was He free to yield? Differently put, is "perhaps" a mere product of human ignorance and/or fickle destiny, or can we also speak of a "God of perhaps," one whose very nature, grounded in a radical freedom, can bend to external pressures, be they changed circumstances or new evidence? In the face of the sailors' and Ninevites' motivations for repentance, what are God's for relenting?

> God is not man to be capricious.
> Or mortal to *change His mind* [*weyitnekham*]. (Num 23:19 NJPS; emphasis added)

Or, perhaps closer to the actual meaning of the Hitpael of *nkhm*:

> God is not a man, that he should lie;
> nor the son of man, that he should *repent*. (v. 19 JB; emphasis added)

Indeed, the projection of human repentance on God Himself was so astonishing that classical commentators such as Ibn Ezra and

---

[5] Uriel Simon, *Jonah: The Traditional Hebrew Text with the New JPS Translation* (trans. Lenn J. Schramm; JPS Torah Commentary; Philadelphia: Jewish Publication Society, 1999), 10.

[6] See also Exod 32:9–14; 1 Kgs 20:31.

Nachmanides proposed that here the Torah was "merely speaking after the manner of human beings."[7]

Rashi offers a creative bridge between the language of the sailors' plea and one of the Toranic texts at the epicenter of biblical repentance. Here is Rashi's exegesis of Exod 32:12:

[Moses to God:] . . . "Turn from your burning anger and *relent* [*hinnakhem*] of this evil against your people."

Rashi: *hinnakhem*. Let him direct a different thought towards them [*hit'ashet*] concerning the evil which he thought to do to them.

Rashi is here glossing a well-known term with the sailors' unusual expression:

The captain approached him and said to him: "How can you be so entranced? Arise and cry out to your god! Perhaps the god will *give us a thought* [*yit'ashet*] and we will not perish." (Jonah 1:6; emphasis added)

Rashi sees *yit'ashet* (to come up with a different thought) as synonymous with the more usual term for changing one's mind, *hinnakhem* in the Niphal.[8]

Other critics have taken the matter even further. Crenshaw speaks of the attempt "to move YHWH to repentance," since "the basis for divine repentance in Jonah is pity for doomed people and cattle."[9] The divine revelation of "I will be who I will be" would thus be the declaration of total unpredictability, with options on whether this veers towards caprice or complete freedom.[10]

---

[7] See Ibn Ezra on Gen 6:6; John T. Willis, "The 'Repentance' of God in the Books of Samuel, Jeremiah, and Jonah," *HBT* 16 (1994): 156–75.

[8] See the apparent contradiction between 1 Sam 15:11, 35, which allows that God may change His mind, and 1 Sam 15:29, apparently patterned on Num 23:19–20, except that the meaning "to change one's mind" occurs elsewhere only in the Niphal. See Jacob Milgrom, *Numbers: The Traditional Hebrew Text with the New JPS Translation* (JPS Torah Commentary; Philadelphia: Jewish Publication Society, 1990), on Num 23:19.

[9] James L. Crenshaw, *Joel*, 139, 137; see also James Limburg, *Jonah: A Commentary* (Louisville, KY: Westminster John Knox, 1993), 84–86, 92.

[10] See Milgrom, *Numbers*, n. to 23:19.

It would thus seem that the Gentiles' desperate wish is reflected in the theology of the book of Jonah, which projects the concept of a God whose changes of mind involve not only regret but perhaps even repentance, indeed provide the model and justification for such human behavior. This bold suggestion may be reflected in the puzzling proof-text quoted above:

> Perhaps God may turn [*yashub*] and repent [*wenikham*] and turn back [*weshab*] from His wrath, so that we do not perish. (3:9)

The use of no less than three verbs to express God's change of mind is problematic, especially the repetition of *shub*, to "turn or return." The latter case is the easiest to explain, since God is turning *from* His wrath. But what would then be the sense of the first? Zechariah may provide the key:

> "Return [*shubu*] to me," says the Lord of Hosts, "and I will return to you." (Zech 1:3)

The thought is that the first step in the process of repentance is an act of will, a (re)turning to a previous state with a changed mind or attitude. Jonah's Ninevites thus provide the complement to Zechariah's, since God is now seen not simply as reacting to human change with His own, but as providing the model that humans may imitate.

In any case, if the book is about God's tolerance of evil (in other words, about His mercy), we must be careful not to read this as focused solely on the Ninevites, since that matter seems decided by God's pardon. It would seem, rather, that in this book God has a greater challenge to deal with: not the foreigners, who return, but one of His own household, who still wants to defect because he has little patience for sinners or for the God who tolerates them. Thus God's curious circumlocution at the end (Jonah 4:10–11) surely refers not to the *kikayon* but to Jonah. God again wants to give an object lesson about dying: the plant can die (so can you!), and if you can have mercy on it, how about having some on yourself? Finally, the last verse comes less to justify God's action of forgiveness toward Nineveh than to convince Jonah to stay alive (or rather to explain why He

is not about to listen to his prayer—again!—and take his life).
After all, Jonah had already asked to die and acted on that wish
(Jonah 1–2). God saved his life then, with Jonah's collusion or
at least acceptance, and is not about to change His mind! Yet
the book's parting glory is that it is open-ended: God pleads but
denies Himself the final word, and this self-denial of power and
majesty is surely an indication that God Himself has repented of
His traditional ways. Contrary to God putting Job in his place at
the end of that book, the ending of Jonah indicates that God has
also come of age, for now He tolerates not only the wicked but
also, as it were, members of His own family. The book of Jonah
narrates God's repentance, not Jonah's.[11]

Jonah?

It is a source of great perplexity that, in a work highlighting
repentance, everyone repents except the hero himself: the sailors, the Ninevites, even God. For does Jonah repent? Of what?
Does he feel any guilt whatsoever? Simon's comment on Jonah
1:12—"For I know that this great storm came upon you on my
account"—seems to me to summarize the issue:

> *For I know* . . . Thus Jonah sidesteps the question of guilt
> while accepting full responsibility for their safety.[12]

In other words, the question remains open.[13]

---

[11] Lest too much be made of God's putative weakness or excessive mercy,
a different perspective may right things a bit. The model of a king who *never*
changes his mind, even when required, is the Ahasuerus of Esther fame. As we
shall later see, Jonah's God does consider new evidence and judges on the basis
of what the evidence shows *now* (see "Not Rereading Jonah . . . ," in chapter 8).
The world changes and people change too, or at least they should if repentance
is to be a possibility. Thus, in the matter of repentance, God can surely be said to
exercise mercy, when compared to the principle of "each person shall die for his/
her sin." That said, to change one's mind when the evidence changes describes
not only a good judge but also a good scientist: God observed what they did,
what changes they made in their behavior (Jonah 3:10).

[12] Simon, *Jonah*, 13.

[13] Not for Steven Weitzman, *Song and Story in Biblical Narrative: The History of a Literary Convention in Ancient Israel* (Bloomington: Indiana University

If Jonah does indeed repent, that may be at the end of chapter 2, where he promises to "pay what I vowed" (2:10). Sasson speculates that "we do not know what Jonah vowed to God."[14] Since Jonah immediately gets up and goes to Nineveh, however, this may in fact be the content of his vow, itself understandable only as indicating a radical change of mind.[15] Change of mind but not submission, however, since, as we saw above, he is now working from the position of a negotiated compromise.[16]

However, in our study of the final chapter we shall argue an even clearer case of repentance for Jonah, and this one in the form of a verbal petition: "Take my life" (4:2). The intensity is surprising, for at this stage a simple return to the death wish would be puzzling. Are we merely back to the start, or is something else going on?

The Narrator et al.

Readers of fiction have a tendency to identify with one of the characters. In Scripture the prejudice is overwhelmingly with God, either because of rightness or, less nobly, because of power, in which case God's collusion with Nineveh is intelligible: both His letting them off the hook and, more suspiciously, His admiration of their size (4:11). A more central collusion, all the more

---

Press, 1997), 111. He, after nicely observing that the entire narrative "represents an exercise in changing one's mind," imagines this as a contrast to the "unyielding" Jonah. Ho hum.

[14] Jack M. Sasson, *Jonah: A New Translation with Introduction, Commentary, and Interpretation* (AB 42B; New York: Doubleday, 1990), 201.

[15] Some critics, searching the high seas for yet another of Jonah's personal failings, suspect that his mission to Nineveh is reluctant and only halfhearted, witness his rushing through the city in only three days. Or, in a total absence of textual evidence, T. Fretheim still speculates that Jonah "makes his message as vague and blunt and as offensive as he possibly can. . . . He delivered a message that would make it almost impossible for the people to respond positively" (*The Message of Jonah: A Theological Commentary* [Minneapolis: Augsburg, 1977], 107–8). We are thus asked to believe that the greatest recorded success in all of prophetic literature was achieved while its single perpetrator was on lunch break! Now that's magical, worthy to be listed in our Tale of the Fantastic discussion below, in chapter 10.

[16] See above, "Back to Square One," in chapter 3.

powerful for being unacknowledged, is the traditional one between God and the all-knowing Narrator. It was in fact against the image of an omniscient God-disguised-as-narrator that led to Sartre's objection against Mauriac: that God is not, and cannot be, a novelist.[17]

The book of Jonah exemplifies the converse, that a novelist cannot be God either—not that our narrator does not strongly represent God's point of view. However, in our book *both* points of view are narrated: God's, with which the narrator agrees, but also Jonah's principled and unreconciled dissent. And it is the narrator's perspectivism, his willingness to represent opposition, that betrays a disposition to reconsider and thus the possibility to change one's mind. One might say that the narrator learned this from his Hero (see above), but such narrative flexibility produces astonishing and humorous results.

For example, there is, in the portrayal of the two protagonists, a blurring of traditional roles. Imagine, on the one hand, an often irascible God, whose anger is taken over by His antagonist, while He does His mightiest to tease, win back, humor His abandoned lover:

Now X was absolutely furious and burned with anger. (Jonah 4:1)[18]

This sounds very much like one of God's chronic upsets, and it is in fact viewed as such by the Ninevites:

God may turn from his rage, so that we do not perish. (3:9)

However, the X-subject is in fact Jonah, and God's response is very much in step: not exactly the prayerful "Turn from your burning anger" of Exod 32:12, but rather the playful attempt both to pacify and, yes, seduce:

"Are you really *that* upset?" (4:4; repeated in 4:9)

---

[17] Jean-Paul Sartre, *Situations I* (Paris: Gallimard, 1947), 52. "God is not a novelist, and neither is François Mauriac!"

[18] Limburg, *Jonah*, 89.

And, for further examples of reversed expectations, what about the huge fish, which was sent to devour and destroy Jonah but ends up saving him! If not a change of mind, we have here at least a dramatic change of direction. Or, in reverse, the *kikayon*, which starts out as a thriving succah of salvation and ends up dried out, and Jonah along with it. It seems that God's entire universe has the potential for making radical turn-arounds, quite in step with the Lord-of-Contradictions Himself.

CHAPTER EIGHT

THE BOOK OF PROPHECY

At the center of Jonah 4, the *kikayon* radiates its magic in two directions: the personal and the social, both Jonah's status with God and post-repentant Nineveh. The first is dealt with, as we have seen, in the Elijah-like epiphany:[1] God and Jonah have become reconciled, and the focus can now move from the highly personal—should Jonah live or die?—to Everyman. For the issue of (the multiple stages of) repentance remains, and here Nineveh's future fate is instanced as a broad theological issue under debate.[2] Folks get confused and even outraged by this discussion for many reasons, the basic one being the historical sequel. Assyria will revert to its evil, notably against Israel, and this is known to everyone: God in his foreknowledge, probably Jonah in his prophetic mode, certainly the generations of readers and rereaders—including contemporaries themselves, assuming the validity of a growing scholarly consensus on a late date for the book's composition—and especially our own post-*Shoah* generations. From such a perspective, our outrage must be aroused not against Jonah but against God: for what theological reasons can the Ninevites be allowed to live?

---

[1] See above, "The *Kikayon* Episode . . . ," in chapter 4.

[2] Gerda Elata-Alster and Rachel Salmon have observed that "chapter four moves to a new genre of relationship, that of the free individual vis-à-vis God. Now a theological rather than a historico-prophetic issue comes to the fore" ("The Deconstruction of Genre in the Book of Jonah: Towards a Theological Discourse," *Journal of Literature and Theology* 3 [1989]: 55). Similarly, Ehud Ben Zvi: "The identity of the city [Nineveh] is at best peripheral to the main theological discussion between YHWH and Jonah in Chapter 4" (*Signs of Jonah: Reading and Rereading in Ancient Yehud* [JSOTSup 367; Sheffield: JSOT Press, 2003], 121).

Note that the discussion now occurs in a different time frame: it is not whether the Ninevites should be forgiven—they already have been (3:10)—but what after? God's answer is that he will let them live like innocent children or animals; that will be okay. But what if they revert to their evil ways? God will now introduce a new theological argument, one typically projected back to the book's beginning but improperly so. For up until Jonah 4 God's requirements are repentance, and these are met. But Jonah 4 is about the sequel: what if there is a relapse? And if this time repentance does not occur, will destruction ensue?

The Theologies of Mere Existence and True Love

He spares His creatures for the simple reason that He likes them to exist.[3]

The Gentiles in the story love life.[4]

Not to be devoured is the most perfect feeling. Not to be devoured is the secret goal of a whole life.[5]

The philosophical discovery of the feeling of pure existence, of just being alive, we recall, may be traced to Jean-Jacques Rousseau's meditations in the *Reveries of the Solitary Wanderer*. Floating deliciously in a small boat on the Swiss Lac de Bienne, Rousseau is conscious that he exists not as a particular this or that but solely as an existent: he has arrived at the simple state of "pleasurably feeling my existence."[6] One wonders, though. A theologian has thoughts about theology and an historian about history, but does everyone who exists—you, me, Jonah—have thoughts about existence in itself? It seems more typically the case that

---

[3] Jacob Licht, *Storytelling in the Bible* (Jerusalem: Magnes, 1978), 121.

[4] Uriel Simon, *Jonah: The Traditional Hebrew Text with the New JPS Translation* (trans. Lenn J. Schramm; JPS Torah Commentary; Philadelphia: Jewish Publication Society, 1999), 34.

[5] Clarice Lispector, "The Smallest Woman in the World," *You've Got to Read This* (ed. Ron Hansen; New York: HarperCollins, 2000), 356.

[6] "sentir avec plaisir mon existence." Jean-Jacques Rousseau, *Rêveries du promeneur solitaire* (Genève: Droz, 1967), "Fifth Promenade."

we think about our existence as such only in its real or projected absence, when disease and death become threatening. But to have before our mind the idea of existence or health as a positive force, as a constant source of enjoyment and strength and vitality, this is perhaps an achievement reserved for enlightened human beings. Indeed, Rousseau's discovery—of great philosophical interest—is colored by his particular personal circumstances, by his feelings, no less than The Smallest Woman in the World, of having escaped danger at the hands of others. Similarly, by the end of Part One Jonah has discovered the most delicious feeling of being back in the world:

And You raised up from destruction my life, Lord my God. (2:7)

Heightened by his landing on shore with a thud, his pleasurable discovery of still being alive can surely be interpreted, like Rousseau's, through tasting its destructive absence: being swallowed alive by the humongous fish and the horrific deep.

Jonah's reaction is now to go to Nineveh and declare his prophetic message, but this decision seems as mysterious as his initial one to flee. For what is his motivation now: to declare the Ninevites' doom and to delight in their destruction? Surely, rather, to save their lives. But, if so, to what purpose? Note that his destination is now twofold: the populous city of Nineveh, on the one hand, and the solitary desert where he then takes up residence, on the other. Are these two oppositional, as usually thought, or are they rather the two poles of a single plan? Whereas Rousseau's escape from his enemies is presented as the backdrop of a pantheistic tranquility, Jonah's feeling for existence is expressed as gratitude, thus a reconnecting with God that forecasts—again like Rousseau—a finer sense of existence, an intimation of what the language of mysticism termed "supreme felicity." In our chapter 4 this sense was described in individual terms, as Jonah's attempt—like Elijah in the desert—to reconnect with God his Beloved. We must now explore how this relates to his broader intentions with the sinful "Ninevites," and how these intentions are viewed by God.

We recall the Ninevites' bizarre method of expressing repentance by involving animals in their rituals of fasting and mourning, the underlying assumption being that humans and animals share a common fate. The surprise is that this assumption is confirmed by God's pardon and explicit declaration at the end:

> And should I not care about Nineveh, that great city, in which there are *more than twelve myriad persons* who do not know their right hand from their left, and *many beasts as well*? (Jonah 4:11; emphasis added)

This is God's first reason for the pardon, that animals and humans have a common fate because they have a shared identity. The Ninevites are allowed to live if they simply correct their evil ways and refrain from evil. Their ritual argues that animal existence is sufficient because it is innocent, and because existence itself is a good.

What then of the command to "turn from evil *and do good*" (Ps 34:15; 37:27, emphasis added)? God's answer is that not only do you not need to be X to be saved, you don't even need to "do good"! Simply refraining from evil deeds will put you on the level of animals, and that is enough for avoiding destruction, for mere existence. This is God's lowest—but sufficient—standard: humans (and animals) are worthy of life through the simple fact of having been made alive. Why? Because existence—*vivere*—in itself is good. Thus existence does not derive from virtue but simply from goodness, and, theologically speaking, this goodness is that of the Creator who created a good universe, once again available through the absence of sin. The Ninevites' triumph is that God ends up agreeing with them!

All this should come as no surprise, however, since the Ninevites' doctrine is well grounded in biblical theology. For example, Ezekiel's list of the qualities defining righteousness (Ezek 18:5–9) has a preponderance of negative commands stressing the mere avoidance and removal of evil. The goal: life, existence, and the enjoyment of its goodness:

> Who is the man who desires life,
> Who loves years in which to enjoy [life]? (Ps 34:13)[7]

---

[7] "To see the good," *lir'ot tob*, is a variant of *lir'ot betob*, both mean "to enjoy"; see T. A. Perry, *Dialogues with Kohelet* (University Park, PA: Penn State Uni-

The Ninevite conception of innocence adds the important comparison to animals but does not deviate much from Ezekiel's norm. The stress on abundance ("*twelve myriad* persons . . . and *many* animals as well") may add another dimension, however. As Zornberg observes, in her study of Jacob's comparisons of his sons to animals, "the basic definition of an animal, a *haya*, is that it can deal unaided with the life-business of procreation. Jacob sees in his children a similar vital competence to . . . tend to sustaining and increasing life."[8] In other words, the prodigious animal vitality of the Ninevites in itself advances the work of creation.[9]

Jonah does not, for all that, totally agree with God. Their differences may be clarified by considering the well-known proverb:

> Those that honor Me I shall honor; but those that despise me shall be of slight esteem. (1 Sam 2:30)

Is such a list all-inclusive? What of those who neither honor nor despise God? God's answer in Jonah is that they will neither rise nor descend but, well, simply be allowed to exist. Such generosity towards the innocent who have either not sinned (animals and children) or, like the Ninevites, sinned and repented their evil ways, was felt as a threat to Jonah, as it was at a later period:

> He used to say: "Everything is given on pledge and a net is spread for all the living. The shop is open and the shopkeeper extends credit; the ledger is open and the hand writes: and all who wish to borrow, let them come and borrow. And the collectors continuously make their rounds every day, exacting payment from people with or without their consent." (Mishnah *Abot* 3:16)

> He used to say: "You are not expected to finish the work, but you are not free to refrain from it." (Mishnah *Abot* 2:16)

---

versity Press, 1993), 73. For gaining life, see Amos 5:4 and Hab 2:4. For commentary see especially Moshe Greenberg, *Ezekiel 1–20: A New Translation with Introduction and Commentary* (AB 22; Garden City: Doubleday, 1983), 334–47.

[8] Aviva Zornberg, *Genesis: The Beginning of Desire* (Philadelphia: Jewish Publication Society, 1995), 368.

[9] The work of fertility and increase occurs in the creation portions of Genesis no less than three times: 1:22, 28; 9:7.

In short, and like the writers of these mishnahs, Jonah wishes to close the gap or escape hatch: only two possibilities exist and there is no third or neutral way out.

These two options, as the wisdom tradition makes repetitively clear, are righteousness and wickedness. But, again, when one stops being wicked, does that person automatically become righteous? And, conversely, does the righteous person who stops being righteous automatically become wicked? What is the status of those betwixt and between? For between the contradictories "good and bad" or "righteous and wicked" there are the oppositionals: "not good" and "not bad."[10] To be sure, neither Jonah nor God has any stock in wickedness, but the real question for both is less the differences between righteous and wicked than between righteous and innocent. God makes a case for the "betwixt and between", i.e., the majority of humans (and Nineveh is a large city), and equates guiltlessness with innocence.

Now Jonah, it is usually supposed, denies this equation and is said to subscribe to the old adage that a person will die for his/her own sin,[11] and does not allow that repentance can atone for *past* mistakes. The question can more accurately be posed, however, by asking why Jonah, after preaching to the Ninevites *and observing their remission* (3:10), takes up residence east of the city. The usual hypothesis is that he wants to observe the destruction or die if this does not occur. Since this appears to be not in keeping with God's plan, Jonah will be kept alive to witness the Ninevites' survival so that he can learn—or relearn—the important lesson of God's mercy. However, since, as we shall see, Jonah's death wish has nothing to do with either a hatred of Gentiles or disbelief in God's mercy,[12] a different hypothesis

---

[10] See T. A. Perry, *Wisdom Literature and the Structure of Proverbs* (University Park: Penn State University Press, 1993), 116. In terms of the Holocaust, for example, between the categories of Nazis and heroes ("righteous Gentiles") would be the bystanders. For reflections on their moral standing see the probing essays by Berel Lang, "For and Against the 'Righteous Gentiles,'" *Judaism* 46 (1997): 91–96 and "Uncovering Certain Mischevious Questions about the Holocaust," annual lecture presented at the United States Holocaust Memorial Museum, Washington, D.C., March 12, 2002.

[11] See Deut 24:16.

[12] See below, "Jonah's Knowledge of God."

recommends itself: Jonah wants to monitor what will be in the long run *after* they avoid destruction.

Jonah was saved from the pit not merely to exist, however, but especially to serve. Should this standard not also apply to the Gentiles? To further characterize the theological debate between God and Jonah, consider the following parable: Jews at Passover sing the song *dayyenu*, "it would have been enough for us":

> If the Lord had given us X but had not given us the Land or the Torah or the Sabbath, etc., it would have been enough for us.

On the surface it is a song of thanksgiving for every single blessing that has been granted the Jewish people. The logic, however, is anything but comforting. For, one might exclaim, how can one possibly imagine being Jewish, even being human, without the Law, the Sabbath, etc.!! The Ninevites embrace the reductivist/surrealistic logic of *dayyenu* at its most primitive level:

> If God gives us only existence, *dayyenu*.

To which Jonah responds in astonishment:

> God calls humanity to His love and service and you [i.e., You] say "*dayyenu* that we are merely alive"!!

There is, then, for the book of Jonah a legitimate theology of survival. But this level, as important as it is, is relativized by other and even deeper motives. For, as Rilke observed, "what tightens into [mere] survival is already inert."[13] What then is the role of prophecy, of the Temple? These reach beyond mere existence to the dimensions of love and service in an outward movement from center to periphery, and directly and intimately towards God in a movement back to the Temple. Jonah thinks that his salvation from the deep implies a return to "the Temple of Your holiness" (twice mentioned: Jonah 2:4, 7), but God has not abandoned the original plan: "Get yourself to Nineveh!"

---

[13] Rainer Maria Rilke, *Sonnets to Orpheus* (trans. Willis Barnstone; Boston: Shambhala, 2004), poem 95.

Let Psalm 1 serve as a summary. Two conditions of happiness are given. The first is reached negatively, through mere avoidance of evil. The second, knowledge of God, requires positive action. But what if only the first is achieved, which would be the case of the repentant Ninevites? Then they would avoid the punishment of destruction that comes upon the wicked, thereby being granted (mere) existence. But "happiness" may be another matter, one that can be added to the mere existence according to Rousseau's understanding.

In exploring the central problem of the book of Jonah—why the prophet runs away from God—I have proposed the *psychological* model of an erotic relationship between God and Jonah.[14] As against the view of Jonah as a law-and-order man angry with God's mercy and who doesn't want to let the wicked Ninevites off the hook, I have suggested that Jonah's upset and rebellion may lie in a different sense of *khesed*, which is the loving bond promised to God's beloved and here offered, unexplainably, to the undeserving or not yet deserving Ninevites. At a second level—and taking *khesed* as mercy or forgiveness—God's mercy seems a questionable compromise if the Ninevites' only goal in life is mere existence and guiltlessness, for should God settle for mere survival?

The psychological issue is thus not *sui generis*, as is usually posited (according to which Jonah is selfish or depressed or somehow personally defective) but based on important *theological* principles. Now if, as an old catechism would have it, the duty of humans in this life is to know, to love, and to serve God, it is fair to say that theological analysis of the book of Jonah has focused almost exclusively on the latter, viewing Jonah as guilty of faulty service: either towards God in his refusal to carry out the divine command, or towards his fellow humans in his reluctance to preach to the Ninevites—indeed, some even speculate, in his

---

[14] Variants to this particular model could be imagined, of course. For example, instead of love one could speak of honor, as in the Rabbinic argument that Jonah's sin was in "seeking the honor of the children (Israel) over that of the Father"—a model that still sees the problem as a family matter, so to speak. If that is the case, however, then the formula would need to be reversed, since Jonah's entire "rebellion" can be viewed as a protest in favor of God's honor, endangered by the latter's reckless compromise of divine Justice.

hatred of Gentiles in general. In the present essay the complement has been advanced: that Jonah's relation to God from start
to finish concerns the nature of our *loving* relationship with God.
We thus pass from blaming Jonah to exploring his sense of either
damaged or unfulfilled intimacy. If both these issues raise powerful questions about God—the nature of His love and the level
of His standards—a third theological issue crowns Jonah's upset
with confusion over the very nature of God. This issue, which we
shall now examine, involves nothing less than Jonah's *knowledge*
of God.

Jonah's Knowledge of God

Jonah is reticent about his motives for fleeing until near the very
end. When he finally does makes his grand disclosure, however, are
we so sure that we understand what is being said? Here is a typical
rendering of Jonah's state of mind at the start of chapter 4:

> But it displeased Jonah exceedingly, and he was angry. And
> he prayed to the Lord and said, "I pray thee, Lord, is not
> this what I said when I was yet in my country? That is why
> I made haste to flee to Tarshish; for I knew that thou art a
> gracious God and merciful, slow to anger, and abounding in
> steadfast love, and repentest of evil. Therefore now, O Lord,
> take my life from me, I beseech thee, for it is better for me
> to die than to live." And the Lord said, "Do you do well to be
> angry?" Then Jonah went out of the city and sat to the east
> of the city, and made a booth for himself there. He sat under
> it in the shade, until he should see what will become of the
> city. (4:1–5 RSV)

It is usually assumed that the initial "it" is actually a "this" (NJPS),
thus establishing a sequence with the previous scene, which depicts God's decision to pardon Nineveh. Such an assumption is
not without its difficulties, however, as even its defenders admit.
Thus, Simon: "Of all the scenes of the story, only this one . . . is
syntactically linked to the previous one: it begins with an elliptical
sentence whose implicit subject was stated explicitly at the end of

the previous scene."[15] How can we be so sure of such a syntactic link, however, when it is equally possible that the implicit subject is what *follows*? In our haste to conclude that it is Nineveh that is the subject and cause of Jonah's upset, we would do well to ponder Sasson's cautionary advice: "Let us keep in mind how easily God reversed Jonah's mood, for it makes us doubt a prevalent opinion that Jonah sulked because Nineveh escaped punishment."[16] In short, it is not all about the Gentiles!

A similar problem of sequence occurs at the end of the pericope. Commentators typically run v. 3 into v. 4, so that God is actually raising the question as to whether Jonah's anger—assumed to be towards the Ninevites—is appropriate. In the MT, however, there is a strong pause or *setumah* after v. 3, in which case God's question in v. 4 applies not to the present subject but rather to the one that follows.[17] Yet another issue is in the meaning of the words themselves: Since the expression *yera' 'el* (4:1) occurs nowhere else in the Hebrew Bible, its usual rendering as some form of "displeasure" is anything but clear. Its reinforcement by *ra'ah gedolah*, "great evil," does give some level of closure, however, since "evil" does occur in our text with very precise meaning:

> . . . for their wickedness [*ra'atam*] has come up before Me. (1:2)

Working backwards, we may then say that the verb strengthens the sense of the noun: "Jonah sinned a great sin."[18]

---

[15] Simon, *Jonah*, 36; cf. Hans Walter Wolff, *Obadiah and Jonah* (trans. Margaret Kohl; CC; Minneapolis: Augsburg, 1986).

[16] Jack M. Sasson, *Jonah: A New Translation with Introduction, Commentary, and Interpretation* (AB 42B; New York: Doubleday, 1990), 316.

[17] The cut in sequence between vv. 3 and 4 is further accentuated by the consequential "now" ("Therefore, *now*, O Lord"; see Simon, *Jonah*, 38), which closes the prayer that began in v. 2. See also above, "Assisted Suicide, Again!" in chapter 6.

[18] As in David's synonymous declaration to Saul (1 Sam 24:11): "Since I [merely] cut off the corner of your robe and did not kill you, know and see that there is in my hand no evil [*ra'ah*] or transgression [*pesha'*], nor did I sin [*hata'ti*] against you." In the preceding passage the root *r'h* occurs in two different senses: the *disaster* that God was to bring upon the Ninevites (3:10), and the Ninevites' evil or *sinful ways* (3:8, 10). The first sense is usually assumed

Here, then, is how the passage would read with these adjustments:

> Now Jonah [became aware that he had] committed a very great sin, and he was distressed [i.e., with himself]. And he pleaded with the Lord, saying:

> "Please, Lord, was this not my issue [with You] while still in my land! And the reason why I arose and fled to Tarshish is because I *knew* that You are a 'gracious and compassionate God, very patient and full of mercy, and who repents of retribution.'

> And now, Lord, please take my life from me, for my death is better than my life." (4:1–3)

But if Jonah's sin is not any putative dislike of the Ninevites, what then is the issue? More pointedly, how indeed did Jonah *know* that God is merciful? One answer is explained by Simon: "[Jonah] is relying on the knowledge vouchsafed to Moses and subsequently consolidated over generations."[19] In more modern parlance, Jonah's awareness is based on quotations from Mosaic tradition, something that you *learn* in Sunday school, or its equivalent. A second answer is based on the salvation at sea, where Jonah personally *knew*, i.e., *experienced*, God's mercy when saved by the fish. Now if Jonah thus has no reason whatever to doubt this knowledge of God as a merciful Being, what was he then to make of God's puzzling command of total destruction?

From the perspective of Jonah's disclosure of his deepest faith in God's mercy in 4:2 (and not at all, as is always claimed, on his rejection of that mercy!), let us try to readjust our focus on the events leading up to it:

1) God commands Jonah to announce impending doom.[20] God would then be acting peremptorily, as in the bad old days of the Flood and Sodom and Gomorrah. Jonah

---

to be carried over in 4:1, but why not the second meaning, especially since it is repeated?

[19] Simon, *Jonah*, 37.

[20] See above, "Back to Square One," in chapter 3, and Simon, *Jonah*, 4.

therefore avoids the cruelty and runs away, fearing that God will not relent even if the Ninevites do.

2) In 3:1 God succeeds in forcing his prophet back only by acceding to Jonah's more precise (and, indeed, merciful) conditions: "forty days *and no less* (or: I will be patient with them for up to forty *more* days). And this time you may preach *to* them (and not upon or *against* them)."[21]

3) When God does relent, scholars like Kaufmann view this as proof that Jonah's belief in a God of punishment was antiquated and that Jonah was thus somehow wrong. But was not Jonah in fact merely taking God's threat at face value?

The Glory of Israel [i.e., God] does not deceive or change His mind, for He is not human that He should change His mind. (1 Sam 15:29 NJPS)[22]

Why then is Jonah so upset? Surely not because the Ninevites have repented and been spared, because after all that is what the prophet wished, even against God's expressed refusal! No, he is angry because he is aware of his great sin in doubting God's mercy: "Since I denied or doubted Your mercy, I do not deserve it. Therefore 'take my life,' for *I knew* all along (I learned, I should have known, I in fact did know) that you are merciful and repent

---

[21] Since Jonah got God to reconsider and negotiate more lenient terms for the Ninevites, it is beside the point to accuse him of not pleading on their behalf, as does Simon, *Jonah*, xxxvii. Further, while it is not uncommon for the prepositions *'al* and *'el* to be interchangeable in the Hebrew Bible, as in God's announcement of retribution: "Behold I am *against* you" (*'al* in Ezek 5:8, but *'el* in Ezek 13:8; 21:8; 29:10), the shift is intended when there is a deliberate opposition, as in God's "Behold, I am against (*'al*) you [i.e., for evil]" (Ezek 5:8), as contrasted with God's "Behold, I am for (*'el*) you [i.e., for good]" in Ezek 36:9. That God's command of "calling *to*" proves to be more effective with Jonah than His "calling *upon*" is a tactic learned from Jonah himself: "I called *to* (*'el*) the Lord and He responded to me" (2:3). See also the interesting discussion in Ben Zvi, *Signs*, 34–36.

[22] If God now does change his mind, however, then this verse is wrong! For a discussion, see John T. Willis, "The 'Repentance' of God in the Books of Samuel, Jeremiah, and Jonah," *HBT* 16 (1994): 156–75, and "Pastoral Pedagogy" in chapter 9.

of evil." That is to say, he is angry only with himself, not with God or the Ninevites; he consequently accepts to die for his sin (4:3), especially since he now *knows* that he knows.

Thus, when Jonah runs away, he has no thoughts of repentance since he does not believe he has sinned. The entire prayer of chapter 2 thus contains petition and possibly thanks but no remorse. He also cannot understand, if God is determined to exterminate the city, why the fact should have to be announced (the inhabitants of Sodom and Gomorrah were not told beforehand, nor was the flood generation). It is only when his prediction does not come true and Nineveh is spared (3:10) that he realizes that he had sinned by doubting the Lord. Thus the narrative immediately declares: "And thus Jonah sinned a great sin and was angry." Not with the Lord, however, but with himself![23]

Jonah does admit to God's merciful nature (4:2), despite appearances to the contrary—in this case God's express prophetic declaration of Nineveh's destruction. This confession, a comforting return to the basic Torah doctrine he always *knew* and which was momentarily threatened, is genuine enough in that it affirms God's right to be Himself, so to speak, in the matter of repentance. It does not, however, indicate understanding and acceptance of the pitfalls of post-repentant or unrepentant humanity, those issues that Sweeney correctly sees as "encapsulating the essential point of the entire book," or at least the culminating and controversial chapter 4:

> YHWH's rhetorical question to Jonah . . . asserts the right to show mercy even to those who have committed (or will commit) evil.[24]

The question remains open, the argument probably still raging, possibly because, as the mathematician Alex Lubotsky once remarked (in a private communication), "some problems cannot be solved, only managed."

---

[23] For Jonah's language of confession, see above, "Thanksgiving or Confession?" in chapter 6.

[24] Marvin A. Sweeney, *The Twelve Prophets* (2 vols.; Collegeville, MN: Liturgical, 2000), 323.

The Structure of Jonah 4

When chapter 3 ends, the plot is over; Nineveh has received God's message and repented. Chapter 4 now returns to the matter of the first two chapters: the ongoing arguments between God and His prophet, and the psychological and theological issues that still separate them. Two dominant questions remain, now to be resolved at the post-Nineveh level. Now that the prophetic mission has been successfully carried out, will Jonah's personal relationship with God revert to its earlier level, despite his renewed desire to die? The second question concerns the Ninevites, no longer seen in their historical reality but rather as an instance of broader theoretical matters of dispute.

The now canonical "13 principles of God's mercy" that Jonah recites in part at the start of chapter 4 are presented as "eternal and noncontingent,"[25] neither making reference to Nineveh nor depending on the latter's repentance:

> "Thou art a gracious God and merciful, slow to anger, and abounding in steadfast love, and repentest of evil." (4:2)

Our observation that the plot of the book of Jonah, Nineveh's salvation from destruction, ends with chapter 3 makes the same point, as does the syntactic break just discussed, namely, that chapter 4 of the book of Jonah is totally independent of the preceding matter of Nineveh. By this I wish to highlight that the focus of the concluding discussion between God and Jonah does not concern Nineveh's repentance as a *past event*, for that is over and done with. Moreover, it would seem silly for Jonah to shriek bloody despair over the most remarkable success in all of prophetic literature and one that he himself preached.[26] Rather, the debate now turns towards the future and how it relates to these past events from a broader perspective. It is crucial to note how carefully such a perspective is laid out.[27]

---

[25] Ben Zvi, *Signs*, 58.

[26] And, as Ben Zvi pungently observes (*Signs*, 63), the prophetic proclamation with the least persuasive appeal (3:4b) in the Hebrew Bible.

[27] One minor but telling signal is the shift in the vocabulary of God's forgiveness from *nkhm* in chapter 3 (3:9–10) to *khus* in chapter 4 (4:10–11). Wolff makes the observation in this way: "In theological usage *nkhm* always

This concluding chapter has three movements or scenes.[28] Each scene is introduced and driven by the notation of Jonah's emotional state, usually imagined to be his burning anger (*kharah l-*) but, more broadly and correctly, as his being "sad, upset, sorry, distressed."[29] Since the first two movements have been dealt with above, a brief description of each will set the stage for the major concluding scene.

Jonah's Acknowledgement of God's Mercy (4:1–3)

Now Jonah had sinned a great sin, and he was distressed. (4:1)

Until this point we had thought that the message of the book is repentance. That focus is now theologically expanded or, more accurately put, bypassed. Jonah has overcome his doubts and now knows that he knows God: Mercy is the Lord's! This means, speaking of the Ninevites of chapter 3, that their repentance is effective only because of the nature of God, who changes his mind about *punishment* (Exod 32:14) because he forgives *sin* (Exod 32:12). Jonah thinks that the issue of God's compassionate nature is now resolved, but God will now use that awareness to expand the definition. The conversation will now move from the real to the generic "Ninevites" (you and me) in order to consider cases of forgiveness where repentance does *not* occur.[30]

---

refers to an earlier act, an earlier plan, or a saying of Yahweh's that has been uttered at some earlier point. . . . *khus*, on the other hand, is directed wholly to the exciter of compassion *here and now*" (Wolff, *Obadiah and Jonah*, 175; emphasis added). Wolff is wrong, however, in assuming that Jonah's rage is attached to God's remission. The consequences of this shift are but one further signal of a change in scene and focus, indicating once again that the matter of Nineveh is to be approached from an entirely different perspective of time and location as well.

[28] For the important issue of the precise boundaries of these sections, see also my remarks at the start of this chapter, "Jonah's Knowledge of God."

[29] On this important issue of Jonah's putative anger, Sasson's remarks (*Jonah*, 273–74) are a must, guided by his sense that "this idiom does not yield a single meaning." The recurrence of the same word with different meanings (a rhetorical figure called *antanaclasis*, see above, n. 17) occurs no less than three times in this chapter, with the words *yashab* (4:5), *khus* (4:10, 11), as well as here. This figure of speech is ideologically part and parcel with the oracular ambiguities to be studied below in the section "The Double Ending . . ."

[30] I thus agree with Leslie Allen, as far as it goes: "It is the greatness of Israel's God that is the burden of the book. Very much of its theology radiates out from

The first verse of the next scene is actually transitional, both to what follows and especially to the final scene:[31]

Now God said: "Are you *sooo* upset?" (4:4; emphasis added)

This verse is part of the preceding, since it responds (with a refusal) to Jonah's request to die. Not explicitly, since God's question leaves the matter up to Jonah, as he also will do in the book's conclusion. However, the tone is one of reconciliation (not a put-down!): "I don't require your life for this, Jonah." This allows the next scene to occur. Jonah understands that the matter of the real Nineveh is now behind them—both their repentance and their merciful pardon—and to everyone's total satisfaction. But what about the future?

The kikayon *Scene (4:5–8)*

Some of the current confusion over chapter 4 arises, once again, by not fully dealing with the implications of verse 4:5 in MT, or by sensing their importance and wishing them away. According to the received MT—and these consequences are rarely noticed or commented upon, even by those who argue to keep 4:5 in its proper place—Jonah left the city and went on to attend to other business only after both the repentance episode of 3:5–10 and Jonah's apology to God in 4:1–4. The matter of the real Nineveh—the one that is here reported to have repented—comes to a close with Jonah's request to die in 4:3. The final scene, no longer in Nineveh but rather in the succah (or in heaven, see below), opens with God's refusal: "Jonah, you need not be *so* upset." This signals that Jonah may be back in God's graces, thus "he builds himself a succah." From this point on,

---

the two credal confessions of Jonah in 1:9; 4:2" (*The Books of Joel, Obadiah, Jonah, and Micah* [Grand Rapids: Eerdmans, 1976], 192). I argue that the concluding scene goes beyond this point.

[31] See Elyakim Ben-Menahem, "Sefer Yona," in *Sefer Tere'asar: im perush "Da'at Mikra"* [The Minor Prophets] (Jersualem: Mossad Harav Kook, 1974–1976), 17: "This verse, according to tradition [as noted by the *setumah*, see above n. 7 in chapter six] begins a new section. Thus, it is not to be understood as a response to Jonah's complaints but rather as the introduction to God's in vv. 9–11. Verses 5–8 explain where the speech is to occur and for what reasons."

Nineveh the city is in the past, and it is the much broader matter of Nineveh—*concerning* Nineveh—that comes to the fore.[32] Wolff, too good a reader to deny the MT positioning of 4:5, verbally retains it but invents a virtual transfer ("flashback"), one more in accord with his theology.[33]

This *kikayon* scene is also parenthetical, in the sense that a *mashal* or parable or sign is merely preliminary to the comparison that follows and that it is called upon to explain. In 4:4 God has taken notice of Jonah's vexation and now takes steps to fix it by sending the *kikayon*. Just as the huge fish dominated Jonah's sea experience, this no less impressive divine appointee hovers over Jonah's desert just east of Nineveh, and both appointees are in response to Jonah's needs and wishes. As a divine appointee it has ambivalent modes of action that, as we have seen, characterize all the others:

> the fish: both destructive and salvatory,
> the worm: both lowly by nature and elevating (by wordplay),
> the east wind: *both v*iolent and quiet.

Like the others, the *kikayon* has great energy, here displayed in its phenomenal rate of growth. It is in fact this vitality that will form

---

[32] Since 4:1–3 (and v. 4) occurs precisely when the Saving Nineveh plot is over, it is transitional to what follows, perhaps moving the plot material to a higher or more theoretical level now. One could thus argue that the troublesome (to some at least) verse 4:5 can therefore be seen as occuring *before the parenthesis of 4:1–4*. But this would still mean that Jonah's departure from Nineveh would still *follow* the Ninevites' actual repentance and God's forgiveness.

[33] Although Wolff acknowledges that what happens *in* the city has already been reported in 3:5–10, he unexplainably both retains the traditional "*in* the city," and, while correctly refusing the relocation of 4:4 to after 3:4, nevertheless (following Lohfink) sanctions such a move as a "flashback," since he assumes that "Jonah has long since left the city . . . after he had fulfilled his assignment there in 3:4" (*Obadiah and Jonah*, 163, 169). However, flashbacks normally occur through real rather than merely "virtual" Hebrew pluperfects, whereas here we have the normal *waw*-conversive indicating sequential action, thus that the action of 4:5 occurs precisely at this point. What is crucial is to explain why. The proponents of the 4:5 switch—either actual or, like Wolff, virtual—not only encourage the charge of Jonah's carelessness about his mission but also intimate his disengagement from the Ninevites' fate. Just the opposite is the case, however. Jonah stayed the course, exposing himself to the possible dangers and departing only after God desists. One thinks of Honi ha-Meagel enclosing himself within a circle until God grants his request. Good job!

an important aspect of God's parting argument with Jonah (see below). Secondly, its action is transient, again like typical divine messengers, who are usually limited to strict business and cameo appearances. But the ambivalence that chiefly affects Jonah is its sudden rise and fall: its rise leads to his great joy because God is now back in touch with him; and its fall, as God will go on to point out, leaves Jonah missing it.[34]

With the miraculous appearance of the *kikayon* of Jonah's great joy, the prophet knows that the relationship is back on course. And from its parallel with Elijah's epiphany we understand that this sign of reconciliation must yield to its demise, in fulfillment of its promise to take Jonah *up*.[35] Jonah's renewed wish to die in 4:8 is of a totally different nature now: neither the death wish of a rejected lover in Jonah 1, nor that of a penitent in 4:3. Rather, Jonah now asks for the Mosaic kiss of death, which, with the arrival of the sun, may in fact now have been granted. For since God now moves on to a different topic, Jonah's prophetic/erotic issue seems resolved. Jonah swoons and is taken up by God, perhaps even by actual death. If this is the case, then the final scene takes on the colors of a *beth-din shel ma'alah*, of a "study-house in heaven," where God and his minions discuss Torah and the book's broader implications. This would allow a possible, albeit literalist, reading of Jonah's final death wish:

> Then God said to Jonah: "Are you right to be angry about the plant?" And he replied: "I am right to be angry, unto death." (4:9)

The kikayon *Comparison and the Ninevehs of the World (4:9–11)*

We noted above that 4:4 is transitional not only to 4:5 but also to this final scene. This is stylistically indicated by a (partial)

---

[34] On Jonah's discovery of transience, see below, "Omni-Presence . . ."

[35] As intimated by those wordplays signaling the positive valence of the worm's destruction of the bush. See above, "The *Kikayon* Episode," in chapter 4, and especially nn. 11, 39. Need we recall that *up* (*'al*) is, according to a Jewish exegetical tradition, one of God's names? See Hos 7:16; 11:7; 2 Sam 23:1; and Radak.

inclusio, setting off the *kikayon* scene as parenthetical to the matter at hand:

God: "Are you right to be angry?" (4:4, 9)

All this is on a personal level, but what about the Ninevites? We have suggested that Jonah's issue with the pardon has nothing to do with either his distaste for God's mercy or his hatred of the Ninevites. But it does have everything to do *with* the Ninevites. Strangely, God raises this issue as a question about the *kikayon*. Let Wiesel's question provide the proper focus:

If Jonah wishes that much to die, why does he cling to life? Why does he seek the coolness of the shade, when he should do nothing to avoid suffering? His is a peculiar combination of life-force and death wish. Which is more real?[36]

While agreeing with Ben Zvi that the issue of the book of Jonah is not about Israel and the nations,[37] the argument is broader and more refined than traditionally defined (as antagonistic). Humankind in its creational possibilities exists at any moment between two diametrically opposite extremes: radical wickedness (Sodomites, Ninevites) and prophetic consciousness (nearness to God/Reality). Jonah and God agree that the former must be utterly removed, either literally or, morally, through repentance. Jonah also thinks that the latter extreme—prophetic consciousness and cleaving to God—implies, ultimately, removal from this world; and, by the end and after Jonah has agreed to do God a favor or two, God seems willing to grant the request. What then of those outside of God's inner circle of lovers? Through repentance they may return to their original innocence and live out their lives.

This elaborate scheme seems to come crashing down, however, in the event that repentance is not effective or is aborted, and the wicked return to their old ways. The case is extremely poignant for

---

[36] Elie Wiesel, *Five Biblical Portraits* (Notre Dame: Notre Dame University Press, 1981), 133.

[37] "The position that the main purpose of the book of Jonah in its primary setting was to address the relations between Israel and 'the nations' should be rejected" (Ben Zvi, *Signs*, 9, n. 24).

Jonah, since in his case it is the Assyrians who will destroy his people! Does Jonah not know this? He is a prophet after all! Or, as Ben Zvi argues, what if the book was actually composed after the destruction of Israel, when the results of God's pardon were painfully visible? All the more so to a modern reader living in a post-*Shoah* environment! Put theologically, how can God, knowing the future, let the Ninevites live? This question is valid not only for the omniscient God and his prophet but for all re-readers down to the present day.

Not Rereading Jonah and the Theology of Post-and Non-Repentance

Summarizing our book up to this point—especially Jonah 3, where the plot is located—God said that the Ninevites would be destroyed and they weren't. Why? Because they turned themselves around through repentance. How can God do such a thing? Because He is merciful to returnees. In all of this, Jonah is no more than a divine appointee, and, we have argued, a willing one. Let us, however and for the sake of argument, agree with those who see Jonah as wanting Nineveh destroyed, and let us try to reconstruct what his outlook might be.

Our book provides Jonah with no less than four different perspectives:

a) The view from the Temple, where God renders Judgment: because of their wickedness the Ninevites should be destroyed;

b) The view of destruction from the belly of the fish;

c) The view from inside the city itself;

d) The view from somewhere east of the city.

Looking from the first view, from the Temple, Jonah sees the results of the Ninevites' *past* actions. This allows at least the theory that Jonah's immediate descent into the ship and the sea and the fish not only enacts a personal suicide; it projects, in a form both prophetic and emblematic, the destiny of the Ninevites as well. The first and second views are thus sequential and deeply related by cause and effect. When the prophet reaches the real, vibrant

Nineveh, however, the destructive prophecy is suspended and, following the same pattern, we would expect the third view, from the city, to project an emblematic and prophetic resolution.

Indeed, the fourth view is most intriguing in its presentation as hypothetical:

> He sat east of the city . . . until he will see what will be in the city. (4:5)

From the future tenses it would seem that all options are open: Jonah does not yet see anything and the Ninevites have not yet done anything.[38] We are thus led to ask: what does the prophet see when he looks into the future?

One answer—the one provided by the first view—is that he sees nothing. Nothing, that is, except what the divine command projects that he must report. That God's words are subject to revision, however, is clear from Abraham's plea in favor of Sodom and Gomorrah, allowing the possibility (unrealized in that instance) that God can change His mind (Gen 18:20–33). Another model would be Moses' decision to kill the Egyptian. Here, according to midrashic interpretation, Moses actually sees into the future and bases his decision on that information. In Rashi's version, intended to complete the thought of Exodus 2:12:

> [Moses] *turned this way and that, and when he saw that there was no man* . . . i.e., destined to issue from him who would embrace the religion of Israel.

Taking a soft reading of this episode, let us say that Moses could "read" the future. Based on his past contacts with the Egyptians, with whom he grew up, he judged this person to be totally wicked (of course, how can you ever know for sure?).

But what if Moses and Jonah were, like God, re-readers? Can it be that prophetic information, in the form of knowledge of the future, can be used to determine present innocence or guilt? Here a second model contradicts the previous one. The case involves the status of Ishmael's future righteousness and relationship with the Israelites:

---

[38] This view, which we reject, is even stronger when 4:5 is transferred to the position following 3:4. See below.

Fear not, for the Lord has heard the voice of the lad *where he is*. (Gen 21:17)

Rashi, quoting the Talmud: "He is to be judged by his present deeds and not by what [evil] he will do in the future." Sweeney gives an excellent synopsis of such a state of affairs:

Although the reader is aware that Assyria will ultimately destroy Israel, in the temporal perspective of the narrative such an event remains in the future and it cannot be certain whether or not such destruction will take place.[39]

In the book of Jonah the narrative's temporal perspective and God's ethical one coincide.

Here then, in a nutshell, would be the concluding difference between God and Jonah: The prophet, looking either from the past or, more dramatically, "from the east" into the ideal future, finds the Ninevites wanting. God, however, is content to see them "where they are," cleared of past guilt and, well, simply existing. No judgment can be made because, as Sweeney continues, "just as Nineveh chose to repent, so it might choose not to destroy Israel. Fundamentally, the choice is up to Nineveh, not YHWH or Jonah."[40] Only the present matters, and it is this ethics of transience, if we can call it that, that spells the doom of the rereading argument.[41]

Up to this point there is agreement. One is to be judged by present status and not by future misdeeds, even if they are likely. And if there is recidivism, what then? The same rule would presumably apply: clean up your act and you will again be forgiven.[42] But when does the straw break the camel's back? And, worse, what

---

[39] Sweeney, *The Twelve Prophets*, 306.

[40] Ibid.

[41] It does so in the practice of reading texts as well, for even when you read the same text for the one hundredth time, it must be read as a fresh text and you must bracket out past readings (as well as reading ahead, e.g., if it is a first reading but you have started by reading the conclusion) as if they do not exist. See my remarks below, Excursus 1, "On Reading Jonah."

[42] Ben Zvi refers to the Targum to Nahum 1:1, which "reaffirms the theological position that when Nineveh repents from its sins, YHWH relents; but when it sins again, a new prophecy against her is proclaimed" (*Signs*, 151, n. 54).

if repentance is *not* performed? In other terms, when repentance is performed, then the forgiveness, while ultimately dependent even then on divine mercy, still can be justified in terms of the penitent's merit (deeds of restitution, etc.). But what happens when there is no merit?

This point needs to be stressed. Typically, Jonah's reaction to Nineveh's escape is reduced to a silly upset of a poor sport: Lord, I am very upset! There is hardly a point to all this, however, since Nineveh has been saved, at least for now. But Jonah has, all along, taken the long view of matters. First he preaches (3:4), observes their compliance (3:5–9) and pardon (3:10), and then stations himself to see not what has already happened but what *will be* in the future. It would seem that Jonah's eyes are already those of a re-reader. The closing argument, therefore, is not at all about what has already happened (Nineveh is not destroyed) but about the future, what will be if Nineveh falls back into its old ways[43]—and, Lord, you know that they will. . . .

It is precisely such a situation that the Jonah ben Amittai of 2 Kgs 14 had to confront, one regarding "those who have not and will not repent."[44] In that incident King Jeroboam II is a sinner who also causes others to sin, yet would escape divine punishment. Although that text gives no reasons for the pardon, traditional Israelite theology had some readily available. For instance, maybe, like the Canaanites, his cup of evil was not yet full; or that God needed him to restore Israel's northern border (1 Kgs 8:65), as Simon speculates. The prophet Ezekiel lays out a sophisticated sequential program for such a state of affairs.[45] First there is issued Ezekiel's final call to repent (33:1–20). As Greenberg notes, the failure of this call marks the end of Ezekiel's "pre-fall theology," one based on retribution grounded on human responsibility. But

---

[43] I am thus uncomfortable with Ben Zvi's argument that the book satirically targets those who question the efficacy of repentance (*Signs*, 22). This position surely cannot be ascribed to the Ninevites ("the Ninevites are described as being unsure of the efficacity of repentance"). To be sure, the Ninevites ask "who can know?" (3:9), but this merely shows proper respect for the unpredictability of the divine will, and they *do* go ahead with their project (3:10), to God's entire satisfaction.

[44] See the important discussions in Simon (*Jonah*, xxxvi) and Ben Zvi (*Signs*, 56–57).

[45] See Ezek 32–37 and especially Greenberg's commentary in *Ezekiel 1–20*.

the destruction still does not occur and Israel is restored (36:16–38), not for their own sake but for God's.

If Israel can be saved not for justice's sake but for family reasons, as it were ("they are my people"), what about everyone else, us Ninevites? This, it may be argued, is precisely God's new and finely structured argument in Jonah 4: they are my creation, to be saved not through their merit but through mine, as a Creator. As far as theology goes, this creation argument can be used to justify God's forbearance even towards the unrepentant. It thus helps us understand God, but it has little bearing on the book's closing *kikayon* argument, since Jonah did not create it. In other words, I can understand God's claim: "I forgive 'Nineveh' because I created them." But what a strange *a fortiori* proposition to put to Jonah: "Now shouldn't you be prepared to forgive the *kikayon*'s departure all the more so because you did *not* create it?" At best, God's argument would run as follows: "You took delight in the *kikayon* which you did not even create; should I not take delight in (and not annihilate) an entire city which I did create?"

The Sign of the *Kikayon*

The *a fortiori* argument is one of the givens of Jonah criticism, so slavishly applied to 4:10–11 and thought to be beyond question, even though this type of argumentation is virtually nonexistent in Scripture. Since it is a standard offering in modern commentaries, one example can pretty much stand for them all. It is commonly thought that the book ends on an *a fortiori* argument of the type, "If you, Jonah, cared about the plant, then should not I, God, care about Nineveh all the more so because . . ." Such an argument is based on a comparison of sorts, although its antiparallelism is "less than perfect," as its more lucid proponents admit. Thus, Simon, with his editorial adjustments or justifications bracketed:

You cared for the plant [the small vine],	And should not I care about
which you did not work for	Nineveh, that great city
and which you did not grow.	[which I nurtured and grew]?[46]

---

[46] Simon, *Jonah*, 45.

Such forced contrasts are of course required by the prevalent pedagogical prejudice that wishes to teach Jonah a lesson by proving
God's superiority. One might have hoped that the prophetic warning had been heeded, however: "To whom shall you liken God?"
(Isa 40:18, 25, etc.), for any comparison with God will seldom
come out well for the persons compared.

The problem with the *a fortiori* hypothesis here, as I said, is
that it leads to the creation of contrasts that don't really exist in
the text. One way to get the discussion back on track is to realize that we are dealing here neither with an *a fortiori* figure nor
with reasoning but with a strict comparison, and the focus of that
comparison is not God/Jonah but rather *kikayon*/Nineveh. How
so? First of all, while a vine, even a large one, is surely smaller that
any large city, in its context the *kikayon* is anything but minuscule.
In fact, it is its prodigious growth, at least to the height of the
roof of the succah, that excites Jonah's joy. Secondly, there is little
reason for God to boast of having nurtured and grown Nineveh
(that may in fact be the reason why, in the text, he does *not* make
such a boast): Nineveh did that on its own! And now God again
dubs Nineveh "that great city," no longer stressing its wickedness
or even its repentance but rather its natural fulfillment of the
Bible's first and repeated command "to be fruitful and multiply"
(Gen 1:22, 28; 9:7). The point is that both the Creator-God and
his prophet take delight in life and vitality.

But, again, it is on the *kikayon*/Nineveh point of view that we
must remain focused, since it is through the comparison (parallel
and not anti-parallel) that we come to understand Nineveh, especially its ability to survive future divine punishments. For his argument's sake, God presents the *kikayon* as having three characteristics:

a) Jonah did not labor at it;

b) Jonah did not cause it to grow;

c) it is ephemeral.

It is to be noted that these represent the three stages of the *kikayon*'s existence, from its birth to its growth to its demise.[47] And

---

[47] The first two are occasionally combined. Wolff (*Obadiah and Jonah*, 174),
for example: "they stress the same point"; Sasson (*Jonah*, 310) refers to a possible

God, through this sign, this creation of the *kikayon*,[48] asserts—
and Jonah does not deny—that it is for these three reasons that
Jonah took delight in it and felt pity at its destruction.

The second thing to be noticed is that the *kikayon* is presented
from two quite different perspectives. Ben-Menahem's simple observation on the first element makes this crucial point:

> "*you didn't labor [in its creation]*: For the Lord appointed it
> and it sprouted forth of its own accord."[49]

This first perspective is the narrator's, who makes it clear that all
of this is from the Lord:

a) the *kikayon* is God's appointee;

b) the rapidity of the growth is somewhat supernatural, as is
   its diving purpose, "to save Jonah from his evil";

c) the *kikayon*'s removal is effected by the worm, again God's
   direct appointee.

Arguing from the narrator's perspective, here are the qualities
of Nineveh as they would be understood to parallel those of the
kikayon:

a) Nineveh is God's creation;

b) it has prodigious growth: more than 120,000 inhabitants;

c) !!

If our theory of the comparison holds and the *kikayon* is a sign for
Nineveh, is Jonah then to learn that Nineveh too is ephemeral?

---

hendiadys, yielding the sense: "upon which you have not labored to cultivate."
However, such a move confuses two distinct levels of creation both in the sign
(the creation of the *kikayon*) and in the Nineveh comparison.

[48] What is the *kikayon*'s status in the book? Just as Nineveh is a *mashal* or
"symbol of the nations" (Sweeney, *The Twelve Prophets*, 303), the *kikayon* may
be viewed as a sign or *'ot* (the two, *mashal* and *'ot*, are compared in Ezek 14:8),
like the Sabbath (Exod 31:13, 17) or Noah's rainbow (Gen 9:12, 17). The function of a sign is to point to something, thus serving as a witness and reminder,
ultimately of some understanding between humans and God. As such, signs do
not require reasoning but rather careful attention and observation of similarity.

[49] Ben-Menahem, *The Minor Prophets*, 19.

Here the dialogue proceeds as dialogue should.[50] God had just expanded the concept of mercy beyond repentance, to include mercy for God's sake; now Jonah will return the favor. Jonah likes the *kikayon* and will not destroy it. The worm, however, is a signal of sudden possible disaster from God. Is this to intimate that, just like the *kikayon*, Nineveh too can be struck down? Jonah asks to die this final time because of the *kikayon*, i.e., because of Nineveh, because he thinks that the message is that God's mercy does not go far enough, that, just as the worm, God's agent,[51] killed the *kikayon*, God will destroy Nineveh because it too has no personal or acquired merit. God therefore comforts him: "Don't worry, Jonah. Just as you cared for the *kikayon*, I too will care for Nineveh."[52] The famous pedagogical argument, according to which the book and especially its conclusion are to teach Jonah a lesson, is thus reversed.[53] And if *a fortiori* reasoning is still felt to be required, perhaps this one can serve: "You, Jonah, took pity on a simple plant; shouldn't I, God, at least do the same for a huge number of humans and animals!"

The second perspective—Jonah's—is more naturalistic. Jonah sees only the agent and the activity, the bush and the worm:

a) the plant appears suddenly, sprouting forth on its own accord;

b) its grows very quickly;

c) it dies just as quickly.

The Jonah of our story is of course not Goethe's Wagner, who cannot see beyond appearances,[54] but a prophet of God who regularly does. How then does all of this occur? Who created the plant and

---

[50] As Plato put it somewhere, when two go together, one [not always the same one] goes before the other.

[51] The *tola'at*; God, again playing on the elevation of '*al*; see above, n. 34.

[52] However, the book's double ending means that God will still keep his options open for the future, that at some point Nineveh may prove to be as ephemeral as the *kikayon*. See below, "The Double Ending . . ."

[53] See Ps 119:99, quoted below, in "Pastoral Pedagogy" in chapter 9: "I have learned most from my students."

[54] "Ich finde nicht den Spur von einem Geist . . ." ; see Johann Wolfgang von Goethe, *Faust* (trans. Carl R. Mueller; Hanover, N.H.: Smith & Kraus, 2004).

generated this burst of energy, God or the plant itself on its own steam, through its own powers of generation and vitality?[55] When God intervenes to explain the *kikayon* parable, however, neither possibility is put forward, only that the cause was not Jonah.

What then happens when both perspectives are combined in dialogue? More concretely, the book until now has offered two possibilities on where things can come from, depending on how you hold to the creation theory:

a) from *God*, as gifts;

b) from their *own merit*, as reward for effort.

The narrator's vote? From God, no question about it. The secularist's choice: from their own effort. Jonah's? We don't know since Jonah doesn't answer God's question at the end. However, there is a third possibility consisting of a combination of the other two, one that seems closer to the total dialogic solution proposed by the book's ending:

c) from *their own natural powers*.

This would typically work through reciprocity.[56] This possibility raises the question of who created Nineveh, the Ninevites or God? Well, it depends on what you mean (above I argued both sides of the coin!). According to biblical theology, God did create the world and the first humans. God also then turned things over to humans so that they too could be creative, God retaining a (permanent?) role in propagation, as per Gen 4:1. But the teeming city of Nineveh achieved that level by simply following the biblical command to be fruitful and multiply and fill the earth. The technical question here is whether their performance of the commandment was due to goodness or to virtue; were they simply "doin' what comes naturally," as the saying goes, or were they working to achieve bonus points? Thus "which you did not

---

[55] Maintenance of such a permanent *équivoque* is characteristic of the fantastical literary genre; see below, "A Tale of the Fantastic," in chapter 10.

[56] Another form of this kind of reciprocity would be prayer, where the petitioner either opens her mouth so that God can listen, or asks that her mouth be opened by God so that His praise can be declared.

grow" (4:10) could mean either "but which God did" or "which it did itself" or most likely *both*.[57]

It is worth noting how chapter 4 moves away from standard notions of *reward* for merit *and punishment* for sin. For one thing, there is a consideration of how punishment can be avoided in the absence of merit. This does not go all the way to the outrageous *rasha' wetov lo* of how good things happen to evil people, but rather how less than righteous folks and sometimes even less than full human beings in a moral sense (animals, children, those who don't use their freedom to choose) can still avoid destruction and merit existence. From the point of view of mercy, this is surely a step up beyond the massive annihilation of Sodom and Gomorrah or Voltaire's Lisbon earthquake and similar *Shoahs*.

Issues of reward and punishment are also circumvented by the book's erotic argument. When God crowns Jonah's shady succah-like hut with His own shade of grace, one might interpret this as a divine response to Jonah's own efforts. God's response is indeed an acknowledgement but can hardly be conceived of as a reward for the prophet's initiative. While God was touched by the attempted seduction, his gracious gift of the *kikayon* is precisely that: "I don't love you *because* you love me." Did Jonah then not get rewarded for building his succah? Yes indeed, by the succah that he built.

In order to detail the close *kikayon*/Nineveh parallelism, we must now jump ahead to the reasons God gives for enjoying/pitying that great city of Nineveh (great, presumably because it repented its sins):

> that great city which has more than 120,000 humans who do not know their right from their left, and many animals as well. (Jonah 4:11)

The reason boils down to size, the large numbers of people and animals. Notice that since God's purpose here is to explain why the

---

[57] Scripture does give instances, however, of where procreation involves real effort and dedication (let's leave the matter of *raising* the kids to another day). Examples would include Judah's son's, who refused to impregnate Tamar (Gen 38), Jacob's rapid multiplication of animals (Gen 30), and the Israelite population boom in Egypt at the start of Exodus (Exod 1:7).

city is to be saved, i.e., *because* of its size, thus the relative *'asher* ("that great city *which* has") has a causative sense: "*because* it has more than 120,000 humans . . . and many animals as well." If so, how does their ignorance of right and left help God's argument? One popular explanation is that this refers to the 120,000 *children* in Nineveh, and it is for their sake that the entire population is saved. However, the Jonah text does not say "children," but rather "human beings," referring to the entire population. The theory can be saved only by taking the term in a moral sense, by the notion that the Ninevites, through their repentance, have recovered the goodness afforded to innocent children.[58]

Thus when the book's end is read not as an *a fortiori* argument but rather as a strict comparison between Jonah's experience with the *kikayon* and God's experience with Nineveh, we have a better chance of understanding what is really being said:

> Then the Lord said: "You [enjoyed and therefore] cared about the *kikayon* which you did not work for and did not grow, which grew overnight and perished overnight."

The usual bland rendering of *'asher* as a relative conjunction "which"—usually understood as "although")—is doubled by a causal meaning, exactly parallel to its dual use in God's reply (4:11) concerning the Ninevites.[59] For, surely, God is not merely reporting what Jonah already knows—the plant's independence from Jonah's nurture and its transience—but rather the motive—secret and perhaps unacknowledged—for Jonah's enjoyment and concern. Jonah has been forced from his doctrine of strict merit; he can now allow himself to enjoy something arising not from his own effort.

This is only half of the verse, however, for the ambivalence continues to the end:

---

[58] Whence the verse sometimes cited to explain the curious expression "right and left" (see Simon, *Jonah*, 47): "your children, who do not yet know good from bad, they shall enter it [the land]" (Deut 1:39).

[59] Paul Joüon and T. Muraoka, *A Grammar of Biblical Hebrew* (Rome: Pontifical Biblical Institute, 1993), 170e; BDB, 83; Robert Gordis, *Kohelet: The Man and His World* (New York: Schocken, 1968), 296, on 8:11.

> Then the Lord said: "You [enjoyed and therefore] cared about the *kikayon because* you did not work for it and did not grow it, because [*sh*-for *'asher*] it grew overnight and perished overnight. . . ."

I wish to stress that these meanings of *'asher* ("which, although" and "because") are both possible; in fact we will later explain why they are both necessary.[60] We have here in the simple ambivalence of the conjunction *'asher* another of those wordplays (like *nehep-paket* in 3:4) that are both viable and can lead one to the other, here from the conjunctive to the causative. Just as the Ninevites solved the word game by realizing the positive possibilities of "turning around," it is in fact this ambivalence that helps Jonah snap to the recognition of God's goodness (it was God who caused it to grow, not his own effort) and the transience of even the most glorious of created things.[61]

Omnipresence: A Morality and Esthetics of Transience

Simply existing is anything but simple, if you think about it. At one extreme are precisely those who do *not* think about it, who merely live day by day and who care as little for the future as the past. Their motto could be Epicurus' *carpe diem*, "seize the day," this day only. At the other extreme would be those who, in a radically different sense, seize the day (!), who achieve what Pascal declared to be impossible: to avoid life's distractions and tugs towards the past and the future and live in the only time we have and, as philosophers have asserted, the only thing in life that is truly our own: the transient present moment that is our heritage.

In brief, this discussion resumes the earlier one concerning virtue versus goodness, effort versus gift. What both Nineveh and the *kikayon* have in common is their absence of personal merit; they exist, literally, through the grace of God. And *through*

---

[60] Necessary from the point of view of prophetic consciousness; see below, "The Double Ending . . ."

[61] Jonah and Qohelet both share a focus on the spiritual value of the present and the discovery of transience, as I hope to show in my forthcoming study *Joyous Qohelet*.

the same grace of the same God, suddenly, they are no more. They both have the gratuity of love, which does not depend on merit but only on itself.[62] This transience, Jonah discovers, is of the very fabric of life: here today, gone tomorrow. Existence, as the medieval parable has it, is like a bird that flies through a room and out the other side. We want God and Jonah to say about the *kikayon*/Nineveh: "Verweile doch, du bist so schön!" But Faust was criticized, certainly not because he loved beauty but because he desired its permanence and thus misconstrued its essence. The bird leaves as suddenly and mysteriously; perhaps another will come, perhaps two will come (Qoh 11:6): Praise be the Lord! For, as Thoreau also argued, "Be it life or death, we crave only reality."[63]

Reality, fine! But *present* reality? And from a prophet, whose professional duty, at least as popularly understood, is to predict the future? Isn't the usual expectation quite the contrary? Marvin Buss puts it well: "The literary form of divine speech is closely associated with ultimacy," one that "often deals with ultimate questions, especially with Origin and End."[64] Yet we have seen how God refuted Jonah's argument of strict merit by getting his prophet to admire something that came to him through no effort of his own. This argument is now supplemented in a surprising way: God creates transience, and this transience is the basis not only of God's ethics as a judge ("where he is *now*") but also of his esthetics as a creator: I will enjoy things as they are now! Tomorrow, who knows? This seems but a variant on God's theology of existence, of goodness instead of virtue alone. The argument is, quite simply, that goodness is humanity's natural state![65]

---

[62] I develop this important point in my forthcoming study of spiritual eroticism. Briefly put, love does not depend on reasons; one can only love "lovingly" but never "because of" (beauty, wealth, even character).

[63] Henry David Thoreau, *The Portable Thoreau* (ed. Carl Bode; New York: Penguin Books, 1982), 351.

[64] Marvin J. Buss, "Toward Form Criticism as an Explication of Human Life," in The *Changing Face of Form Criticism for the Twenty-First Century* (eds. Marvin A. Sweeney and Ehud Ben Zvi; Grand Rapids: Eerdmans, 2003), 312–25.

[65] Jewish and Christian theologies are irreconcilable on this issue, since the former, in the absence of the theory of original sin, believes that natural innocence was never permanently corrupted and can be regained. Nor, for that matter, does it put much stock in the Christian dogma of the three evils intrinsic

Both Jonah's complex emotion over the *kikayon* and God's pity for the Ninevites are rendered by the Hebrew *khus*, which, as Wolff observed, "always refers to the here and now."[66] While some translators are satisfied with "show compassion or mercy" when referring to God's feeling for the Ninevites, most are more relaxed when it comes to Jonah's reaction. Thus Jonah is said to "fret" (Sasson), "care" (Simon), "be sorry" (Scott; Vulgate), "be concerned" (NRSV).[67] The issue in both cases, however, is one of emotional attachment to this world, the one of self-sustaining and teeming cities, abundant cattle, and also glorious vines and trees. God loves this world and (oops!) so does Jonah. Indeed, God seems to justify His own love through Jonah's admiration of the *kikayon*. Wiesel expresses surprise that Jonah should have contradictory desires, perhaps like Faust's two souls or urges: one towards heaven and one towards *Liebeslust*. But the opposite would be more astonishing. It is through the *kikayon*'s beauty and protectiveness and vigor that Jonah is reminded how the world still clings to him. It is through Nineveh—even Nineveh, who would imagine?—that we are reminded that God loves all the world, and not at some future or ideal time but here and now.

What Jonah "remembered" in the fish's belly—that he still wanted to live—recurs, at a different level, under the *kikayon*. Now this is a matter we had thought solved, Jonah's renewed and now explicit desire to die, here expressed no less than three times.

> Please, Lord, take my life from me, for my death is better than my life. (4:3)

> He requested from his soul to die, saying: "My death is better than my life." (v. 8)

---

to creation (the world, the flesh, and the devil). Jews hold that human beings, through their wrong choices, are quite capable of inflicting damage on their own, thank you very much!

[66] See n. 26 above and the next note.

[67] Sasson, *Jonah*, 300; Simon, *Jonah*, 44; R. B. Y. Scott, "The Sign of Jonah," Int 19 (1965): 16. On this third example of *antanaclasis* in this chapter, see above, nn. 17, 28. I like T. Fretheim's rendition of God's parting use of *khus*: "May I not, am I not allowed?" except that for him the stress is on God's sovereign right to spare Nineveh rather than on His love for it (*The Message of Jonah: A Theological Commentary* [Minneapolis: Augsburg, 1977], 236).

"I am distressed unto death." (v. 9)

Note carefully the language of his explicit death wishes and their finely nuanced presentation. The first two are petitions and are based on rhetorical forms particularly important in wisdom writing: the "better-than" saying. As we shall see in greater detail in Excursus 2 below, these two sayings do *not* assert that death is good and life is bad, rather that *both* are good but, given Jonah's life situation, death with God's or the soul's approval would be better than life without it. But life itself remains a positive value. This is important because it indicates that Jonah retains the lesson of life learned at the instinctual level. This lesson is now supplemented and reinforced, this time in the external world and again quite spontaneously, by Jonah's esthetic reaction to the *kikayon*, notably its protective shade and vitality and even, paradoxically, its extreme transience. In the final wish to die (4:9), however, the "better-than" has been dropped and Jonah has made his decision to die. Either God will "take" his soul (4:3), as a spouse takes a bride; or, unlike the death of common humanity where the body removes itself from the soul, Jonah's soul (4:8) will separate itself from the body and the world it inhabits.[68]

There is more. Jonah's love for God *to the exclusion of all other loves* is tested, as was the case of Abraham (Gen 22) and very nearly so in the case of Job ("take all *except* his life," Job 1:12), only by the offer of life itself. The drama of Part One is that, exactly the obverse of Abraham and Job, the test is reversed: it is Jonah who tests God by offering his own life. This is the only, the ultimate, test of love: Jonah offers and God backs down. The conclusion of Part One, then, is Abraham's: "*Now I know that you fear God*" (Gen 22:12). Jonah is in love only with Eternity.

The culmination of Part Two proposes a very different Jonah, one now in love with what "appeared overnight and perished

---

[68] See T. A. Perry, *Erotic Spirituality: The Integrative Tradition from Leone Ebreo to John Donne* (Tuscaloosa: University of Alabama Press, 1980). In the book of Jonah the former death, that of common humanity, is enacted symbolically by the Ninevites' ritual of penance, when the body "dies" through fasting and mourning.

overnight" (4:10).[69] But do we want to say that Jonah has only been "tricked" so that God, one final time, can show off His superior knowledge and strength and reasoning? If this movement is regarded as a sequel, however, then the problem vanishes: beyond death all becomes possible. Just as the "death of love" (the death of all things, including the self, required by love) opened the door to Eternity, now—only as a complementary movement—Eternity falls in love with the works of time. Jonah knows this beforehand, however, and does not need to have it pointed out. What God now reveals in the final moment is that, just as humans imitate God, God now, as it were, seems to imitate humans: the Eternal too, like Jonah with his *kikayon*, is revealed as in love with the works of time. And I fancy that God is as delighted with His *kikayon* as he is with His Nineveh.

Jonah the Prophet

The intimate chat that crowns this book at the end has shown God's true colors, and Jonah does not disagree. But his failure to reply to God's closing question is itself a question to God: I grant your point about the present and goodness and transience. Do you grant mine about the future?

One is surprised that the more favorable view of Jonah is not at least occasionally glimpsed: that, far from hating the Ninevites out of some putative exclusive love for the Israelites, Jonah—the book's prophet to the Gentiles—hopes for their complete restoration, one which would include not only mere existence but much more as well. For is it not more probable that Jonah, far from the usual view that he is an Israelite exclusivist, projects *devekut*—the soul's ardent clinging to God—as a universal possibility?[70] To approach the issue from another line of argumentation: if Jonah was exceedingly concerned with his

---

[69] A modern and secular parallel might well be Meursault's rage against the priest who came to hear his confession before his execution: "Aucune de ses certitudes ne valait *un cheveu de femme*." See Albert Camus, *L'Etranger* (Paris: Gallimard, 1967), 185.

[70] For example, Moses (Num 11:27) resists Joshua's desire to restrict the prophecy of Eldad and Medad: would that others could reach their level!

standing as a prophet, then his extraordinary success must have been gratifying, to say the least. Could the furthering of this success not have been foremost in his mind as he withdrew to the east, in order "to see what will be with/in the city"?[71] If Jonah's renewed desire to die in chapter 4—based on his complaint that God is too merciful—seems problematic, however, this is true only according to the usual (and false) hypothesis of Jonah's hatred of the Ninevites. According to our view, however, Jonah's complaint is not against the Ninevites but rather against God's willingness to settle for less than full love, and this with regards to the Ninevites as well as to himself.

Jonah's upset with God in chapter 4 can now be further clarified. The issue now is not *whether* the Ninevites will repent (they already have!) but rather, as per Kimhi,[72] whether the Ninevites will persevere in their repentance by living out the wider consequences of that change of mind. According to the usual understanding, Jonah now stations himself nearby so that, when the Ninevites do backslide, he can gloat and tell the Lord "I told you so"—a rather hollow victory for a prophet, to say nothing of God's gullibility! We suggest a different motivation, one which may merely amount to a fuller understanding of Kimhi's concept of repentance. Jonah is upset with God's mercy not because it allows the Ninevites to repent but because it allows them to repent *only* for the purpose of staying alive. For Jonah feels that averting destruction is merely a first step to a higher life, to a loving relationship with the *qadmono shel 'olam*, that Being who is the most origin-al or "east-erly" of all that exists. For even if the Ninevites stay alive, their lives will still be filled with the vanities that distract from true Life. As the prophet says pointedly at the end of his prayers and forecasting God's "mercy":

Those who care for empty vanities
Forsake their love. (2:9–10)

---

[71] Here, the meaning of the preposition *b*- is not "*concerning* the city," referring to what God's decision would be, but rather "*in* the city," to see what the inhabitants would do.

[72] See Simon, *Jonah*, 40.

In such a state of affairs, where Jonah's message is devoted to mere subsistence, then, indeed, his "death is better than his life." For if life does not lead to Life, if Genesis does not lead to the Song of Songs, then "why am I alive" (Gen 25:22)?

The end thus returns to the beginning, but without itself being negated. For Nineveh is always to be viewed from two perspectives. To view Nineveh from the *sea*-desert is to raise the question of origins, of existence itself. To view the metropolis from the desert "east" of the city is to raise the issue of goals, of "the ends of being and ideal grace." What this all means for the serious erotic and theological argument between God and Jonah can be summarized by a reading of Psalm 116, which speaks to the ideological core of the book of Jonah:

> The Lord preserves the simple [Ninevites].
> [But] precious in the sight of the Lord is the death of His pious ones. (Ps 116:6, 15)

And Jonah the Dove is the one who takes genius and vocation seriously. As Ruth Reichelberg put it in her beautiful meditation on Jonah,

> Isn't the dove the bride of the Song of Songs? She thus represents the mystical union between God and His people. As soon as the Dove appears, we are totally in a beautiful love story.[73]

Some have read in Jonah the dangers of living in a cocoon instead of reaching out. This is an important point, for in Part One Jonah had to show approval for outreach by reaching out against his will. But now God must—and does—reciprocate. By now taking Jonah to Him, God acknowledges that Jonah too was right, that the final goal of all of this is, beyond even service, intimate friendship with God. From Jonah's and God's perspective too, the Ninevites' innocence, recovered through repentance and salvation—were it to occur in Eden itself—would be a fool's paradise if not oriented towards reunion, if the Father of Mercy did not lead to the Loving Spouse. God and Jonah: the positive

---

[73] Ruth Reichelberg, *L'Aventure prophétique: Jonas, menteur de vérité* (Paris: Albin Michel, 1995), 85.

tension between innocent beginnings and ideal ends, between divine goodness and human effort.

The Double Ending, Oracular Ambiguity, and Prophetic Consciousness

> You showed compassionate concern for the *kikayon* plant, although you did neither work for it nor grow it, which arose in a single night and perished in a single night.

> And will I not show compassionate concern for that large city Nineveh, although it has more than one hundred and twenty thousand persons, since they cannot discern between their right and their left hand—and much cattle besides? (Jonah 4:10–11)

One of the book's most astonishing feats is its conclusion, or apparent lack of one. Put differently, why is God's closing question to Jonah left unanswered? To end a book in this manner is untypical of biblical narrative, and the surprise is compounded theologically by the fact that it is God who asks a question that remains unanswered! Seen from the vantage point of the book as an ongoing dialogue, God's question avoids the closure of monologic discourse, in favor of further exchange and respect for one's partner. Instead of simply slamming down His point of view, God invites reaction, discussion, argument.[74] Alternatively and as suggested above, Jonah's silence is itself an answer, a triumphal instance of his dialogue of silence.[75] Other current explanations include the following:

    a) the answer does not need to be explicit because it is obvious from the *a fortiori* structure of God's question. This view allows the midrash[76] to fill the void by projecting Jonah's positive response to God's mercy.

---

[74] See above, "The God of Perhaps," in chapter 7.

[75] See my Conclusion, "The Ongoing Dialogue." For the "Dialogue of Silence," see above, Introduction. For a more midrashic approach, see below, chapter 10, "Concluding Midrash II."

[76] Sasson, *Jonah*, 320.

b) The book requires the reader to provide the answer,[77] thus effectively removing Jonah as an active participant.

The common reading of this concluding episode strains belief, however, for we are asked to believe that Nineveh is worthy of salvation merely because it is a *large* city and has a large *animal* population! From Lot's reasoning in Gen 19:20, one would have drawn the opposite conclusion. There Lot seeks refuge from God's destructive wrath in a neighboring town because of its *small* size, presumably because it does not have the quantity of evil requisite for destruction.[78]

All popular readings of the book's conclusion formulate God's closing remarks as a question, but the grammar in no way justifies such unanimity.[79] Although the *waw* connective can occasionally be used as an interrogative particle,[80] it can more typically be employed as a contrastive conjunctive:

You showed concern, compassion for the *kikayon* plant, although you did neither work for it nor grow it, which arose in a single night and perished in a single night.

But I will *not* show compassionate concern for that large city Nineveh, although it has more than one hundred and twenty

---

[77] Simon, *Jonah*, 46; Claude Lichtert, "Récit et noms de Dieu dans le Livre de Jonas," *Biblica* 84 (2003): 251.

[78] Thus, Rashbam: "*Isn't it* [the city] *small?* Since its population is small, you can overlook them, since there are not many sinners there." The follow-up thought here is that one should keep a low profile, stay below God's radar detection: "Don't be friendly with those in power" (Mishnah *Abot* 1:10)! This is how the widow of Zarephath reproached Elijah (1 Kgs 17:18). Further problems with the usual reading of Jonah's conclusion are discussed in Yvonne Sherwood (*A Biblical Text and Its Afterlives: The Survival of Jonah in Western Culture* [Cambridge: Cambridge University Press, 2000], 268–80).

[79] Even to raise an alternative possibility would seem tantamount to removing the question in Job 2:10, which would yield little sense. For dissenting views, however, see Alan Cooper, "In Praise of Divine Caprice: The Significance of the Book of Jonah," in *Among the Prophets* (ed. Philip R. Davies and David J. A. Clines; JSOTSup 144; Sheffield: JSOT Press, 1993), 144–63; Thomas M. Bolin, "'Should I Not Also Pity Nineveh?' Divine Freedom in the Book of Jonah," *JSOT* 67 (1995): 109–20. Of the few instances of omission of the interrogative particle cited in GKC (150a), the closest to our text would be 2 Kgs 5:26, where the negative *lo* is presumed to be a shortened form of the interrogative *halo*.

[80] See Joüon and Muraoka, *A Grammar*, 161a.

thousand persons, since they cannot discern between their
right and their left hand—and much cattle besides! (Jonah
4:10–11; emphasis added)

While such a reading will surely shock traditional ones,[81] it
yields perfect sense within the total context of the book. It suggests that God is now sticking to His original decree against a
wicked city (as He will in the future). The order of progression of
God's ideas would be as follows:

a) Nineveh is doomed and must be "overturned." To be sure,
   there is a double-entendre here, and both God and Jonah
   know it: either that Nineveh, like Sodom, will be destroyed,
   or that, through its being "overturned" through repentance,
   it will be saved.[82] It is commonly assumed both that Jonah
   is unaware of the ambiguity and possibility of repentance,
   and also that God will easily cave in at the slightest sign of
   repentance—that is in fact what He proceeds to do!

b) Because of their repentance, the city is now spared.

c) Jonah requests and obtains a delay on the final verdict, as
   indicated by his withdrawal east of the city, in order to
   monitor their *sincere* compliance.[83]

d) God, who has already shown his ability to change his mind,
   now does so again. His reasons are that, upon probation,

---

[81] It in fact totally reverses the popular view, according to which "we see
human self-love [i.e., Jonah's] contrasted with divine compassion" (Kenneth
Craig, *A Poetics of Jonah: Art in the Service of Ideology* [Columbia: University of
South Carolina Press, 1993], 81). For the view of Jonah's positive view of divine
compassion, see above, "Jonah's Knowledge of God."

[82] The notion of being "overturned" [*hpk*] through repentance, of change of
personality and spiritually upgrading one's actions, is not only a conceptual pun
on God's part but is also grounded in an identical linguistic usage that one can
assume was familiar both to God and to Jonah. I refer to Samuel's announcement to Saul: "The spirit of the Lord will pass over you and you will prophesy
with them, and you will be *(over)turned [into another person]*" (1 Sam 10:6). Or,
referring to Pharaoh's possible change of heart (but in the wrong direction):
yehafek lebab Par'oh (Exod 14:5).

[83] Or, alternatively, in order to negotiate terms that are more lenient or at
least clearer. See above, "Back to Square One?" in chapter 3.

their repentance was not sincere. They still do not know their fundament from their elbow and they continue to behave like animals.

This revised reading counters the common assumption that Nineveh represents *all* of non-Israelite humanity. Why should we not, rather, posit that they represent the opposite extreme, not only from their portrayal in the Hebrew Bible but also in Greek and other texts?[84] To also argue, *a fortiori*, that God is all-merciful because He will pardon even the extremely wicked Ninevites is to admit that God has no standards whatsoever. Is God willing to go even that far? No, the book concludes: God will accept repentance *if it is sincere*; but if the Ninevites return to their evil ways, then *no way!*[85]

Bolin argues that, in addition to negative views of Nineveh in Nahum, etc., a late dating of the book of Jonah—after the city's destruction—leads to a reformulated basic question: "not so much 'Why does God forgive the wicked Ninevites?' but rather 'Why were the Ninevites destroyed if God had forgiven them?' "[86] Bolin's answer is essentially the sailors': "For You are the Lord, You do as You wish," understanding by divine freedom God's ability not only to be merciful (as is usually assumed) but, more radically, to do *anything* He wishes to do.[87] Of course, by reading God's closing statement as a declarative rather than a question, Bolin has his answer from the text itself. And, in this case and while not denying God's total freedom, the motive of

---

[84] Bolin, " 'Should I Not Also Pity Nineveh?' "

[85] Sweeney finds this aspect of God hinted in the placement of the book of Jonah in the Book of The Twelve Prophets immediately preceding Nahum, which "celebrates YHWH's destruction of Nineveh for its crimes against Israel, YHWH, and the world at large, and thereby points to the necessary interrelationship of YHWH's justice together with YHWH's mercy. YHWH can show mercy to Nineveh when it repents, but YHWH will punish Nineveh when it sins"; see *The Twelve Prophets*, 303.

[86] Bolin, " 'Should I Not Also Pity Nineveh?' " 119.

[87] Craig declares God's absolute freedom to be the central ideology of the book of Jonah: "The unified position of this narrative world is that *God controls everything and is free to command not only the natural elements but the prophet as well, free to forecast impending doom, and free also to alter plans*"; see *A Politics of Jonah*, 145. I prefer to argue that God both does have standards and also grants Jonah a full measure of human freedom.

justice is also operative, for in this reading God does not so much do whatever He wishes all the time, merely what He says He promises to do—which may be considered a proof not only of freedom but of character as well.

It seems to me that one can not only allow the possibility of a different ending but that, in a sense important to the prophetic consciousness at the book's center, one must maintain *both* possibilities presented in the conclusion: the text affirms *both* that God will forgive *and* that he will not (and, don't forget, Jonah has been asked to weigh in, implying that his opinion does matter). This matter can of course be settled sequentially; for example, He will let them live in the eighth century but destroy them in the seventh. At a deeper level, however, we end up with one of those situations of oracular ambiguity that occur elsewhere in the Bible and in ancient literature as well.[88] For God can easily reject your reading by observing: "You heard a question, but I made an assertion." Or, precisely, vice versa. The principle of divine foreknowledge is thus protected, and at least God does have the option of reading ahead and thus rereading.

In sum, the Jonah story argues that Nineveh averted destruction. We, and everyone after Assyria's downfall in the seventh century—including God and Jonah, who have prophetic foreknowledge of events—know that they did not. While some have argued that this circumstance alters our reading of the story,[89] it seems to me that such arguments are questionable as reading perspectives in general and also miss the point of the book, at least as it is offered as the product of a prophetic consciousness. It may surely be argued that, even if Jonah cannot predict the future, he surely can, by merely projecting from his own human experience, know the potential of evil and read the possibilities on the wall. For the Jonah text, however, the question is not the historical one of what did or did not actually happen but rather—rendered through theological and prophetic concepts—what all the possibilities are and as they may occur at whatever point in history.

---

[88] See T. A. Perry, "Cain's Sin in Genesis 4:1–7 and Oracular Double-Talking," *Prooftexts* 25 (2006): 259–76.

[89] Ben Zvi, *Signs*.

Ben Zvi avidly pursues our text's multiple or potential meanings and offers the following explanation:

> Given that these texts were read, reread and studied, it is
> likely that all these readings would occur at some point. . . .
> And since one may assume that the authors of prophetic
> books knew that their work was supposed to be read and
> reread, it is likely that some of these multilayered meanings
> were intended by the actual authors.[90]

While agreeing with the thrust of these remarks,[91] I would start
from a different set of assumptions and describe multilayered
meanings from a theoretical perspective more in tune with those
of the original prophets and their authors. The point of attribut-
ing a text to Jeremiah or Jonah, for example, is due to the authors'
concept of prophetic consciousness, the goal of which is not so
much to predict the future, as the popular notion goes, but rather
to describe the seeds of the future in which all is eventually possible. Lévinas, in a different context and not referring to prophecy
as such, nevertheless furnishes a stunning description of such a
project:

> One must go back to the primordial phenomenon of the time
> when the phenomenon of the "not yet" takes root.[92]

For, from that point, all rereadings of future events—at least all
those inscribed in the text—are available.

The rabbis had an exegetical equivalent for this concept: "The
[inscribed] deeds of the Ancestors are indicators of what will happen to their children."[93] To take this concept seriously, one should
disregard the common view of Jonah as a dolt who understands
the divine word poorly if at all. Rather and as we have endeav-
ored to explain, he is, like the Ancestors all regarded as prophets,

---

[90] Ibid., 59, n. 68.

[91] But not at all with either Ben Zvi's excessive concessions to the now popular ridicule theory or his notion of Jonah's "serious theological errors" (ibid.,
113), since the book of Jonah is conducting a debate rather than an inquisition.

[92] Emmanuel Lévinas, *Totalité et infini* (Paris: Livre de poche, 1971), 277.

[93] *ma'asey abot syman lebanym.* "Such is the character of the written words
of the prophets, that they apply to the present and also to the future" (*b. Megillah* 14a).

thought to have understood everything. For Jonah, this includes both the merciful nature and freedom of God,[94] the difference between preaching *against* Nineveh (1:2) and *to* Nineveh (3:2), the *two* syntactical possibilities of the book's oracular closing, where God can either forgive or not, or both. This suggests that each "word of God" disclosed through prophetic consciousness is both a concrete reference and a reflection on itself as omniscient discourse.[95]

---

[94] Prophetic ambiguities are necessary to protect God's freedom (contrast the ludicrous rigidity of the king's decrees in Esther) and to make available to God's creatures a future that is truly free and open to human creativity. The presence of multiple voices (Ben Zvi, *Signs*, 119) within the book of Jonah reproduces the broader intertextual debate in the biblical corpus, and "*only* such a global, large perspective may shed true light on YHWH and YHWH's attributes" (ibid., 114).

[95] Ben Zvi refers to all this, I think, in his concept of the book's genre as "meta-prophetic," which he defines as one that "deals with or is even devoted to issues that are of *relevance for the understanding of the message of other prophetic books*" (*Signs*, 85; also 19, n. 16). Ben Zvi adds that, in his opinion, which I share, Jonah is the only prophetic book "that can be considered meta-prophetic in its entirety." He goes on to argue that "the centrality given to the characterization of Jonah within the book reinforces the characterization of the book itself as a meta-prophetic book" (87), and this is partly the case because God's words "are associated directly with prophets" (89). Thus the main issue of our book is "prophecy and prophet" (93).

PART FOUR

NEW LITERARY PERSPECTIVES

We now return to the perennial puzzle of Jonah's literary genre. I have argued that its primary allegiance is to its canonical prophetic underpinnings, although its deviations have provoked numerous other theories. And while some of these do not appear to me successful—I am thinking especially of the current vogue of seeing Jonah as a humorous or satirical figure—it is readily admitted that its prophetic mode is itself of a deviant sort. Traditional Jewish exegesis has viewed Jonah as a figure for Israel, thus minimizing the personal drama between the prophet and God. Others, at the opposite extreme, have focused too narrowly on the personal aspect, neglecting Jonah's universalism, his strong desire that everyone seek prophetic intimacy.

Up to this point we have considered Jonah's activities as prophetically turned inward and especially upward: intra se and supra se, as Bonaventura loved to say. His entire project to this point has been the prophetic one of the pursuit of intimacy with the Holy One: for himself, to be sure, but also for all those—indeed, the entire world—who would embrace God's love. For this more universalistic aspect of his theology to succeed, however, Jonah has to take on an additional orientation, what Bonaventura, completing the triad, referred to as extra se or outward bound. Jonah now has to become a pedagogue, a mediator between God and humans. Parallels with well-known modern literary genres such as the pastoral and the literature of the fantastic may help clarify his perspective of sitting on the edge where different worlds intersect and are thus susceptible to mediation.

To complete the complex picture of our prophet, then, we must now consider those literary aspects of our book through which his pedagogic mission can be carried out. Here Jonah, the biblical John of the Cross, as it were, turns momentarily from his one-on-One burning love for God and says, like Abraham by the terebinths of Mamre (Gen 18:3, see Rashi): "Please wait, Lord, I'll be right back, just as soon as I service the good folks at the door." Now, to relate successfully to his hardened Ninevite clients, Jonah must devise appropriate outreach strategies. This hardly comes as a surprise for a master strategist who, in order to recover his Lover, invented the genre of a dialogue of silence. If the Gentiles would only—continuing my allegorical reading of Gen 18:4—just take some water and bathe their feet (compare Moses at the burning bush in Exodus 3:5) and rest a bit under the tree, that is to say, under the kikayon, the divine shade of reconciliation. . . . It may not seem preposterous to suggest that even in his moment of greatest intimacy with God under the enclosing shade of the kikayon, Jonah's extra eye (his gaze extra se) was turned outward, engaged in a pedagogic performance for the Ninevites' benefit.

CHAPTER NINE

LIFE ON THE EDGE I: A
PASTORAL PERSPECTIVE

> The only hope then lies not in identification with
> either pole of opposition, but in discovering
> . . . some larger grammar in which the words
> *culture* and *wilderness* may both be spoken.
>
> John Elder[1]

Jonah, the wandering prophet, ups and leaves home—the Temple, his cherished workplace—and heads for the boonies of Tarshish. He of course never arrives at his destination—did anyone ever think that he would? For, contrary to a frequent misinterpretation, Jonah was not sailing *to* Tarshish as a destination but rather *in the direction of* Tarshish, since he was, as Uriel Simon observes, "not merely seeking to leave the Land of Israel by sea . . . but in fact was trying to sail to the farthest point possible from his assigned destination."[2]

---

[1] John Elder, *Imagining the Earth*; quoted in Lawrence Buell, *The Environmental Imagination: Thoreau, Nature Writing, and the Formation of American Culture* (Cambridge, MA: Harvard University Press, 1995), 1.

[2] Uriel Simon, *Jonah: The Traditional Hebrew Text with the New JPS Translation* (trans. Lenn J. Schramm; JPS Torah Commentary; Philadelphia: Jewish Publication Society, 1999), 5. To render Tarshish as the sea itself, as the Targum consistently does (see above, n. 1 in Part One on p. 1), could yield either the tepid reading "to set sail" or, more metaphorically, such notions as biological death and rebirth. In both cases, of course, the primary stress is on escape.

Clues to Jonah's meanderings are hinted by their particular nature and structure. As regards time, our text takes special pains to specify the precise length of Jonah's visits. The first notation records his stay in the belly of the fish: three days and three nights (2:1). His second assignation—Nineveh—was also to last for three days at best (3:3) but was shortened to a single day (3:4).[3] His third stay, under the *kikayon*, lasts but a single night (4:10). This clear process of reduction amounts to a focusing on time as durations, the time it takes Jonah to get from one "place" to another.

Now, God appears to Jonah in three places:

a) the Temple, which is "before the Lord" (1:3);

b) the *yabashah* or dry land (2:11);

c) the desert "east of the city" (4:5).

Of the three, only the first is, to some extent, a "place" in Qohelet's sense of the goal of one's desire and pursuit (Qoh 1:5, 7); rather, they are borders between two categories of place. Precisely speaking, these are the borders that join the three dimensions of the entire universe one to another: the heavens, the seas, and the dry land (Jonah 1:9). Thus the Temple is the gateway to heaven (Gen 28:17), and the edge of dry land where Jonah is deposited by the fish is also the sea's lip.

What, then, are we to make of that third place of revelation, that desert outpost outside of Nineveh? For if, on closer inspection, our wandering prophet does have a method to his madness, if indeed his seemingly random peregrinations do have a structure, then his whisking through the city and withdrawal to a place "beyond" should give us pause. Our question in this chapter is to ask, in Part Two—in countless ways parallel to Part One—what direction he was headed when he left Nineveh. Was his desert outpost indeed a destination, or was it rather a direction, perhaps a stopover on the way to something else? And if, like Tarshish itself, that other deserted place was never really Jonah's final destination, what sort of attraction did it hold so as in some crucial way to fashion the very nature

---

[3] Other possibilities are explored throughout this study (see Index below). For further thoughts on the theme, see also below, Excursus 3: "Three Days."

of that desert outpost? To look at it another way: If, with Calvino,[4] we have viewed Nineveh as defined by the two deserts it opposes, what is the nature of that desert stopover itself, now seen as located between Nineveh and . . . where?

Pastoral Landscape, Common Misanthropy

Jonah's ongoing debate with God may indeed have something to do with landscape and living environment. Recall that the pastoral as a literary genre is without fail set in the country, as the polemical title of a popular Renaissance apology proclaims: "Down with town, in praise of graze!"[5] Thus, when Jonah is commanded to leave his contemplative environment for . . . Nineveh, he responds, in deed, that, as the popular saying goes, he would rather go to hell than there.

One aspect of the prophet's objection, unnoticed by critics, may be the city's size: "Go to Nineveh, that *large* city" (1:2). Critics like to interpret "large" as important or, ironically referring to the city's wickedness, as "great." And, of course, the stylistic tic of greatness is rampant throughout our text.[6] The prophet Jonah, however, shows a sustained and one might even say a principled preference for solitude. Consider his self-imposed isolation during the storm when, if ever, all hands should be on deck and all hearts directed to their gods. Or, his rushing through the large city at breakneck speed, taking joy only with solitude regained. It may be added that Jonah's "great" joy (the only one expressed in the entire book) occurs not only in recovered solitude but under the *kikayon*: the only organic image in the entire book and a required stage prop for creating a minimalist pastoral environment. We have, then, a pastoral

---

[4] Italo Calvino, *Invisible Cities* (trans. William Weaver; New York: Harcourt Brace, 1974); see above, "Jonah and the Ninevites: A Tale of Two Cities," in chapter 3.

[5] Antonio de Guevara, *Menosprecio de corte y alabanza de aldea* (Valladolid: n.p., 1539). This is admittedly a free rendition of the original title. Our translation does highlight, though, an additional reason for Jonah's flight from Nineveh, a place where animals are forced to fast in order to atone for human guilt.

[6] See below, "The Mediating Narrator," in chapter 10.

hero who hates crowds, loves nature and solitude, and, in the current vernacular, "good ol' country livin'."[7]

These withdrawals in both cases project the appearance of misanthropy. One thinks of Thoreau:

> After spending a week in town "mixing in the trivial affairs of men, . . ." he is overcome by a sense of "fatal coarseness," as if he had "committed suicide"; but then a walk through the fields enables him to recover his "tone & sanity—& to perceive things truly and simply again."[8]

One might say that, in addition to his "suicide" motivated by erotic abandonment, his withdrawal can also be read as a distaste for the "fatal coarseness" of normal social involvement. Again, Molière seems to have said it best, in describing his misanthrope's desire "to flee to a desert from any human access."[9]

The Thoreau example also suggests, however, less a flight *from* something than *toward* something else. The book of Jonah is set, as we have seen, on the sea and the dry land, and each setting is also the object of our hero's purpose. Jonah's two voyages can thus be described as a return to those two forms of biblical wildness: that of the ocean that precedes creation itself, and that of the eastern desert where love is found. For it is clear that Jonah does not intend to complete these voyages beyond the edges of existence. Rather, they are directions towards which he seeks a kind of equilibrium. Thus Jonah neither jumps into the water, nor

---

[7] From this perspective, God's concluding response can be seen as an ironic rejoinder to Jonah's knee-jerk pastoralism: As for size, it doesn't matter. I can love Nineveh *even if* (not: because) it is large!

[8] Leo Marx, *The New York Review of Books* 46, no. 11 (June 24, 1999): 64.

[9] ". . . de fuir dans un désert l'approche des humains" (Molière, *Le misanthrope* [London: Bristol Classical Press, 1996], I:1, line 144); see also above, "East of the City . . . ," in chapter 5. It would thus seem that Jonah's two social pullbacks have common, misanthropic motivations. The second, however, is explained in the text as desire "to see what will be in the city" (4:5). To some critics, this desire betrays a bare remnant of a social bond, since Jonah's goal is merely to see whether he has been a successful prophet (see Deut 18:21–22). He will thus sit there in the desert and see whether Nineveh will be destroyed, in which case his words of prophecy are confirmed as true. In this reading, Jonah is more cruel in the second withdrawal, since, among the sailors, he does propose his own life ("throw me overboard") to save them.

does he push all the way to the howling desert (Deut 32:10). In the first case, he enters a ship, real in itself and also a place where he can negotiate both his relations with the sailors and, through them, his original relation with God. Similarly, his desert succah becomes both a spot from which to monitor what is going on in Nineveh and also a makeshift Temple.

Pastoral Pedagogy

This refusal is not in fact, though it is in depiction, a withdrawal; it is a confrontation, a return, a constant turning upon his neighbors. This means, first, that he [Thoreau] has had to establish himself as a neighbor; which next means, to establish himself as a stranger; which in turn means to establish the concept and the recognition of neighbors and strangers.[10]

In our preface we floated the possibility of a didactic and symbolic Jonah, building a Thoreau-like hut on the outskirts of Nineveh. According to this hypothesis, Jonah does not merely pause in order to see what will become of the city in the short run. On the contrary, he sees his mission as of much longer duration. Thus,

He went out from the city and *sat* to the east of the city and made a booth there and *sat* under its shade. (4:5; emphasis added)

This repetition of "sitting" is hardly superfluous; rather, it portrays two different actions: a *sitting* in the booth and a *settling down* and *dwelling* east of Nineveh. Thus,

---

[10] Stanley Cavell, *The Senses of Walden* (New York: Viking, 1972), vi. Similarly, Lawrence Buell, *The Environmental Imagination*, 12: "[Wordsworth] stood in a no-man's land between town and country."

> Now Jonah left the city and *settled* to the east of the city. (4:5; emphasis added)[11]

I have suggested above that the projection of an extended desert stay can be read either as a waiting for God or as hope that the Ninevites will, having stopped their evil deeds, progress further in their quest for the divine. In this latter regard, the prophet's intention is not only to see but especially to *be seen*, to picture, for their benefit and by his very visible presence, the image of a visible saint.[12]

Jonah's new home environment can be defined by what it is not: not only not the sea, but also not the teeming civilization of Nineveh and not the empty expanses of the desert either. Rather it is a typical pastoral retreat, located precisely at the border or frontier where wild nature and high nurture meet and from which both can be observed and brought into confrontation and, hopefully, reconciliation. To describe Part Two of the book of Jonah as a pastoral would of course be an exaggeration. Yet it is important to project the setting as pastoral in order to interpret Jonah's attitudes and motivations. His pastoral place has the important pedagogical mission of both seeing the civilized with fresh eyes and also integrating the wild into the civilized. East of the city is the place of both canopies, the hut and the *kikayon*, the place where art (makeshift civilization) and nature have common ground; better yet, where God's own artifact (nature) replaces humanity's (the hut).

That the Ninevites are the most obvious beneficiaries of Jonah's pastoral pedagogy does not preclude self-education as well, especially if, as Tigay postulates, the theme of the book of Jonah is

---

[11] "Settled" is the correct translation of the usual "sat" in Simon, *Jonah*, 39, n. This meaning is common; see, e.g., Gen 37:1; Josh 6:25. For use of the same word with different meanings, the rhetorical term for which is *antanaclasis*, see Judg 6:3, where *'lh* means alternately "to rise up" and "to attack." For a close parallel to our verse, see Exod 2:15, where the same verb is repeated with different meanings within the same verse: "Moses *settled* in Midian and *sat* down next to the well."

[12] Cavell applies this phrase—a favorite of Puritan Congregationalists to designate one of their own—to Thoreau's withdrawal to Walden: "This is one way I understand the writer's placing himself 'one mile from any neighbor.' It was just far enough to be seen clearly" (*The Senses of Walden*, 11).

"the *education of a prophet*."[13] From what we have seen, one might equally argue that its theme is to educate God. For if, like Hosea's graphic acting out the meaning of the behavior of others, Jonah is performing for humans, he may also have an additional audience in mind.[14] One scenario might be the following:

> I, Jonah, will cause myself to be cast into the sea (the primeval chaos of nature) so that You, God, can *see and understand* the meaning of Your command to go to Nineveh.

In brief, in its attempt to mediate and teach the opposition between culture and wildness, the book of Jonah may also be considered a pastoral document. That God Himself may have learned a thing or two from the experiment gives a delicious twist to that dictum much loved by the rabbis: "I have learned most from my students" (Ps 119:99).

Of course, at the end of the day Jewish theology cannot admit an authority higher than God. And while it does cast the human/ divine relationship in erotic and marital terms—and thus egalitarian in some sense—on a pedagogical level the idea of God being taught and educated by humans seems inadmissable. Yet, it is surely time to shake off the usual pedagogical interpretation of Jonah, that Jonah must be taught a lesson. That God is a pedagogue cannot be doubted, but in a sense quite different from the one usually supposed. For, parallel to Jonah's acting out the word of God (like Hosea), God has his own methods of making actions palpable and thus available as learning tools. Just as God always answers prayer (see above, chapter 2), He models—or, in a negative sense, mimics—human behavior. Willis gives a plausible explanation, grounded not in God's freedom but rather in the openness of human history, Lévinas' "le pas encore":[15]

---

[13] Jeffrey Tigay, "The Book of Jonah and the Days of Awe," *Conservative Judaism 38* (1985/86): 69; also Meir Sternberg, *The Poetics of Biblical Narrative* (Bloomington: Indiana University Press, 1985), 320: "Jonah evolves before our eyes into a story of a prophet's education."

[14] Aviva Zornberg, in *Genesis: The Beginning of Desire* (Philadelphia: Jewish Publication Society, 1995), 70, projects the concept that God has to learn to live with creatures that are not up to His expectations.

[15] Emmanuel Lévinas, *Totalité et infini* (Paris: Livre de poche, 1971), 277.

The Bible teaches that God does not know how man will respond to his circumstances, and therefore his own actions are determined by what humans do.[16]

This concept can be described as a pedagogical application of the principle of measure for measure, God in effect saying: "You destroy others, I destroy you; you repent, I repent" (see Jer 26:13). Note that this solution diverts the discussion from God's attributes of mercy versus judgment, God modeling the formula for perfectly spoiling a child: "I want only what you want." The pedagogical aspect comes into play in God's follow-up question: "Now, what exactly do you want?"

We began by positing the book of Jonah as a salvational narrative, and surely everyone gets saved, if that overworked word is the right one. Like all the classical prophets, Jonah ben Amittai is God's agent of salvation, thus true to his mythical forebear, Noah's *jonah* or dove, who delivered the crucial message of God's restoration or resurrection of humankind, along with all the animals as well. Picture Jonah, ostentatiously perched in his hut on the edge of civilization, so anxious for the Ninevites' complete restoration that he tries to broker with God. Read as the gates are about to close (and reopen!) at the end of the Day of Repentance, the book becomes a direct instrument of transformation. Like pastoral *Walden*, it may be considered a "Fable of the renewal of life" (Sherman Paul).[17] Or, like many prophetic tales such as Nathan's critique of David (2 Sam 12:1–6), it is a parable—this one acted out with full staging.[18]

---

[16] John T. Willis, "The 'Repentance' of God in the Books of Samuel, Jeremiah, and Jonah," *HBT* 16 (1994): 169.

[17] Sherman Paul, *The Shores of America: Thoreau's Inward Exploration* (Urbana: University of Illinois Press, 1958), 301.

[18] See Mordechai Cogan's remarks in *1 Kings* (AB 10; Garden City: Doubleday, 2001), 472, on the prophetic condemnation of Ahab in 1 Kgs 20:35–43.

CHAPTER TEN

LIFE ON THE EDGE II:
A TALE OF THE FANTASTIC

T he Jonah story has long projected the impression of being "strange":[1] the great fish, popularly domesticated as a whale, the storm that conveniently rains only on Jonah's ship, its numerous folkloristic stage-effects.[2] Ben Zvi notes that even "the hyperbolic character of the repentance in the story of Jonah also connotes a sense of 'uniqueness' to the event that makes it somewhat similar to the appointment of the great fish or the mysterious and gigantic plant."[3] The ambience of mystery created by such side effects and stage props do suggest parallels with a wide range of literary genres. The following proposal is intended to address one of the major issues for modern readers: the ways that the book of Jonah negotiates between the "real" (natural, historical, concrete) world and the supernatural.

The *conte fantastique* or fantastical tale is a specific literary genre of broad distribution made popular by such writers as

---

[1] See Leslie Allen's interesting comments and bibliography on the possible relationship between what I call the fantastical and NT parables, where "the realistic is combined with the the the extraordinary and the improbable" (*The Books of Joel, Obadiah, Jonah, and Micah* [Grand Rapids: Eerdmans, 1976], 177).

[2] Hans Walter Wolff, *Obadiah and Jonah* (trans. Margaret Kohl; CC; Minneapolis: Augsburg, 1986); *Studien zum Jonabuch* (Neukirchener-Vluyn: Neukirchener, 2003), 84.

[3] Ehud Ben Zvi, *Signs of Jonah: Reading and Rereading in Ancient Yehud* (JSOTSup 367; Sheffield: JSOT Press, 2003), 28n.

Edgar Allan Poe and Maupassant.[4] In a typical narrative situation, a reporter is sent from a metropolis, where the supernatural
is thought not to exist, to an area (a remote province or castle or
even a river) where it seems to. There the reporter experiences or
hears of some terrifying event, which he then reports back to the
city and the curious reader. The upshot is that the supernatural
may still not be true, but who knows? How else can such happenings be explained? The fantastical tale thus occupies a precise
locus between its two neighboring competitors and components.
As Todorov explains:

> As soon as one chooses the one or the other response, one
> leaves the fantastical and enters a neighboring genre: the
> strange or the marvelous. The fantastical is the hesitation
> experienced by a being who knows only natural laws when
> confronted by an event supernatural in appearance.[5]

The Jonah story, whether transmitted as a prophetic work or
a legend, is typically thought to project a magical world in which
the normal laws of physics and nature no longer apply.[6] Thus,
while the opening prophetic tag, "Now the word of the Lord . . . ,"
lays claim to a prophetic and therefore historical discourse, it
deliberately avoids any of those indications—such as who was
the reigning king at that time—that would give even the trap-
pings of historicity.[7] More interesting, to moderns at least, is the
Job-like prologue in heaven that, when followed by thunder and

---

[4]See Daniel Couty, *Le Fantistique* (Paris: Bordas, 1986); Pierre-Georges
Castex, *Le Conte fantastique en France* (Paris: José Corti, 1974); Tzvetan Todorov,
Introduction à la littérature fantastique (Paris: Seuil, 1970); W. R. Irwin, *The
Game of the Impossible: A Rhetoric of Fantasy* (Urbana: Illinois University Press,
1976). With particular reference to Jonah see Yvonne Sherwood, *A Biblical Text
and Its Afterlives: The Survival of Jonah in Western Culture* (Cambridge: Cambridge University Press, 2000), 183–96.

[5]Todorov, *Introduction*, 29.

[6]See Uriel Simon (*Jonah: The Traditional Hebrew Text with the New JPS
Translation* [trans. Lenn J. Schramm; JPS Torah Commentary; Philadelphia: Jewish Publication Society, 1999], xviii–xxi), who refers to "nonrealistic" writing
and discusses the Job prologue's relevance to Jonah.

[7]"Striking . . . is the absence of an exposition that would anchor the plot
in a given place, time, and circumstances" (Simon, *Jonah*, 4), as one comes to
expect from similar texts.

creatures of the deep and what-not, seems closer to the model of the *merveilleux* or fairy tale: "Once upon a time . . ." The critical debate has consequently pivoted on whether the events in Jonah— in particular the large fish and the prodigious gourd tree—are historically plausible or rather miraculous.[8] The rabbis were especially fond of the text's miraculous virtualities. In their reading, for example, the horrific storm is seen as supernatural because the sailors are able to see adjacent areas of the sea that remain perfectly calm.[9] Or, when Jonah is lowered into the water up to his ankles, the storm suddenly stops, only to start up again stronger as soon as he is pulled back on board.[10] Where some feel amusement at the childlike fantasy, older readers, like the sailors during the storm or like Jonah himself in the belly of the sea monster, probably experienced goose bumps of terror. The main point is that both possibilities are but opposite extremes of the fantastical spectrum. For, on the one hand, how do you smile when an otherworldly monster has you by the *nefesh*, or "throat"? But also, on the other, the terror veers not to the desperate but rather to a kind of lightness of being through the controlling powers of dominant presences: a trickster God, a mediating narrator (the reporter of our example) who tries to remain factual, and a whiz kid (Jonah) who always manages to land square on at least one foot. Thus, whereas we moderns naturalize the superordinary, so that divine interventions are seen primarily as either literary or ideological devices, earlier readers supernaturalized the ordinary, as it were. As a result, a modern reader who tries to restore older

---

[8] See Jeffrey Tigay, "The Book of Jonah and the Days of Awe," *Conservative Judaism* 38 (1985/86): 69–70. The claim of the prophetic tradition, of course, is that they are both. In Rabbinic literature there is a concept of creatures or divine artifacts that are neither quite natural nor quite supernatural. These are the ten things that were created on Sabbath eve at twilight (Mishnah *Abot* 5:6). For example, the "mouth of the earth" that swallowed up Korah; or the manna in the desert (Exod 16); and even, as some say, the tongs that made the tongs (cf. 1 Kgs 7:49; Isa 6:6). To this list Jonah's strange fish and *kikayon* would be worthy additions.

[9] See *Pirkei de-Rabbi Eliezer*; also Radak, Rashi, and others quoted in M. Zlotowitz, *Jonah: A New Translation with a Commentary Anthologized from Midrashic and Rabbinic Sources* (Brooklyn: Mesorah, 1980), 92–93.

[10] Zlotowitz, *Jonah*, 103.

presuppositions finds herself, much like the reporter in the *conte fantastique*, mediating between competing claims and disclaimers.

In such a case, it would appear that the state of suspended belief peculiar to the fantastical tale is but a modern projection, that such hesitations are inconceivable in a culture that believes only in the legendary or supernatural (presumably the Middle Ages) and become possible only when Enlightenment and/or skeptical views emerge. One could also surmise, however, that one reason why the rabbis' midrashic readings found favor was because they felt that the "miraculous" events in our text might very well be construed as, if not natural, as merely strange. And, in point of fact, the fantastical hesitations between natural and supernatural readings are sponsored by the Jonah text itself, as we shall now see.

Jonah's God: Trickster? Naturalist?

Forget, for a moment, the notion of an All-Powerful God who always gets His way in the end and imagine instead a strong character very much in need of Jonah's help and reluctant, for all that, to resort to "*les grands moyens*," perhaps out of love or respect. Thus when Jonah asks to die, He obliges; when he changes his mind, God again accedes.[11] Couldn't Jonah respond in kind and, the second time around, go to Nineveh? It would seem that Jonah's God, rather than supreme Will, has needs, and His approach must therefore be, rather than *force majeure*, persuasion and negotiation. To do so, God enlists the help of the *natural* world, while retaining a hint of some higher force of appeal (He *is* God after all!). Indeed, one paradox of the book of Jonah is that God, the epitome of the supernatural, always acts in rather natural ways. His first action is to "*cast* a great wind" (1:4), an expression that occurs only here in all of Scripture. Now if the use of this verb anticipates three further occurrences in this chapter (1:5, 12, 15), the explanation cannot be limited to the stylistic one of "unifying an entire sequence by means of a key word."[12] The stress, rather,

---

[11] See above, chapter 2.

[12] Simon, *Jonah*, 8.

is to humanize God's action by making it comparable to the sailors' own activity in the three other instances. Thus when God attempts to reason with Jonah, the exchange seems as natural as the latter's conversations with the sailors.

God's major coup as a *super*natural actor in Jonah's drama—at least in the eyes of some children and believers—is the production of a large fish, somehow transmogrified by popular will into a whale or leviathan. Against this backdrop, one must always insist that this act of "appointment" is but one of four, projecting a grouping rather modest in its power—certainly no splitting of the sea! Here is the series of the Lord's appointees:

a large fish (2:1);

a *kikayon* plant (4:6);

a worm (4:7);

a quiet easterly wind (4:8).

Each emissary is taken from a different order of nature and does not act, at least not egregiously,[13] beyond natural possibility. It would seem, at least from the latter three, that God's approach avoids grandeur in favor of an economy of means. One way that the supernatural possibility is at least retained is in the modest and unassertive manner that has been employed since Genesis, less in the action itself than in the timing, in the seemingly fortuitous but timely occurrence of these events.[14]

---

[13]Joseph Blenkinsopp has described their ambivalence as follows: "a plant that grew overnight with preternatural rapidity; . . . a worm uncharacteristic of its kind in size and habits; . . . a scorching east wind. . . . There is something distinctly sapiential about this appeal to the world of nature to make a point about divine causality and divine freedom and then apply it to God's action in history" (*A History of Prophecy in Israel* [rev. and enl. ed.; Louisville, KY: Westminster John Knox, 1996], 242).

[14]See the "chance" happenings in Gen 24:12; Ruth 2:3. Jack M. Sasson got it just right: "I want . . . to emphasize the fortuitous—yet God-directed—nature of the event [in 2:1], just as major moments in the previous narrative have also depended on seemingly chance occurrences and split-time arrivals: the appearance of a Tarshish-bound ship just as Jonah gets to Jaffa; the sudden outbreak of the huge storm, and its sudden end as well" (*Jonah: A New Translation with Introduction, Commentary, and Interpretation* [AB 42B; New York: Doubleday, 1990], 148).

One might argue that there is yet a fifth divine appointee: the sun (4:8), whose appearance is even softer than that of the quiet east wind. This lack of specification can sponsor contradictory readings. On the one hand, we should notice another kind of progression in Jonah's successive revelations, one from the (almost) miraculous to the (almost) natural. At the start, the *kikayon*'s meteoric growth is quite incredible but could be explained by eager naturalists, I suppose (so could the huge fish, by the way). Next comes the destructive worm, more akin to the natural world, were it not for the breakneck speed with which it causes the plant to wither. As for the wind, its paradoxical qualities have already been mentioned. Finally, the sun rises and heats up naturally, so much so that the text does not need to insist yet again that God is the Appointer since He seems no longer directly part of the picture.

In sum, the text maintains the *possibility* of supernatural direction. And while the worm or wind may not cause that *frisson* associated with Edgar Allan Poe, it also may, if one suspects a larger consciousness or purpose lurking below the surface. In such a case, that state of suspended belief that is the fantastical's trademark renders magical power, rather than neutralized, even more threatening. Indeed, in going out of its way to stress that these magical features come directly from God, the text, far from allaying our anxieties, increases them. Thus when Jonah, out of the midst of the storm, declares himself to be one who *fears* God, the word retains its primary sense of awe and dread, at least to the sailors, who now begin trembling in their life jackets.[15]

The Mediating Narrator

If Jonah's God acts almost naturalistically, however, how is His supernatural aspect represented? Differently put, if God's method is to make the supernatural look (almost) natural, how does our text make the natural supernatural? How, beyond the use of seemingly fortuitous "happenings," is the doubt maintained

---

[15] When the storm hits, the sailors are naturally afraid (1:5). When they discover that it comes from God, however, their fear is upgraded to a "*great* fear" (1:10, 16). See also Simon, *Jonah*, 42.

that makes the supernatural even possible to imagine? One of the prime requirements of the classic fantastical tale is the presence of a reporter/narrator who is also a character in the story and who, as it were, brokers the connection between the real and the supernatural. In the Jonah tale and in the absence of a mediating character, some of the narrator's functions are taken over by the very manner of narration, which maintains a sense of the *un*natural less in the content of the tale than in its stylistic choices.

Consistent with Todorov's observation that "l'exagération conduit au surnaturel,"[16] Jonah's narrator attempts to make the shift from naturalism/historicity to the unnatural (either strange or supernatural) through an emphasis on abnormal sizes. First among these is the gigantic fish that gobbles up our prophet, projecting the reader back to "the days when giants inhabited the earth."[17] And, to be sure, gigantism must be registered as among those narrative techniques and habits closely related to a sense of the fantastical. These are usually noticed by readers, since their sheer preponderance is quite remarkable, but explanations veer strongly towards the trivial (stylistic tics, keyword unity, etc.). Consider, however, the sketch of Jonah the Giant, for his single-day trek across a three-day space can be accomplished only by taking, literally, giant steps.[18] These seem required by the environment itself, by Nineveh's whopping size—carefully underscored at all three points articulating the book's structure—the beginning, the midpoint and the end:

Get up and go to Nineveh, *that great city.* (1:2; emphasis added)

Get up and go to Nineveh, *that great city* . . . (Now Nineveh was a gigantic city requiring three days to cross). (3:2–3; emphasis added)

And shall I not have mercy on Nineveh, *that great city which has in it more than one hundred and twenty thousand persons.* . . . (4:11; emphasis added)

---

[16] Todorov, *Introduction*, 82.

[17] Gen 6:4; Num 13:32–33.

[18] Some argue, taking a more realistic tack, that Jonah covered only a third of the city, but this leaves unexplained how the entire city was brought to its knees.

By the end, the tag "that great city" has taken on the aura of an epic epithet, although its repetition is of a piece with a broader elaboration:

> Now the Lord brought a *big wind* upon the sea and there was a *big storm* on the sea. (1:4; emphasis added)

> Now the sailors feared a *great fear*. (v. 10; emphasis added)

> For I know that it is because of me that this *large storm* is upon you. (v. 12; emphasis added)

> And the men feared the Lord [with] a *great fear*. (v. 16; emphasis added)

> Now the Lord appointed a *great fish* to swallow Jonah. (2:1; emphasis added)

> And a *great evil* came upon Jonah. (4:1; emphasis added)

> And Jonah was joyful over this *kikayon with a great joy*! (v. 6; emphasis added)

One way to think about such exaggeration is in its relation to other forms of the unusual that lead towards the mysterious by blurring distinctions. The ideological archetype here might well be God's concluding argument, according to which Nineveh's moral regeneration is supported by its sheer size—a total non sequitur according to normal ways of moral thinking.

One problem with consistently translating *gadol* as large or great is that it blurs the stylistic subtlety that is one of the text's glories. Take, for example, Moses' first vision, the episode of the burning bush:

> And the angel of the LORD appeared to him in a flame of fire out of the midst of a bush; and he looked, and lo, the bush was burning, yet it was not consumed. And Moses said, "I will turn aside and see this *great* [*gadol*] sight, why the bush is not burnt." (Exod 3:2–3 RSV)

Whatever the bush is, it is quite likely not large in size. Tending to the opposite extreme from such realism, NJPS opts for Moses' later decision that it is a supernatural vision and translates accordingly as "marvelous." But the ambiguity of Moses' perplexed on-site hesitation can surely be better grasped by a more neutral (let's say "fantastical") adjective:

"I will turn aside and see this *strange* sight."

Another stylistic feature of the fantastical is the narrator's love of prosopopoeia (personification), creating the cumulative feeling that inanimate objects have a mysterious (and thus scary) life of their own. Jonah's escape route is the sea, to which he descends and finds a ship bound, so we are instructed by most translators, for Tarshish. Wherever that location is—and opinions vary greatly—there is consensus on its great distance, so much so that the general meaning seems to be no more than "setting out to sea"—indeed, as we have seen, the Targum consistently renders Tarshish simply as "the sea." An equally possible understanding of the phrase, however (and the one preferred here), is that the ship is coming *from* Tarshish, i.e., *from* the sea.[19] Since this is rather obvious (would it be coming from dry land?), one is led to imagine a different level of reference, perhaps that the ship is, in some way, a creature of that deep. This is surely suggested by references to the ship's "innards," literally its "loins" (1:5), into which Jonah descends, as well as by the curious notation that sees the endangered ship as "having a mind" to break up (1:4).[20] Such anthropomorphisms create that hesitation between the natural and the miraculous/magical explanation that is the proper domain of the fantastical. In this case, the suggestion arises of an organic continuity between Jonah's naturalistic dungeon (the ship's hold) and the (*almost*) supernatural prison of the fish's belly.[21] The ship is thus both the symbolic and the real echo or parallel of the great

---

[19] See also Sasson, *Jonah*, 83; Ben Zvi, *Signs*, 78n.

[20] Anthropomorphisms, needless to say, are typically glazed over in modern translations. Thus, for example, the RSV renders "loins" as the ship's "inner part," while the ship itself merely "threatened" to break up.

[21] This ship shares an essential characteristic with Noah's (Gen 6:14–21): it is meant not to destroy but, in times of extreme crisis, to save a remnant of life in order to regenerate the world. The symbolism of Jonah's ship is thus ambivalent, expressive of his contradictory wish—quite typical of lovers—both to die and to live.

fish itself. On the one hand, it is the human or artistic counterpart to the natural. On the other, the ship already foreshadows the huge fish by its almost conscious and strange vitality.

In the book of Jonah yet other inanimate things seem to have lives and minds of their own:

the sea ceases from the storm's turmoil by "curbing its anger" (1:15);[22]

the *she'ol* to which Jonah descends has a belly (*beten*) (2:3);

the *kikayon* has prodigious powers of growth that recall Jack and the beanstalk (4:6).

At a higher level on the scale of beings, the (possibly hermaphrodite) fish "vomited" Jonah onto dry land (2:10).[23] And in the great city of Nineveh, a level of surrealism is reached when animals not only fast but put on clothes of mourning (3:8).

Jonah the Magician

Rabbi Eliezer taught: Jonah ben Amittai was the son of the widow of Zarephat.[24]

As in the fantastical tale, our hero Jonah is widely perceived as the victim, not the conqueror, of the supernatural, always in fact defeated by—if not submissive to—God's controlling hand and multiple tricks. Thus Simon observes that "the story of Jonah is

---

[22] The waters seem also to have taken on a thicker consistency, since the sailors attempt to escape the sea's rage by "digging" (*khtr*) themselves out (1:13). Those who look for humor at every turn in this book might enjoy the image of the sailors' imaginative transfer to dry land while still at sea. Strangely, Simon regards the sailors' newfound agricultural methods as merely "applying the techniques of their craft" (*Jonah*, 14).

[23] Hermaphroditism is surely one possible interpretation of the shift in the fish's gender. Thus the fish may have "vomited" Jonah onto dry land out of disgust but, also plausibly, from either morning sickness or birth pangs at her delivery.

[24] Yalkut Shimoni 2, 550, quoted in Simon, *Jonah*, 38. The reference is to 1 Kgs 17:24, and the meaning is that Jonah entered paradise without suffering death. See Sasson, *Jonah*, 86; also Louis Ginzberg, *The Legends of the Jews* (6 vols.; Philadelphia: Jewish Publication Society, 1968), 4.350, n. 38.

full of miracles, but the prophet is always their object, never their initiator."[25] But is this in fact entirely true? Did not Jonah, against all odds, convert the entire Ninevite population? And he who persuaded the recalcitrant Ninevites, may he also not be able to persuade God Himself?

This may be said to constitute the essence of the fantastic: that one escapes death itself, seen as the epitome of the inevitable. One thinks of Houdini's magical escapes, all projecting the illusion of doing the impossible, of beating the system. One gets the impression that Jonah's book focuses on a hero who delights in this kind of challenge. From the very start—and this sets the tone for the entire book—Jonah challenges God's patience in the most blatant way possible and still, at book's end, lives to tell of it! This on a supernatural level. But even on more natural levels, things are no different. Consider the horrific storm: all the sailors are prepared to die, yet Jonah somehow comes up with the magical formula. Of course, the incident that most strikes our imaginations and challenges our credulity is Jonah's survival *below* sea level. Just think: three whole days in the belly of a fish?![26] And this story has far broader implications as well. The entirety of Jonah 2 has been dubbed a "psalm" and is usually considered from the single perspective of a prayer. That it is a prayer—or, as argued above, prayers—is certainly the case. Yet it is also nothing less than a personal narration of a trip to hell (*She'ol*) *and back!* Its meager ten verses report a fantastic journey that spans the entire range of creation between the absolute depths of nonexistence (the base of the mountains) and the peaks of Jonah's universe, the "Temple of Your holiness" where dwells the divine Presence. Further, it spans not only physical creation but also the moral and spiritual range of humanity, the range or gulf between those who have abandoned hope (2:9) and those who remember God (2:8) and, through sacrifice, look to salvation (2:10). In the parallel Part Two, a journey to yet another world takes place, sketched only in delicate outline, yet unmistakable. From the lonely desert hut to which he has withdrawn, Jonah is rapt up into what he takes to be

---

[25] Simon, *Jonah*, xx.
[26] See Excursus 3, "Three Days."

a tree of paradise but which, from its powers of prodigious growth, also projects the fairytale world of Jack's beanstalk.

None of these miraculous (i.e., magical) escapes is without physical and even psychological consequences for their practitioner, of course, and Jonah is anything but unscathed. His first escape is at the expense of a generic screech for delivery; he does indeed return to dry land, but rather unceremoniously: he is vomited![27] Later, the protective *kikayon* comes crashing down on his head as quickly as it sprang up; and God taunts him to the very end. But such, one supposes, are the costs of plying a risky trade. The importance of such unpleasantries is that they help maintain that pervasive ambivalence on which the fantastical depends. Thus, on the one hand, especially from the start to the end of chapter 3, Jonah has the sense—or is it an illusion?—of being in control, whether for life or death. On the other hand, however, especially from the appearance of the worm onward, things finally spin out of control and Jonah seems to lose his sense of independence. Yet this certainty is also upset, and in a most unexpected way, by the book's ending, or rather the absence of one. Todorov, again: "Deprived of its ending, where hesitation is always resolved, the book is squarely in the fantastical genre."[28]

Consider this. When Jonah is spewed back onto dry land, his motto is that of Job's messengers: Only I am left to report the disaster (Job 1:16, 17, 19). For, as we have seen, he has no reason to expect that the sailors have been saved. And the dry land to which he returns is only that: an empty space without identity, a mere negation of total destruction that bears all its violence and terror. Similarly, Jonah's withdrawal east of Nineveh is to an observation post from which Nineveh is to be monitored. Again, however, there is opportunity for Jonah The Magician. For in both cases the story projects that both disasters may be averted, with Jonah's permission. This is surely his conviction regarding the sailors: you can be saved if—and only if—I am removed. At

---

[27] One should not get too excited about this action here, as many have done, arguing God's displeasure if not loathing. After all, while Jonah was indeed *ing*ested, being vomited indicates that he was not *di(e)*-gested.

[28] "Privé de sa fin, où l'hésitation est [toujours] tranchée, le livre relève pleinement du fantastique" (Todorov, *Introduction*, 48).

Nineveh, the impression is conveyed that God has already decided not to destroy the repentant Ninevites. But perhaps this is only conditional. For what if, in the final scene, Jonah refuses to grant God's argument?[29] It is thus possible that the situation posited above may be reversed, maybe God is the magician and Jonah is the trickster. For the question is very much the following: who in fact gives the impression of supernatural power and who is merely the master of illusion? Or perhaps each is both, that God is the magician and Jonah is His assistant/fall guy, the one that agrees to have the knives thrown at him because, given the Magician's expertise, he cannot possibly be hit.

Interrogation

The book of Jonah is the site of sustained interrogation.[30] The book opens with a strong puzzle, one that continues to grip readers all the more powerfully for being implicit: what are Jonah's motivations for fleeing from God? The book ends with another question—this one explicit—that gives God's hypothesis on the matter. Between these two extremities of the text, questions remain a dominant mode of conducting dialogue, as the tale takes on, for its interlocutors, a series of puzzles or mysteries asking to be solved. Perhaps "asking" is too tame a word, since in the book of Jonah questions are typically asked under tremendously urgent circumstances.

The first instance is the storm: so strange in its extreme fury that Jonah's psychology becomes incomprehensible to the sailors. It is accessed through a question that is also an exclamation:

"What are you doing sleeping?!" (1:6)

---

[29] According to this view, Jonah's silence at the end indicates not capitulation but precisely the reverse. Compare Elie Wiesel's reading of Job's silence at the end. See his "Job Our Contemporary," in *Messengers of God* (New York: Touchstone, 1976), 234–35.

[30] See Kenneth Craig, *A Poetics of Jonah: Art in the Service of Ideology* (Columbia: University of South Carolina Press, 1993), 161–65.

When the lots fall to Jonah, the ensuing interrogation, by its pro-
lific intensity, compounds the mystery and urgency:

> Because of whom has this evil come upon us?
> What is your business?
> Where have you come from?
> What is your country?
> From what people are you? (v. 8)

Such an interrogation hints at the known connections between
the fantastical tale and the detective novel, that literary genre
that is "dedicated above anything else to the methodological
and gradual discovery, through rational means, of a mysterious
event."[31]

No less intent on investigating (criminal?) intent is The Grand
Inquisitor Himself. In chapter 4 God twice responds to Jonah's
request to die with a question:

> "Are you *so* upset?" (4:4; emphasis added)

> "Are you *so* upset about the *kikayon*?" (v. 9; emphasis added)

It is regularly assumed that these are not really questions but
rather, well, put-downs, attempts to humor a depressed person.
In no way do they seem to allow the possibility of granting the
request. What does in fact happen, however, is that in the first
instance Jonah does not even bother to reply except, as he likes
to do, by physically removing himself to another location. In the
second instance, he does indeed reply, but by merely restating his
plea—thus a non-answer, a refusal to engage further discussion.
For, really, once the decision to die has been bridged, what is there
further to say?

It is thus quite likely that the deafening silence of Jonah's initial flight and his refusal to answer God's query at the end are both
of a piece with his death wish. And whether the traditional view is
held—that Jonah cannot conceive of a world without Justice—or
the alternative presented above, of a God out of touch with His

---

[31] Couty, *Le Fantastique*, 107.

beloved, the upshot in both cases is again an interrogation, this one on the mystery of God's own nature.

At many levels, then, mysterious events and motivations seek solution though interrogations that, in every case, assume criminal intent as a working hypothesis. When the precise nature of guilt is examined, however, modern readers, we would argue, pursue a fantastical reading of their own, one quite out of touch with the text itself.

A Modern Fantastical Reading

[Chekhov's] writing, which is strewn with unsolved details, is a kind of newspaper of the intimate fantastic. In this respect, his stories are like tales of crime in which nobody is a criminal.[32]

For critics without number, the book of Jonah has only two characters, although their identity can vary. For some, the Gentiles are sidestepped and only God and His prophet exist, eyeball to eyeball from start to finish.[33] For others, God is at best a minor character and the real drama concerns only Jonah and the Gentiles.[34] Both views agree in this, however: that regardless of their prominence or lack thereof, the Gentiles' evil does not exist (the sailors) or, if it does (the Ninevites), it is nothing in comparison to Jonah's wicked refusal to service them. We thus have the strange situation of a universe full of crime but without criminals (except, of course, Jonah himself!). From Augustine's noble advice to "hate the sin but love the sinner,"[35] we have thus progressed, so the critics would imply, to a need to love

---

[32] James Wood, *The Broken Estate: Essays on Literature and Belief* (New York: Random House, 1999), 65.

[33] Meir Weiss, *The Story of Job's Beginnings: Job 1–2, a Literary Analysis* (Jerusalem: Magnes, 1983); Ben Zvi, *Signs*; myself.

[34] Elias Bickerman, *Four Strange Books of the Bible: Jonah, Daniel, Qohelet, Esther* (New York: Schocken, 1967). A third possibility: the book is "a punitive affair between God and Nineveh, temporarily interrupted by the go-between's recalcitrance" (Meir Sternberg, *The Poetics of Biblical Narrative* [Bloomington: Indiana University Press, 1985], 320).

[35] Saint Augustine, *The City of God* (trans. Marcus Dods; New York: Modern Library, 2000), 14.6.

the sinning Gentiles by denying the sin, to a world in which sin has almost no weight, at least in comparison with Jonah's.

Such a view is entirely a creation of readers and theologians, with scant basis in the text of Jonah. For, indeed, what becomes of Jonah in such a reading? A kind of negative "lamb of God who bears the sins of the world" upon his shoulders—without even getting any credit for so doing. Now if Chekhov is right that an essential and neglected element in the fantastic is a brooding sense of causeless guilt—a feeling that Job struggled valiantly to deny—then the joke here is on the critics and theologians, since Jonah seems perfectly oblivious to guilt of any kind! The tricky aspect of this popular reading is to incriminate the person least expected: the one who is sent out to right all wrongs!

Our story does project a crime nevertheless (*lèse-majesté*, one supposes), and the fact that it opens with this crime brings it to the fore of our attention. In this respect the book of Jonah can be regarded as an interesting variant of the detective novel, with this difference: that whereas the latter attempts to identify the criminal, here the criminal is known from the start and it is the mystery of his motivation that must be solved. The mere fact that an attempted solution—the hero's own confession—is postponed until the last chapter makes this quite clear. But when readers take that confession at face value, they merely repeat the sailors' error of accepting self-incrimination as evidence of guilt.

A Rabbinic Fantastical Reading

Our story is launched squarely in the supernatural:

The word of the Lord unto Jonah. (1:1)

If this is history—as it is purported to be—it is also a history of the supernatural, of the eruption of the divine into human affairs that characterizes the Hebrew Bible from Gen 12:1:

The Lord spoke to Abram: "Get yourself out of your land . . ."

Where is Jonah at this moment? "Before the Lord," probably meaning in the Temple and surely in a prophetic state. Suddenly and to the prophet's great surprise, the contact is broken and Jonah is exiled, the cleaving to the supernatural is disrupted and Jonah must sojourn in the normal world and among a wicked people. Now if the literary fantastical describes a situation in which "a being who knows only natural laws is confronted with an event that is apparently supernatural,"[36] *from Jonah's point of view* the situation is exactly the reverse: "The fantastic is the hesitation experienced by a being [Jonah] who knows only supernatural laws, confronted by apparently natural events." The book of Jonah, were it not reported as history, could be described as the allegory of a prophet exiled. As it stands, it is the (reversed from the usual) fantastical account—from the hero's point of view—of a miraculous being exiled into the real or natural world.

The Jonah story in its present form reveals essential elements of an underlying fairy-tale plot, a modern counterpart of which might well be Voltaire's *Candide*.[37] Exiled from a paradisical home, the hero undergoes multiple trials, traversing all levels of existence and hardship until he finally returns home (again, paradise). This would suggest that the concluding conversation between God and His Beloved takes place when Jonah is again in heaven. That is to say, God has finally acceded to Jonah's ongoing wish and Jonah is now, literally, dead to the world. In keeping with the structural symmetry that characterizes our book, the opening prologue in heaven is now complemented and closed at the end.

The rabbis posited not one but *two* encounters with death for Jonah ben Amittai. On the one hand, he was the widow of Zarephath's son, who died and came back to this world (1 Kgs 17:17–24). On the other, he went to the next world without suffering death. Both positions, reinforcing one another, project a magical hero who overcomes the ultimate challenge, a person of the edge, a negotiator between worlds.

Our erotic reading has enabled us to see the underlying theme of the book of Jonah as a debate with God over where prophets such as Jonah "belong": on earth or in heaven? In this reading

---

[36] Todorov, *Introduction*, 29.
[37] Voltaire, *Candide, or Optimism* (trans. Peter Constantine; New York: Modern Library, 2005).

the book's true plot cannot be limited to the Nineveh events of chapter 3 but rather engages dialogic actions between the two contenders that span the entire book. Thus Jonah's two personal voyages—the ones that he directs *away* from Nineveh, first to Tarshish and then to the desert—share the same characteristics:

a) Jonah initiates the voyage by approaching the site (the sea, the desert, the love nest) and entering the conveyance (the ship, the succah, the *kikayon*).

b) God continues and almost completes the journeys for Jonah, taking him below the sea and under the *kikayon*.

c) Jonah is, rather unceremoniously in both cases, brought back to earth, literally in Part One and metaphorically (perhaps) in Part Two. It is thus the case that Jonah does not set out for either the depths or the desert (the two wildernesses) as final destinations. Rather, he is content, in the first instance, to board a ship and, in the second, to station himself "east *of the city*." What Jonah begins,[38] however, the Lord completes: From the ocean's surface the fish takes him to the outer edge of physical existence, the "base of the mountains" (2:7), where the flood of primeval chaos (a negative transcendence, as it were) enwraps him. From a point that approaches the desert, God takes Jonah up into the magical realm of the *kikayon*, that instantaneous and miraculous simulation of total divine shelter and enclosure.

The magical: isn't this precisely the world of trance (in the fish and under the *kikayon*)? And also prayer? If prophecy, like prayer, establishes contact with the divine or supernatural, the directions are, like Jacob's ladder, opposite but also complementary. While prayer reaches up to God, prophecy reaches down to humans.[39] The modern emotional reaction to both may fairly be described as fantastical.

---

[38] Stressing Jonah's (as opposed to the fish's) desire for escape, Lévinas' term "excendance," the urge to "sortir de l'être," may be more appropriate. See Emmanuel Lévinas, *De l'évasion* (Paris: Livre de poche, 1982), 97–98.

[39] See Nahum Sarna, *Songs of the Heart: An Introduction to the Book of Psalms* (New York: Schocken, 1993), 27.

Conclusions

The Ongoing Dialogue

The book of Jonah is "about" God and Jonah and, beyond that, about the multiple or complex relationships between humans and the divine. The ideal model proposed here is the prophetic one, for what more attractive exemplar can one imagine than that of friends knowing one another and talking with one another?[1] Roles traditionally assigned to our protagonists include the authoritarian hypothesis, focused on the question of "who is in charge here?" and yielding the inevitable answer: Why God of course![2] Another favored approach is the didactic or pedagogical one. Here Jonah is seen as in need of training, for aren't all humans defective, even (and perhaps especially) the great among us, and none so pathetically, of course, as poor Jonah himself?

Traces of these answers are retained in my theses developed above. Jonah is a typical prophet in the perennial tradition, which has one central goal or ideal to teach and reach: the knowledge of God. For Jonah this means pursuing a dialogue or conversation (in Montaigne's sense) by "asking the hard questions" so that an *adult* relationship (neither the child, authoritarian one, nor the

---

[1] See Martin Luther's engaging remark on Jonah 4:1: "God chats in such a friendly fashion with him and gives him a sign and behaves like a man who speaks and acts with his neighbor like a friend" (*Oeuvres 14: Explication du prophète Jonas et du prophète Habaquq 1526* [trans. Pierre Jundt; Geneva: Labor et Fides, 1993], 67).

[2] Thus, Craig, *A Poetics*, 142 (cf. 152): "The silence at the end signals that the Lord is supremely authoritative."

adolescent, pedagogical one) can continue to develop. There is of course yet another stage, the one between adolescence and full adulthood. That is the one of, let us call it, early adulthood, the stage at which one falls in love and marries and lives only for the beloved. Our story begins precisely at this stage (can there ever be another, as even God rhapsodizes in Jer 2:2?) and, even with the entanglements of solid adulthood and social responsibilities, still clings to the erotic ideal as giving meaning to all the others. God does the same, by the way, if the opening chapters of Hosea are of any relevance. At a different but related level of the prophetical calling, Jonah is again not the passive object of education but rather its conveyance. Rather than poor Jonah needing to be taught a lesson, as is usually imagined, he is the conveyance of saving knowledge. In his role of visible saint and through his symbolic actions, it is the prophet who is the teacher.

The dialogic situation pits God and Jonah at opposite ends of a spectrum that spans the entire universe and its narrative. At one extreme is the Temple, where Jonah wants to be; at the other is Nineveh, where God wants Jonah to be. The book of Jonah can thus be described as dialogic in its attempt to negotiate a compromise between these diametrically opposing positions. As was the case in the Hebrew Bible since Abraham,[3] this spiritual dialogue can be plotted geographically: on the one hand, a vertical voyage from the peaks of the Temple to the bases of the mountains; on the other, a horizontal trek from ultimate exile in Nineveh to the restored nuptial bliss of the succah. In both cases Jonah proposes what looks like a decent alternative. In Part One he heads to the ocean and back to the Creator/God who can restructure things. In Part Two Jonah heads for the desert, that locus of betrothal with the God of Salvation.

In neither case does the prophet go all the way by himself, however. In the first, he enters the boat and awaits the fish; in the second, he builds a hut and hopes for the *kikayon*. In both cases, the man of God waits upon God's good wishes and God responds positively: the fish takes him to the very base of the created world;

---

[3] When Abraham leaves his land (Gen 12:1), one understands it as a spiritual journey that also includes real geographical separation, since, as the rabbis argued, the text never entirely departs from its *pshat* or "literal meaning."

the *kikayon*—somewhat analogous to Jack's beanstalk—simulates a return to heaven. And then, quite dramatically, the situations are reversed. On the one hand, Jonah is vomited back to dry land and dried out to Nineveh; on the other, his protective roof dries out and he is again exposed to the elements. The message seems to be that historical existence must be played out: Nineveh will be saved and returned to the human family not by God but rather by His designated servant.

For if God must always have it His way, why then do we need dialogue at all?! One popular answer is, again, the pedagogic one, namely, that Jonah (and we too) must be taught a lesson. This is the answer of the book of Job: we simply do not have all the pieces of the puzzle (Job 38:1–42:6). A deeper answer is that the historical enterprise itself is dialogic, comprehensible, and justifiable only from a perspective that is truly outside. For just as God is in love with the works of creation,[4] Jonah's dialogue with God stands as an emblem for the works of time in love with eternity. For, ultimately, Jonah's love must reach through but also beyond the God of both salvation and full creation to . . . God—thus a pursuit detached even from God's most beneficent powers, a totally disinterested love. In Jonah's conception, God's love for Nineveh and its myriads has as its final destination the Ninevites' burning love for God that the prophet Jonah exemplifies from the start.

Jonah designates himself as one who fears God (1:9). At what may be called a negative level—which has nothing but positive ramifications—to fear God means *not* to fear any other thing, since "what can man do to me" (Ps 56:12; 118:6)? The corollary would go something like this: to *love* God would mean *not* to love any other thing. Or, alternatively: to love things for themselves and not for any benefit I might derive. If one objects that this separation (between a thing and its benefit to me) is impossible to live, is this separation any less difficult when what is loved is God?

It has seemed appropriate to some to term Jonah a comedy and Job a tragedy, but the reverse is closer to the truth. For in Jonah reigns the bitter nostalgia of a lost lovers' paradise; in Job,

---

[4] A love that Jonah came to take on as his own: "You showed love towards the *kikayon*, . . . which arises and perishes in a single day" (4:10). Or, perhaps, it is a lesson that God learned from Jonah, as we shall see below.

the sarcastic and wry humor of challenge. And where Job can think only of difference, the book of Jonah is a protracted dream of reconciliation. For Job is a comedy of the intellect, the driving urge—always frustrated, always renewed—to uncover the cosmic joke that baffles our suspicion,[5] our deep desire for meaning and translating events into story. For although Job does begin in myth, the rambling, repetitive, and reasoning monologues (disguised as dialogues) pulverize this promise and preclude any return to legend.

At the end of Jonah, God's questions have been viewed as having all the rhetorical finality of His questions to Job: were you there when I made the *kikayon*? Were you there when I made the animals? Yet the ending may be anything but a capitulation, and this peculiarity may extend to both texts as well. For, as Wiesel has sensed, Job's beatific acceptance may actually conceal a rejection: "Job discovered a novel method to persevere in his resistance: he pretended to abdicate before he even engaged his battle,"[6] so that his final refusal to speak out (imagine Job refusing to speak!!) speaks volumes. Similarly, God's concluding question to Job cannot be interpreted only as a going one better than Jonah's own "he sat at the east to see what will be" in Nineveh.[7] For Jonah's silence does not mean that he has nothing further to say but rather that he has already said enough. Thus we return to the dialogue of silence and, as the old proverb goes, if speech is silver, silence is golden.

Israel and the Nations

God's counterargument, which forms the substance of Jonah 4, can be sketched as follows: Merely being alive is a good (if not a virtue) because in itself it declares the goodness of the Creator. Innocence is thus not merely a no-man's land or void between good and evil; it is a positive space given as a gift. Further, by

---

[5] See Milan Kundera, *The Joke* (trans. David Hamblyn and Oliver Stally-brass; New York: Coward-McCann, 1969).

[6] Wiesel, "Job Our Contemporary," 234–35.

[7] Ibid.

destroying the *kikayon*, God reminds His prophet that the erotic clinging to God in this life involves a luxury tax that can be assessed at any time.

These two levels—existence and love—are clearly represented in Jewish thought. Let one example stand for many, Sforno's exegesis of Deut 11:26:

> Look and see, that your eyes not see things in a middling way, as is the custom among other peoples of the earth. For, indeed, *I set before you today a blessing and a curse*. And these represent two extremes: for the *blessing* is success far beyond the sufficient—the best! And the curse is misfortune that can never reach sufficiency.

On Sforno the *Torat Hayyim* comments:

> *Look!* This points to something new, as in Qohelet 1:10: "*Look! This is new.*" And the newness is this: that among Jews the path must not be the golden mean but rather the extreme, either the blessing or (God forbid!) its opposite.[8]

What God has proved in the book of Jonah is that the Gentiles do care for their lives, but in so doing they have also proved Jonah's point that they do not love God without motive. For God their creator, this means that they deserve to live, provided they stay out of trouble. For Jonah it means that, at the very least, they do not *currently* deserve a spot in the inner circle of lovers. Just who will occupy that inner circle in the future is not a foregone matter, however, if Isaiah's projection is to be credited:

> In that day shall Israel be third with Egypt and Assyria. (Isa 19:24)

For, although God's gift system remains currently in force, in the long run Jonah's pedagogy of merit will alone prevail. In that day, so Jonah argues (with God's delayed approval?), humanity's coming of spiritual age will prove that Mercy and Justice are twins, and that *all* Beloveds are sons of Truth.

---

[8] *Torat Hayyim*, ad loc.

Concluding Midrash I

> When I am far from You, my death is in my life;
> But if I cleave to You, my life will be in my death.
> (Yehuda Halevi)[9]

Jonah the Dove was sent out of Noah's ark no less than three times.

The first time he found no rest and returned to the ark.

The second time he returned with an olive branch, showing that God had renewed His covenant of existence with the human race.

He then went out yet a third time, but this time he did not return.

When Jonah died the first time, he could find no rest in Tehom.

When he approached death a second time, an opening was offered: hope to the human race.

Why then did Jonah go out yet again? Because the rest denied both in Tehom and in the ark of Nineveh was now available.

The ark of humanity is suspended between Tehom and Heaven, the deaths of annihilation and ecstasy.

Concluding Midrash II

After death, according to the Rabbinic conception, what does everyone do, sit around and sing praises? Study Torah! How? Why, in the best way possible: in the style of Resh Lakish.[10]

---

[9] *Berakhaqi mimka moti bekhayyai we'im 'edboq beka khayyai bemoti.*

[10] "When Resh Lakish died R. Johanan was sad, etc." This midrash is based on the death of Resh Lakish, as recounted in *b. Baba Metzia* 84a.

Thus God—the ultimate pedagogue not because He has all the answers but because He models questions—terminates the book of Jonah with a question.

And if the Infinite God is indeed in love with the works of time, it is in a time that intimates the Infinite. For what Jonah is reminded of by God's final question, which is anything but a conclusion or ending, is the lesson of the *question as question*. Lévinas suggests the following:

> When Knowledge, becoming Philosophy, wants to give satisfaction to the Desire for the Infinite, when one wants to give answer to a question in the process of gaining knowledge, the Question emerges once again, in philosophy it always emerges again from behind the answers. It is the question that has the last word, thus revealing its forgotten birth in the Desire for the Infinite.[11]

Through the paradox of a concluding question, God sanctions Jonah's own quest, which is to suggest that the Infinite God wants to be desired. For, indeed—returning to Rilke's exclamatory question—what would God do if Jonah were no longer around to ask Him questions?[12]

---

[11] Emmanuel Lévinas, *De L'Existence à l'existant* (2d ed.; Paris: Vrin, 1990), preface to the second edition. One might offer an additional sense, with a slight emendation: "in philosophy *and in exegesis* it [the question] always emerges again from behind the answers."

[12] See Rilke's question above in the preface, xiii, n. 5.

Excurses

EXCURSUS 1: On Reading Jonah

A colleague from a major European university once noticed my interest in Shakespeare. "I did doctorate exams in Shakespeare," he trumpeted. "Well," I eagerly started, "why do you think Lear rejected Cordelia?" He replied without hesitation: "I can tell you what my *professor* thinks since he wrote a book on that. I simply read *his* book and passed my exams." This foolish story becomes disturbing when we reflect that most of us approach works of literature more or less like my acquaintance read *King Lear*, through another's reading and authority. But what if that reading were partial or even wrong? How can I judge unless I have another standard? But whose? Some other authority's whose reading may have the same defects? How many of us practice Mary Moody Emerson's "defiant right of the individual reader to bring all texts to judgment?"[1]

The moral of the tale: Do you wish to understand the book of Jonah? Then you, yourself, *read*, study the book of Jonah! Not that the rich body of writing on Jonah is irrelevant, nor that your own naive reading is exempt from error—far from it. But how do we come to be able to judge readings of others except through our own developing sense of the text? And when critics read one another more than the text itself, the average study—Jonah is very

---

[1] Quoted in Robert D. Richardson, *Emerson: The Mind on Fire* (Berkeley: University of California Press, 1995), 27.

much a case in point—reads more like an anthology of opinions than a critical evaluation.

And it is the case, too, that even the popular exercise of anthologizing is sadly truncated: Lutherans read Lutherans, academic critics do not range far from academia, and the *nihil obstat*s from all quarters prevent us from looking over the fence into our neighbor's garden, with the sad result that the possibly greener grass excites less envy than distrust. I posit, from personal experience, that the greatness of a critic is, often by pointing out difficulties in the text, to lead the reader to ask his or her own questions.

From these brief observations I offer a few hints on how to read Jonah, or how to avoid mistakes, or, better, how to learn from mistakes already made. These simple rules are of course well known to students of literature, but even we tend to set them aside when entering the realm of Scripture.

a) The primacy of reading. Another personal anecdote may clarify this point. A colleague wished to prepare a course on wisdom literature and complained that von Rad's *Wisdom Literature* was simply putting him to sleep. My colleague's teacher (Moshe Greenberg) suggested that he *first* sit down and study the primary texts (Proverbs; Qohelet; Job), whereupon von Rad's study became full of interesting ideas.

b) The centrality of simple reading (the act of reading is of course anything but simple). The Bible, whatever else it is (history, religion, revelation, philology, psychology), is also a literary work, written in words and using a wide range of stylistic conventions. As such, the first (and, I would add, fundamental) mode of access is through careful study of its literary features.

But what of theology? Is not the book of Jonah part of Holy Scripture? Of course, but theology—if that is what you wish to call it—is better brought along as a companion to reading, rather than imported from without or above (or below). Indeed, it seems preferable to come from the opposite direction: the search for spiritual meanings must be an integral part of our reading of any book, not just Scripture. Thoreau expressed well the companionship we must pursue between reading and our own intimate intuition of existence: "We must laboriously seek the meaning of each word and line, conjecturing a larger sense than common use permits out of what wisdom and valor and generosity we have."[2] Such conjectures can arise either from the text or the reader; in either case—as in a true interpersonal relationship—they must be tested and either confirmed or rejected or modified by the other member of the dialogue.

    c) The avoidance of simplistic or univocal readings of whatever persuasion, especially at the start. I refer to those traditional approaches to Jonah that, while expanding the work's meaning and interpretive range, must be avoided as totalizing ways of reading, at the level of simple reading. Among these are the following:

allegorical, wrenching the "whale" episode away from its plain sense of descent to real corporeal death and then return to physical life.

plain-sensical, believing that the literal whale is the real point of the story. Might as well believe that a fable about the Fox and the Lion is also about real animals!

canonical, attempting to explain that, since Jonah is included in the Prophetic books, its entire meaning is prophetic, often with only superficial knowledge of what prophecy is about.

theological and apologetic:

    1) Jewish in the communal sense, as having a message to the entire Jewish people. The problem is that the Jewish people are not mentioned in the book.

    2) Christian, that Jonah is an allegory of Christ's descent into hell and that the book criticizes Jonah's narrowness. This stunning allegory, if accepted, still must be

---

[2] Henry David Thoreau, *The Portable Thoreau* (ed. Carl Bode; New York: Penguin Books, 1982), 353.

understood. Referring one allegory to another is not the end of discussion but rather the beginning; it reminds one of Montaigne's complaint on the current definition of a human as a rational animal: "Fine! I began with one question and now I have three!"[3] As to Jonah's Jewish or partisan narrowness, it remains to be seen whether Jonah is so comic as all that or whether his theological point is at all parochial. To over-theologize the book by stressing God's mercy, for example—that this element is present in a communal sense is not to be doubted: His mercy is upon all His works, including the Ninevites—may be to compromise other aspects of God that such critics would be loath to do.

Finally, two kinds of reading must be clearly distinguished, for their strengths as well as their weaknesses: the synchronic and the diachronic. The first sees the entire text entirely at any point of the reading. Midrashic exegesis proceeds exactly in this vertical way. It assumes that the entire text (in reading Bible, the entire Bible) is before the mind and is implicit in each word and at each moment. By contrast, diachronic reading is horizontal and can proceed only in a direct line from start to finish. The cardinal rule here is: don't read ahead! This prohibition applies not only to reading the last page of a detective novel first. It means also not interpreting chapter 1 of Jonah in terms of what will be disclosed in chapter 4 (even though that may be known from a previous reading, that knowledge must be bracketed and a fresh reading produced). Roland Barthes' model of free versus classical reading seems to reproduce this distinction, namely, that linear reading is classical whereas synchronic reading (which Barthes prefers) allows entrance into the text at whatever point and thus approximates midrash.[4]

The prohibition against reading ahead has a stronger warning as well, the avoidance of deciding beforehand what the text

---

[3] Michel de Montaigne, *The Complete Essays of Montaigne* (trans. Donald Frame; Stanford: Stanford University Press, 1976), 819.

[4] Roland Barthes, *Image-Music-Text* (trans. Stephen Heath; New York: Hill & Wang, 1978); *Mythologies* (trans. Annette Lavers; New York: Hill & Wang, 1972).

says, of eisegesis (reading into) as opposed to exegesis (or reading out). Thus, to take an ongoing example, politicians decide beforehand what conclusions they wish and then arrange the evidence to reach those conclusions. The method must always be exegesis over eisegesis, science before politics.

EXCURSUS 2: Better-Than

Jonah is suicidal, he wants to die. Attention is usually paid to the first part of his statement, his plea for death, whereas the more interesting part may be the prophet's express motivation. Usually translated as "I would rather die than live," the literal rendering gives an important clue:

> . . . for my death is *better than* my life. (Jonah 4:3, 8)

This expression occurs only twice in the Hebrew Bible and is unique to Jonah. What we would like to focus on is the form of "*better-than*," especially common in wisdom texts and proverbs.[5] Briefly put, such statements are neither simple assertions of preference such as "red is better than yellow," nor do they suggest that "red is good" and "yellow is awful" or that, in Jonah's case, life is no good at all. Notice that, when Jonah asserts that his death is better than his life, his working assumption is that *normally* the reverse would be true, that his life is better than his death. What changes things is the life context, just as, more generally speaking, better-than statements typically contextualize the values or preferences in order to reveal a wisdom insight. Thus, to cite another example, "a tail is better than a head" flies in the face of normal perceptions, which would assert the opposite. How then can such a statement be advanced? By a contextualization such as occurs in the rabbis' saying:

> Be a tail of a lion rather than a head of a fox.
> (Mishnah *Abot* 4:15):[6]

---

[5] See T. A. Perry, *Wisdom Literature and the Structure of Proverbs* (University Park: Penn State University Press, 1993), 40–44.

[6] The saying is attributed to Rabbi Mathya the son of Charash.

Or, stated in better-than terms:

A tail of a lion is better than a head of a fox.

Beyond the contextual issue is that of the (positive or negative) values of the individual members. In the culture projected by *Abot*, they would be expressed as follows:

tail (-) of lion (+)
head (+) of fox (-)

Now such better-than statements assert comparative values *within* a hypothetical total structure that states no less than the four available possibilities. In descending order of value, from best to worst, the following quadripartite is implied:

1) head of lions   (++)

2) tail of lions   (-+)

3) head of foxes   (+-)

4) tail of foxes   (- -)

The better-than proverb, comprised of propositions 2 and 3, thus presents the exception that proves the rule, according to which it is understood that heads are better than tails, except under the specified condition.

Returning to our Jonah text, it is now possible to observe that Jonah's death wish, saying that death would be good, is *not* also an assertion that life is no good. Rather, his normal belief is that life is indeed better than death, and his assertion to the contrary is a relative one, since his paradoxical valuation of "death over life" is only better than propositions 3 and 4 but certainly not better than proposition 1. Thus, through the simple wisdom structure of better-than, it is clear that Jonah does not go all the way towards suicide, since he still asserts that his life is good (simply that his death would be better).

As for the contextualization in Jonah that makes this claim possible, I would propose an erotic model such as the following quadripartite:

my life (+) with You (+)

my death (-) with You or by You (+)

my life (+) without You (-)

my death (-) without you (-)

To repeat, Jonah's death wish is comprised of statements 2 and 3 (as are all better-than proverbs): my death with or by You would be better than my life without You. But best of all would be my life with You.

If this analysis argues that Jonah's death wish does not totally negate or deny his life wish (because the desire to die is only "better than" but certainly not the best), then we are encouraged to conceptualize the paradoxical situation in which death but also life are possible. We might thus be led to another erotic commonplace, perhaps the most familiar of them all: that for lovers, life is a a living death, the emblem for which could again be the Cressida text:

"I could live and die in the eyes of Troilus."
(*Troilus and Cressida* 1.2.242)

The strong reading of this text is also the argument of Jonah: that lovers both live and die at the same time. This is the opposite of *Liebestode*, of the loving and pursuit of death, however, since the living death of lovers is acknowledged and accepted:

For love is as strong as death. (Cant 8:6)

According to a strong reading of this text, too, love and death, despite or even through their very antagonism, coexist and may even be mutually supportive. So long as they are with You.

EXCURSUS 3: Three Days

Landes regrets the absence of a satisfactory treatment of the three days/three nights motif.[7] This excursus is an attempt in that direction.

In the creation narrative things take three days to emerge from ideal existence to activity, from natural habitat to habitation by its inhabitant, so to speak. Thus light is spoken forth on the

---

[7] George M. Landes, "The Kerygma of the Book of Jonah: The Contextual Interpretation of the Jonah Psalm," *Int* 21 (1967): 10, 12.

first day (Gen 1:3–5) but does not become active until the fourth, through the creation of the luminaries (vv. 14–19). The precondition of the winged creatures' appearance on the fifth day (vv. 20–21) is the stretching out of the firmament on day two (vv. 6–8). And, to complete the double and parallel triad, the dry land (day three, vv. 9–10) awaits its quadripeds and bipeds on the sixth (vv. 24–25). In short, for all creatures to emerge in days four through six, there is a requisite three-day hatching or incubation period.

One can detect a distant but eery parallel in Jonah's own "incubation," if that is the right term.[8] One might say that Jonah's three days in the belly of the fish is nothing short of an emergence from darkness (the ship's hold) and watery chaos (shades of Gen 1:2) and return to dry land. We have seen how the entire plot of Part One, while in some sense a static journey or mere reversion to square one, is also a necessary precondition for Jonah's return to active life.

Jonah's three days' journey into Nineveh (3:3) constitutes the second triad that was prefigured in the first. This time, however, Jonah is not going all the way in, as he did in the fish. Thus not three but rather one = three, the figure for shortcutting nature, for shortcircuiting the normal process and jumping directly into the sabbath, as it were.

The number three as a figure for completion can of course point in opposite ways: either to another such cycle, thus a continuity, as we saw above in the three/four figure.[9] Or, the completion could signify termination. In this latter case, renewal could come about only through a miraculous or magical resurrection. This gives added poignancy to the Rabbinic identification of Jonah with the lad resurrected by Elijah: "Rabbi Eliezer taught: 'Jonah ben Amittai was the son of the widow of Zarephat.'"[10]

The *kikayon* epiphany provides yet another possible application of this figure, at least according to those who see the *kikayon*'s

---

[8] See T. H. MacAlpine, *Sleep, Divine and Human* (Sheffield: JSOT Press, 1987), 158–59.

[9] See above, "The *Kikayon* Episode," in chapter 4.

[10] Yalkut Shimoni 2, 550, on 1 Kgs 17; quoted in Uriel Simon, *Jonah: The Traditional Hebrew Text with the New JPS Translation* (trans. Lenn J. Schramm; JPS Torah Commentary; Philadelphia: Jewish Publication Society, 1999), 38. See above, "A Tale of the Fantastic," in chapter 10.

demise as occurring on the second (rather than the first) night.[11] Recall that, in our reading, this entire scenario was staged by the prophet as a kind of prenuptial, as initiating his return—now that the Nineveh business has been dispatched—to God's sanctuary. Hosea provided the perfect prophetic text for this possibility: "After two days he will revive us; in the third day he will raise us up, and we shall live before Him" (Hos 6:2). Rashi takes this as a reference to the Holy Temple, probably understanding *le-fanav*, "before Him," as "in His Presence," i.e., the Sanctuary.[12]

Finally, with reference to the *forty* days within which the Ninevites must repent, Moberly studies the textual variant Septuagint reading "*three* days."[13] While, it is argued, the shorter period is more congenial to the "swift movement of the story," such esthetic notions may find little encouragement among theologians interested in divine mercy. More strenuous arguments are put forth to explain not why three is so good but rather why it had to replace forty, which had inherent defects. Thus forty has no sense of urgency, providing yet another occasion for blaming Jonah, now for being casual: "the time for repentance is far off." Such a claim fails to recall that, even with the number three, the length of the delay is God's command, not Jonah's. A second complaint about forty is that it is too long to fast. But, surely, although the repentance ritual may have lasted in some form, the focus, at least in the midrash, is rather on the behavioral requirements of repentance, deeds such as making restitution of stolen goods.

EXCURSUS 4: Male and Female Fish

Here we step from the merely fanciful or fantastic to the outrageous. We do so with some sense of alibi, however, since the exegete's defensive claim is that outrageous readings never arise without some form of textual provocation. The one that concerns us here is that, of the four references to the huge fish in Jonah,

---

[11] See above, n. 17 in chapter 4.

[12] See especially above, "Life at the Center: Love's Canopies," in chapter 5.

[13] R. W. Moberly, "Preaching for a Response? Jonah's Message to the Ninevites Reconsidered," *VT* 53 (2003): 156–67.

three are male and one (the third) is female, as indicated by the feminine ending -*h*, the Hebrew letter *he*:

dag/dag/daga*h*/dag (Jonah 2:1; 2:1; 2:2; 2:11).

None of the literal explanations make sense, and the text therefore seems to cry out: *darsheni*, "Give me a midrashic explanation!" Whence the delightful Rabbinic speculation that in fact Jonah was swallowed by *two* fish of different gender.[14] Here are a few more suggestions.

There is an old tradition of midrashically interpreting the shape of Hebrew letters. The first and perhaps best known occurs at the very start of the Hebrew Bible, addressing the question "Why does the Bible begin with the letter *bet*, '*In* the beginning' rather than, say, *aleph*, the first letter of the alphabet?" The proposed answer notices that the shape of the first letter—reading from right to left—allows an opening only in a forward direction and excludes reading/interpretation in the other three directions: above, before, and below. Thus, it is argued, just as reading can only occur *after* the first letter, speculation on what occurred before creation or in the higher or nether worlds is to be avoided.

Jonah's fish seems to be male, and the added letter "*he*" to the third mention seems superfluous and thus in need of interpretation. The letter's shape may give a clue. Here is Rashi's explanation of Gen 2:4, where the letter *he* stands out in MT by its smaller-than-usual size:

> These are the generations of the heavens and the earth when they were created [*behibar'am*].

Rashi:

> This verse teaches that this world was created by means of "*he*," suggesting that all [created beings] must descend "to behold the pit" [*shakhat*]; like this letter "*he*" which is closed on all sides but open at the bottom so that they may all pass down through there.

Rashi's use of "pit" adds an interesting reading to Prov 26:27:

---

[14] Cited above, "Jonah's Suicide," in chapter 1.

He who digs a pit [*shakhat*] will fall into it.

It is possible that the word *shakhat* has two meanings in this same verse, the second meaning strongly suggested by the letter he: "will fall into *it*," into the letter *he*. In view of the above, it is not much of a midrashic stretch to read as follows:

He who digs a pit will fall into it, i.e., *she'ol*.

This brings us to Jonah, who thanks God (2:7) for bringing his life up from *shakhat*, the pit, which from the context can only mean *She'ol*. The explanation is as follows: In the three references to the male fish, the perspective is God's:

The Lord appointed a great *dag* or fish (2:1);

and Jonah was in the belly of the fish (where God has placed him) (2:1);

And God commanded the fish . . . (2:11)

Why God saves Jonah, however, is because of the latter's distress that leads directly to *She'ol* or "death, "symbolized here by the *he* of the fish (2:2). As Simon observes, Jonah calls out not only "from" the fish's belly but "because of it" as well.[15]

Alternatively, in the Land of Israel God "speaks" to Jonah. Outside the Land words are not used, but that does not mean that God does not have other means at His disposal: the fish or *dagah*, the barely disguised inverse—and thus complementary mode—of speaking (*hgd* 1:8, 10)! Thus, the three male fishes are active but silent: they swallow, preserve, and vomit. Only the female fish sponsors speech, in the form of prayer.

The book of Qohelet presents a curious and unexplained parallel, where the author/hero's name "Qohelet" occurs four times: three in the male gender (1:1, 2; 12:10) and once in the female gender (7:27).[16]

---

[15] Uriel Simon, *Jonah*, 19.

[16] See the preliminary remarks in T. A. Perry, *Dialogues with Kohelet* (University Park, PA: Penn State University Press, 1993), 184. Also of interest is the occurence of the feminine variant in the third position of four.

BIBLIOGRAPHY

Abarbanel, Don Isaac (1437–1508). See *Torat Hayyim*.

Abot. See Mishnah.

Ackerman, James A. "Jonah." Pages 234–43 in *The Literary Guide to the Bible*. Edited by Robert Alter and Frank Kermode. Cambridge, MA: Harvard University Press, 1987.

Allen, Leslie C. *The Books of Joel, Obadiah, Jonah and Micah*. Grand Rapids: Eerdmans, 1976.

Andersen, Francis I., and David Noel Freedman. *Hosea: A New Translation with Introduction and Commentary*. Anchor Bible 24. Garden City: Doubleday, 1980.

Auerbach, Eric. *Mimesis: The Representation of Reality in Western Literature*. Translated by Willard Trask. Garden City: Doubleday, 1957.

Augustine, Saint. *The City of God*. Translated by Marcus Dods. New York: Modern Library, 2000.

Babylonian Talmud. Edited by I. Epstein. London: Soncino, 1935–1948.

Balentine, Samuel E. *Prayer in the Hebrew Bible*. Minneapolis: Fortress, 1993.

Barthes, Roland. *Image-Music-Text*. Translated by Stephen Heath. New York: Hill & Wang, 1978.

———. *Mythologies*. Translated by Annette Lavers. New York: Hill & Wang, 1972.

Becker, Ernest. *The Denial of Death*. New York: Free Press, 1973. Repr. Free Press Paperbacks, 1997.

Ben-Menahem, Elyakim. Sefer-Yona. Pages 1–19 in *Sefer Tere'asar: im perush "Da'at Mikra"* [The Minor Prophets]. Jerusalem: Mossad Harav Kook, 1974–1976.

Ben Zvi, Ehud. *Signs of Jonah: Reading and Rereading in Ancient Yehud.* Journal for the Study of the Old Testament: Supplement Series 367. Sheffield: JSOT Press, 2003.

Bickerman, Elias. *Four Strange Books of the Bible: Jonah, Daniel, Qohelet, Esther.* New York: Schocken, 1967.

Blenkinsopp, Joseph. *A History of Prophecy in Israel.* Rev. and enl. ed. Louisville, KY: Westminster John Knox, 1996.

Bolin, Thomas M. *Freedom Beyond Forgiveness: The Book of Jonah Re-examined.* Journal for the Study of the Old Testament: Supplement Series 236. Sheffield: JSOT Press, 1997.

———. "'Should I Not Also Pity Nineveh?' Divine Freedom in the Book of Jonah." *Journal for the Study of the Old Testament* 67 (1995): 109–20.

Bowling, Robert G., and G. Ernest Wright. *Joshua: A New Translation with Notes and Commentary.* AB 6. Garden City: Doubleday, 1982.

Brettler, Marc Zvi. *The Book of Judges.* London: Routledge, 2002.

Buell, Lawrence. *The Environmental Imagination: Thoreau, Nature Writing, and the Formation of American Culture.* Cambridge, MA: Harvard University Press, 1995.

Buss, Martin J. "Toward Form Criticism as an Explication of Human Life." Pages 312–25 in *The Changing Face of Form Criticism for the Twenty-First Century.* Edited by Marvin A. Sweeney and Ehud Ben Zvi. Grand Rapids: Eerdmans, 2003.

Calvino, Italo. *Invisible Cities.* Translated by William Weaver. New York: Harcourt Brace, 1974.

Camus, Albert. *L'Etranger.* Paris: Gallimard, 1942.

———. *Le Mythe de Sisyphe.* Paris: Gallimard, 1942.

Carson, Anne. *Glass, Irony and God.* New York: New Directions, 1995.

Castex, Pierre-Georges. *Le Conte fantastique en France.* Paris: José Corti, 1974.

Cavell, Stanley. *The Senses of Walden.* New York: Viking, 1972.

Chalier, Catherine. *Lévinas: L'Utopie de l'humain.* Paris: Albin Michel, 1993.

Christensen, Duane L. "The Song of Jonah: A Metrical Analysis." *Journal of Biblical Literature* 104 (1985): 217–31.

Chow, Simon. *The Sign of Jonah Reconsidered: A Study of its Meaning in the Gospel Traditions.* Coniectanea Biblica NT 27. Stockholm: Almqvist & Wiksell International, 1995.

Cogan, Mordechai. *1 Kings: A New Translation with Introduction and Commentary*. Anchor Bible 10. Garden City: Doubleday, 2001.

Cohen, Abraham D. "The Tragedy of Jonah." *Judaism* 21 (1972): 164–75.

Coomaraswamy, Ananda. *The Dance of Shiva*. New York: Noonday, 1957.

Cooper, Alan. "In Praise of Divine Caprice: The Significance of the Book of Jonah." Pages 144–63 in *Among the Prophets*. Edited by Philip R. Davies and David J. A. Clines. Journal for the Study of the Old Testament: Supplement Series 144. Sheffield: JSOT Press, 1993.

Corrozet, Gilles. *Le Compte du rossignol*. Edited by Ferdinand Gohin. Paris: Garnier, 1924.

Couty, Daniel. *Le Fantastique*. Paris: Bordas, 1986.

Craig, Kenneth. *A Poetics of Jonah: Art in the Service of Ideology*. Columbia: University of South Carolina Press, 1993.

Crenshaw, James L. "The Expression *mi yodea'* in the Hebrew Bible." *Vetus Testamentum* 36 (1986): 274–88.

————. *Joel: A New Translation with Introduction and Commentary*. Anchor Bible 24C. Garden City: Doubleday, 1995.

Cross, Frank M. "Studies in the Structure of Hebrew Verse: The Prosody of the Psalm of Jonah." Pages 159–67 in *The Quest for the Kingdom of God: Studies in Honor of George E. Mendenhall*. Edited by H. B. Huffmon, F. A. Spina, and A. R. W. Green. Winona Lake, IN: Eisenbrauns, 1983.

Daube, David. "Death as Release in the Bible." *Novum Testamentum* 5 (1962): 82–104.

Davenport, Guy. See Carson, Anne.

Day, John. "Problems in the Interpretation of the Book of Jonah." Pages 32–47 in *In Quest of the Past: Studies on Israelite Religion, Literature and Prophetism*. Edited by A. S. van der Woude. Old Testament Studies 26. Leiden: Brill, 1990.

Eagleton, Terry. "J. L. Austin and the Book of Jonah." Pages 231–36 in *The Book and the Text*. Edited by Regina Schwartz. Cambridge, MA: Basil Blackwell, 1990.

Elata-Alster, Gerda, and Rachel Salmon. "The Deconstruction of Genre in the Book of Jonah: Towards a Theological Discourse." *Journal of Literature and Theology* 3 (1989): 40–60.

Emerson, Ralph Waldo. *The Portable Emerson*. Edited by Carl Bode. Rev. ed. The Viking Portable Library. New York: Penguin Books, 1981.

Epictetus. *Enchiridion*. Pages 482–537 in *The Discourses and Manual*. Translated by W. A. Oldfather. 2 vols. Cambridge, MA: Harvard University Press, vol. 2, 1966.

Even-Shoshan, Abraham. *A New Concordance to the Torah, the Prophets and the Writings* [Hebrew]. Jerusalem: Kiryat Sefer, 1992.

Fisch, Harold. *A Remembered Future: A Study in Literary Mythology*. Bloomington: Indiana University Press, 1984.

———. *The Holy Scriptures: English text revised and edited*. Jerusalem: Koren, 1992.

Fretheim, Terence. "Jonah and Theodicy." *Zeitschrift für die alttestamentliche Wissenschaft* 90 (1978): 227–37.

———. *The Message of Jonah: A Theological Commentary*. Minneapolis: Augsburg, 1977.

Friedrich, Hugo. *Montaigne*. Paris: Gallimard, 1968.

Ginzberg, Louis. *The Legends of the Jews*. 6 vols. Philadelphia: Jewish Publication Society, 1968.

Goethe, Johann Wolfgang von. *Faust*. Translated by Carl R. Mueller. Hanover, N.H.: Smith & Kraus, 2004.

Goldin, Judah. New Forward to *Hebrew Ethical Wills*. Edited by Israel Abrahams. Philadelphia: Jewish Publication Society, 1976.

Gordis, Robert. *Koheleth: The Man and His World*. New York: Schocken, 1968.

Govrin, Michal. *The Name*. Translated by Barbara Harshav. New York: Riverhead, 1998.

Greenberg, Moshe. *Ezekiel 1–20: A New Translation with Introduction and Commentary*. Anchor Bible 22. Garden City: Doubleday, 1983.

———. *Ezekiel 21–37: A New Translation with Introduction and Commentary*. Anchor Bible 22A. Garden City: Doubleday, 1997.

Guevara, Antonio de. *Menosprecio de corte y alabanza de aldea*. Valladolid, 1539.

Hacham, Amos. *Commentary to the Book of Psalms* [Hebrew]. 2 vols. Jerusalem: Mossad Harav Kook, n.d.

Halpern, B., and R. E. Friedman, "Composition and Paronomasia in the Book of Jonah." *Hebrew Annual Review* 4 (1980): 79–92.

Hauser, Alan Jon. "Jonah: In Pursuit of the Dove." *Journal of Biblical Literature* 104 (1985): 21–37.

Ibn Ezra, Abraham (1080–1164). See *Torat Hayyim.*

Joüon, Paul, and T. Muraoka. *A Grammar of Biblical Hebrew.* Rome: Pontifical Biblical Institute, 1993.

Joyce, James. *The Portable James Joyce.* New York: Penguin Books, 1976.

Jung, Carl G. *Symbols of Transformation.* Translated by R. F. C. Hull. London: Routledge and Keegan Paul, 1956.

Kaufmann, Yehezkel. *The Religion of Israel.* Translated by Moshe Greenberg. Chicago: Chicago University Press, 1960.

Keil, Yehudah. *1 Samuel* [Hebrew]. Jerusalem: Mossad Harav Kook, 1981.

Keller, Carl-A. "Jonas." Commentaire de l'Ancien Testament XIa. Edited by Edmond Jacob, Carl-A. Keller, Samuel Amsler. In *Osée, Joël, Abdias, Jonas, Amos.* Genève: Labor et Fides, 1992.

Kilmer, Joyce. "Trees." Page 19 in *Trees and Other Poems: Candles that Burn,* by Joyce Kilmer and Aline M. Kilmer. Atlanta: Cherokee, 1994.

Kundera, Milan, *The Joke.* Translated by David Hamblyn and Oliver Stallybrass. New York: Coward-McCann, 1969.

La Fontaine, Jean de. *Fables choisies.* Mont-Royal, Québec: Modulo-Griffon, 2004.

LaCocque, André. *Romance She Wrote: A Hermeneutical Essay on Song of Songs.* Harrisburg, PA: Trinity Press International, 1998.

LaCocque, André, and Pierre-Emmanuel Lacocque. *The Jonah Complex.* Atlanta: John Knox, 1981.

———. *Jonah: A Psycho-Religious Approach to the Prophet.* Columbia: University of South Carolina Press, 1990.

Laín Entralgo, Pedro. *The Therapy of the Word in Classical Antiquity.* New Haven: Yale University Press, 1970.

Landes, George M. "The Kerygma of the Book of Jonah: The Contextual Interpretation of the Jonah Psalm." *Interpretation* 21 (1967): 3–31.

Lang, Berel. "For and Against the 'Righteous Gentiles.'" *Judaism* 46 (1997): 91–96.

————. "Uncovering Certain Mischievous Questions about the Holocaust." Annual Lecture presented at the United States Holocaust Memorial Museum, Washington, D.C., March 12, 2002.

Laytner, Anson. *Arguing with God: A Jewish Tradition.* Northvale, NJ: Jason Aronson, 1990.

Lévinas, Emmanuel. *De l'Existence à l'existant.* 2d ed. Paris: Vrin, 1990.

————. *De l'évasion.* Paris: Livre de poche, 1982.

————. *Totalité et infini.* Paris: Livre de poche, 1971.

Levine, Eytan. *The Aramaic Version of Jonah.* Jerusalem: Jerusalem Academic Press, 1978.

Lewis, Haim. "Jonah—A Parable for our Time." *Judaism* 21 (1972): 159–63.

L'Heureux, John. "Departures." Pages 308–19 in *The Vintage Book of Contemporary American Short Stories.* Edited by Tobias Wolff. New York: Vintage Books, 1994.

Licht, Jacob. *Storytelling in the Bible.* Jerusalem: Magnes, 1978.

Lichtert, Claude. "Récit et noms de Dieu dans le livre de Jonas." *Biblica* 84 (2003): 247–51.

Lifshitz, Ze'ev Haim. *The Paradox of Human Existence: A Commentary on the Book of Jonah.* Northvale, NJ: Jason Aronson, 1994.

Limburg James. *Jonah: A Commentary.* Louisville, KY: Westminster John Knox, 1993.

Lispector, Clarice. "The Smallest Woman in the World." Pages 349–58 in *You've Got to Read This.* Edited by Ron Hansen. New York: HarperCollins, 2000.

Luther, Martin. "On Habakuk and Jonah." In *Oeuvres 14: Explication du prophète Jonas et du prophète Habaquq 1526.* Geneva: Labor et Fides, 1993.

Lys, Daniel. *Le Plus beau chant de la création. Commentaire du Cantique des Cantiques.* Paris: Cerf, 1968.

Magonet, Jonathan. *Form and Meaning: Studies in Literary Techniques in the Book of Jonah.* Sheffield: Almond, 1983.

Maimonides, Moses. *Eight Chapters* [Hebrew]. Jerusalem: Mossad Harav Kook, 1968.

Marx, Leo. *The New York Review of Books* 46, no. 11 (June 24, 1999): 64.

Masson, Michel. "L'Expérience mystique du Prophète Elie: 'Qol Demama Daqqa.'" *Revue de l'Histoire des Religions* 208/3 (1991): 243–71.

McAlpine, T. H. *Sleep, Divine and Human*. Sheffield: JSOT Press, 1987.

McCarter, P. Kyle, Jr. *I Samuel: A New Translation with Introduction, Notes, and Commentary*. Anchor Bible 8. Garden City: Doubleday, 1980.

Meschonnic, Henri. *Jona et le signifiant errant*. Paris: Gallimard, 1981.

Mekhilta of Rabbi Ishmael. Edited by Haim Horovitz and Israel Rabin. 2nd ed. Jerusalem: Wahrmann, 1970.

Menahem Ha-Meiri. *Perush 'al Sefer Mishlei* [Commentary on the Book of Proverbs]. Edited by Menachem Mendel Zahav. Jerusalem: Otsar ha-Poskim, 1969.

Milgrom, Jacob. *Numbers: The Traditional Hebrew Text with the New JPS Translation*. The JPS Torah Commentary. Philadelphia: Jewish Publication Society, 1990.

Mishnah. Translated by Jacob Neusner. New Haven: Yale University Press, 1988.

Moberly, R. W. "Preaching for a Response? Jonah's Message to the Ninevites Reconsidered." *Vetus Testamentum* 53 (2003): 156–67.

Molière. *Le misanthrope*. London: Bristol Classical Press, 1996.

Montaigne, Michel de. *The Complete Essays of Montaigne*. Translated by Donald Frame. Palo Alto, CA: Stanford University Press, 1976.

Moore, George Foot. *Judaism in the First Centuries of the Christian Era: The Age of the Tannaim*. 3 vols. Harvard University Press, 1966. Reprinted 3 vols. in 2. Peabody, MA: Hendrickson, 1997.

Morrison, Toni. *Beloved*. New York: A. A. Knopf, 1998.

The New Oxford Annotated Bible: Revised Standard Version. New York: Oxford University Press, 1977.

Opgen-Rhein, Hermann. *Jonapsalm und Jonabuch*. Stuttgarter Biblische Beiträge 38. Stuttgart: Katholisches Bibelwerk, 1997.

Paul, Shalom M. *A Commentary on the Book of Amos*. Minneapolis: Fortress, 1991.

Paul, Sherman, *The Shores of America: Thoreau's Inward Exploration*. Urbana: University of Illinois Press, 1958.

Perry, T. A. "Cain's Sin in Genesis 4:1–7 and Oracular Double-Talking." *Prooftexts* 25 (2006): 259–76.

———. "The Coordination of *KY / 'L KN* in Cant. 1:1–3 and Related Texts." *Vetus Testamentum* 55 (2005): 528–41.

————. *Dialogues with Kohelet*. University Park, PA: Penn State University Press, 1993.

————. *Erotic Spirituality: The Integrative Tradition from Leone Ebreo to John Donne*. University: Alabama University Press, 1980.

————. "Metaphors of Sacrifice in the Zohar." *Studies in Comparative Religion* 16 (1986): 188–97.

————. "A Poetics of Absence: The Structure and Meaning of Chaos in Genesis 1:2." *Journal for the Study of the Old Testament* 58 (1993): 3–11.

————. *Wisdom Literature and the Structure of Proverbs*. University Park: Penn State University Press, 1993.

Pirkei de-Rabbi Eliezer. Warsaw: n.p., 1852.

Rabelais, François. *Le tiers livre*. Genève: Droz, 1964.

Radak. Rabbi David Kimhi (1157–1236). See *Torat Hayyim*.

Rashbam. Rabbi Shmuel ben Meir (1080–1158). See *Torat Hayyim*.

Rashi. Rabbi Shlomo Yitzhak (1040–1105). See *Torat Hayyim*.

Reichelberg, Ruth. *L'Aventure prophétique: Jonas, menteur de vérité*. Paris: Albin Michel, 1995.

Richardson, Robert D. *Emerson: The Mind on Fire*. Berkeley: University of California Press, 1995.

Rilke, Rainer Maria. *Rilke's Book of Hours: Love Poems to God*. New York: Riverhead, 1996.

————. *Sonnets to Orpheus*. Translated by Willis Barnstone. Boston: Shambhala, 2004.

Robert, André, Raymond Tournay, and André Feuillet. *Le Cantique des cantiques: Traduction et Commentaire*. Paris: Gabalda, 1963.

Rofé, Alexander. *The Prophetical Stories*. Jerusalem: Magnes, 1988.

Rousseau, Jean-Jacques. *Lettre à d'Alembert sur les spectacles*. Genève: Droz, 1948.

————. *Rêveries du promeneur solitaire*. Genève: Droz, 1967.

Rudolph, Wilhelm. *Joel-Amos-Obadja-Jona*. Kommentar zum Alten Testament xiii/2. Gütersloh: Gerd Mohn, 1971.

Saint-Exupéry, Antoine de. *Oeuvres*. Paris: Gallimard, 1959.

Sarna, Nahum M. *Exodus: The Traditional Hebrew Text with the New JPS Translation*. JPS Torah Commentary. Philadelphia: Jewish Publication Society, 1991.

————. *Songs of the Heart: An Introduction to the Book of Psalms*. New York: Schocken, 1993.

Sartre, Jean-Paul. *Situations I*. Paris: Gallimard, 1947.

Sasson, Jack M. *Jonah, A New Translation with Introduction, Commentary, and Interpretation.* Anchor Bible 42B. New York: Doubleday, 1990.

———. *Ruth: A New Translation with a Philological Commentary and a Formalist-Folklorist Interpretation.* 2d edition. Sheffield: Sheffield Academic Press, 1989.

Scève, Maurice. *La Délie.* Edited by I. D. McFarlane. Cambridge, MA: Cambridge University Press, 1966.

Scott, R. B. Y. "The Sign of Jonah." *Interpretation* 19 (1965): 16–25.

Sforno, Obadia ben Ya'akov (1475–1550). See *Torat Hayyim.*

Sherwood, Yvonne. *A Biblical Text and its Afterlives: The Survival of Jonah in Western Culture.* Cambridge: Cambridge University Press, 2000.

———. "Cross-currents in the Book of Jonah." *Biblical Interpretation* 6 (1998): 49–79.

Simon, Uriel. *Jonah, Introduction and Commentary* [Hebrew]. Tel Aviv: Am Oved, 1992.

———. *Jonah: The Traditional Hebrew Text with the New JPS Translation.* Translated by Lenn J. Schramm. JPS Torah Commentary. Philadelphia: Jewish Publication Society, 1999.

Spangenberg, I. J. "Jonah and Qohelet: Satire versus Irony." OTE 9 (1996): 495–511.

Sternberg, Meir. *The Poetics of Biblical Narrative.* Bloomington: Indiana University Press, 1985.

Stevens, Wallace. *The Necessary Angel: Essays on Reality and Imagination.* New York: Vintage Books, 1951.

Sweeney, Marvin A. *The Twelve Prophets.* 2 vols. Collegeville, MN: Liturgical, 2000.

Targum. See Levine, *The Aramaic Version of Jonah.*

Taylor, Dennis. "The Need for a Religious Literary Criticism." *Religion and the Arts* 1 (1996): 124–50.

Thoreau, Henry David. *The Portable Thoreau.* Edited by Carl Bode. New York: Penguin Books, 1982.

Tigay, Jeffrey H. "The Book of Jonah and the Days of Awe." *Conservative Judaism* 38 (1985/86): 67–76.

———. *Deuteronomy.* The JPS Torah Commentary. Philadelphia: Jewish Publication Society, 1996.

Todorov, Tzvetan. *Introduction à la littérature fantastique.* Paris: Seuil, 1970.

Torat Hayyim. Chumash [the Five Books of Moses], *with Classical Commentaries.* Edited by Mordechai Breuer et al. 7 vols. Jerusalem: Mossad Harav Kook, 1986–1993.

Trible, Phyllis. *Rhetorical Criticism: Context, Method, and the Book of Jonah.* Minneapolis: Fortress, 1994.

Vercors. *Le Silence de la mer.* Paris: Club des Librairies de France, 1964.

Voltaire, *Candide, or Optimism.* Translated by Peter Constantine. New York: Modern Library, 2005.

Walsh, Jerome T. "Jonah 2,3–10: A Rhetorical Critical Study." *Biblica* 63 (1982): 219–29.

Weiss, Meir. "Psalm 27 [Hebrew]. *Tarbiz* 64 (1995): 323–30.

———. *The Story of Job's Beginning: Job 1–2, a Literary Analysis.* Jerusalem: Magnes, 1983.

Weitzman, Steven. *Song and Story in Biblical Narrative: The History of a Literary Convention in Ancient Israel.* Bloomington: Indiana University Press, 1997.

Whybray, R. N. *The Book of Proverbs: A Survey of Modern Study.* Leiden: Brill, 1995.

———. *Proverbs.* The New Century Bible Commentary. London: Marshall Pickering, 1994.

Wiesel, Elie. *Five Biblical Portraits.* Notre Dame: Notre Dame University Press, 1981.

———. "Job Our Contemporary." Pages 211–35 in *Messengers of God.* New York: Touchstone, 1976.

Willis, John T. "The 'Repentance' of God in the Books of Samuel, Jeremiah, and Jonah." *Horizons in Biblical Theology* 16 (1994): 156–75.

Wolff, Hans Walter. *Obadiah and Jonah.* Translated by Margaret Kohl. Continental Commentaries. Minneapolis: Augsburg, 1986.

———. *Studien zum Jonabuch.* Neukirchener-Vluyn: Neukirchener, 2003.

Wood, James. *The Broken Estate: Essays on Literature and Belief.* New York: Random House, 1999.

Yeats, W. B. *The Collected Works of W. B. Yeats: Volume I, The Poems.* Edited by Richard J. Finneran. Rev. 2d ed. New York: Scribner, 1996.

Zakovitch, Yair. "The Pattern of the Numerical Sequence Three-Four in the Hebrew Bible." PhD diss. The Hebrew University, 1978.

Zlotowitz, M. *Jonah: A New Translation with a Commentary Anthologized from Midrashic and Rabbinic Sources.* Brooklyn: Mesorah, 1980.

Zornberg, Aviva. *Genesis: The Beginning of Desire.* Philadelphia: Jewish Publication Society, 1995.

Index of Names and Subjects

INDEX OF ANCIENT SOURCES

INDEX OF HEBREW WORDS